Leo Frobenius 1873—1973

1973 Inter Nationes
Bonn–Bad Godesberg

Leo Frobenius
on African History,
Art and Culture
An Anthology

With a Foreword by
LÉOPOLD SÉDAR SENGHOR

Edited by
EIKE HABERLAND

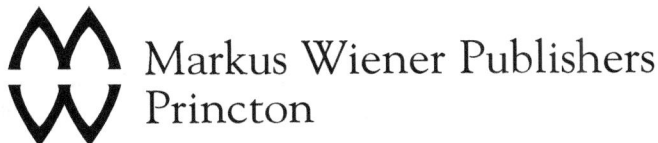 Markus Wiener Publishers
Princton

Second printing, 2014.
First American Edition 2007 by Markus Wiener Publishers.

For information write to:
Markus Wiener Publishers
231 Nassau Street, Princeton, NJ 08542
www.markuswiener.com

Copyright © 1973 by Franz Steiner Verlag, Stuttgart /Frobenius Institute,
Frankfurt am Main

Library of Congress Cataloging-in-Publication Data

Frobenius, Leo, 1873-1938.
  [Leo Frobenius, 1873-1973]
  Leo Frobenius on African history, art, and culture : an anthology /
edited by Eike Haberland ; preface by Léopold Sédar Senghor.
    p. cm.
  Originally published: Leo Frobenius, 1873-1973 : an anthology.
Wiesbaden : F. Steiner, 1973.
  Essays translated from the German by Patricia Crampton.
  ISBN-13: 978-1-55876-425-5 (hardcover : alk. paper)
  ISBN-13: 978-1-55876-426-2 (pbk. : alk. paper)
  1. Ethnology—Africa. 2. Frobenius, Leo, 1873-1938. I. Haberland, Eike.
II. Title.
  GN645.F7615 2007
  306.096—dc22
                          2006024212

Markus Wiener Publishers books are printed in the United States of America
on acid-free paper, and meet the guidelines for permanence and durability
of the Committee on Production Guidelines for Book Longevity of the
Council on Library Resources.

Leo Frobenius - An Anthology

The Lessons of Leo Frobenius

Now, to celebrate the centenary of his birth, we have a Leo Frobenius anthology. The great German ethnologist has thoroughly deserved this memorial in the second half of the 20th century, of which one of the characteristic features will be the emergence of the African countries on the international scene. For no one did more than Frobenius to reveal Africa to the world and the Africans to themselves.

I cannot do better than to speak here of the lessons we have learned from reading the work of Frobenius, and above all his two fundamental works, which have also been translated into French: *Histoire de la Civilisation africaine* (The History of African Civilization) and *Le Destin des Civilisations* (The Destiny of Civilizatons). When I say "we", I refer to the handful of black students who launched the *movement of the Négritude* in the 1930s in the Quartier Latin in Paris, with Aimé Césaire from the Antilles and Lyon Damas from Guyana.

I still have before me, in my possession, the copy of the *History of African Civilization* on the third page of which Césaire wrote: "décembre 1936". A year earlier, when I was teaching at the Tours Lycée while preparing my doctor's thesis on "Verbal Forms in Languages of the Senegal-Guinea Group" – never to be finished, owing to "going into politics" – I had started to attend courses at the Paris Institute of Ethnology and at the Practical School of Advanced Studies. So I was intellectually on familiar terms with the greatest Africanists and above all the ethnologists and linguists. But suddenly, like a thunderclap – Frobenius! All the history and pre-history of Africa were illuminated, to their very depths. And we still carry the mark of the master in our minds and spirits, like a form of tattooing carried out in the initiation ceremonies in the sacred grove.

We knew by heart Chapter II of the first book of the *History*[1], entitled "What Does Africa Mean to Us?", a chapter adorned with lapidary phrases such as this: "The idea of the 'barbarous Negro' is a European invention, which in turn dominated Europe until the beginning of this century".

*

Leo Frobenius was the one, above all others, who shed light for us on concepts such as *emotion, art, myth, Eurafrica*.

Firstly, the word *emotion*. Up to that time our masters, who had been

---

[1] I shall in most cases refer in future to Frobenius' two authoritative works simply as "History" and "Destiny".

trained in the school of rationalism – not that of Descartes, who was less unequivocal than has been claimed – but that of the "scientific" 19th century, had taught us to despise *emotion* and to be guided only by discursive reason. "Taught us"? More accurately, tried to teach us. For when we went "up" to Paris from the bush it was, of course, because we intended to disarm the colonists, but also, dialectically, to challenge the effectiveness of their arms and discover the secret which would enable us to sharpen our own.

But had our ancestors left us only the weapons, I mean the *values* of civilization? The Father Director of my college in Dakar denied that they had left us those. But Louis Armstrong's trumpet had already sounded across the French capital like a judgment, Josephine Baker's hips were vigorously shaking all its walls and the "fetishes" of the Trocadero were accomplishing the "Negro revolution" in the Ecole de Paris. Nevertheless, in our painstaking essays at the Lycée of Louis le Grand and the Sorbonne, where to the astonishment of our teachers we referred to "black values", we lacked not only "vision in depth", but also the basic philosophical explanation. It was Leo Frobenius who gave us both the vision and the explanation, at the very moment when, having completed our studies, we were entering upon active militant life, with the concept and the idea of *Négritude* under our belts. It was Frobenius who helped us to give the word its most solid, and at the same time its most human significance.

As he told us in the *History:* "More than any other living organism, man is capable of 'receiving reality' . . . receiving reality means the faculty of being *moved* by the essence of phenomena – not by the facts but by the reality which gives rise to them, or, in other words, by the essence of the facts"[2]. Many are the passages, in this work and others, where Frobenius compares and contrasts the *real* and the *fact*, the *sense* and the *sign*. "The essence of facts", that is their significance, which we perceive symbolically in the tangible qualities of the things and beings which underlie those facts. Hence the primordial importance which Frobenius attributes to intuitive reason. "In civilization," he writes, "that is in feeling, sensitivity is thought . . . what we call civilization is often the expression of the spirit, the language of the spirit, at least when it concerns men whose thought is still and primarily *intuitive*"[3]. It was Frobenius who, more than any other, more even than Bergson, reinstated intuitive reason in our eyes

[2] *History*, p. 25.
[3] *Destiny*, p. 114.

VIII

and restored its position as pre-eminent. He it was who inspired us to re-read the philosophers, to discover that the Greeks had given precedence to intuitive reason and that Descartes himself regarded "feeling" as an aspect of reason.

And it is from feeling, that is to say from emotion, that *art* takes its inspiration. This idea may now be universally accepted, but it was not so at the beginning of the century. "It is superfluous," Frobenius states in *History*[4], "to explain that art is the sense of life and that by penetrating life styles we also approach the essence of these styles". This means that art is primarily the perfection of the essence of life, of that spiritual energy in the Other which causes emotion. And note that man, when moved, begins to "act", to relive the Other – plant, animal, star, etc. – first to dance it, then to sculpt it, paint it, sing it. The "essence of life", I said, which is characterized by the internal structures of the Other, its external forms and its behaviour: its *rhythm*. It is this "possession" of the ego by the Other and the reaction of the ego to the Other which explains the differences in style between different artists and – this is what interests us here – between different races.

For every race possesses its own *Paideuma*, that is its own peculiar capacity for and manner of being moved: of being "possessed". Nevertheless, the artist, whether dancer, sculptor or poet, is not content to relive the Other; he *recreates* it in order the better to live it and make it live. He recreates it by rhythm and thus makes of it a higher, truer reality, one that is more real than the factual reality[5].

This brings us to the *myth*. As the dictionary tells us, the myth is "a fabulous story, often of popular origin, involving beings who embody the forces of nature and aspects of the human condition in symbolic form"[6]. From here we shall have to go back to the famous distinction which Frobenius made, not between the mind, but between the *understanding*, and the *spirit*. "It is a question," he explains, "of the limitation of the faculty of human perception, which is on the one hand intellectual and conditioned by the senses and on the other paideumatic . . . and conditioned by feeling. This opposition between the most important organs which unite us with life may correspond to a fission of the world which surrounds us into a *realm of factual phenomena* and a *realm of real phenomena*"[7]. Look, for instance, at boys being initiated into a civilization

[4] History, p. 39.
[5] Cf. in The Destiny of Civilizations the chapter entitled "The Real in Civilization".
[6] Petit Robert (Société du Nouveau Littré, Le Robert).
[7] History, p. 25.

under the influence of the Bull. They will undergo, among other things, a ceremony in which, possessed by the essential reality of the Bull, they will dance, perhaps wearing the mask of the Man-Bull-Moon, as I have seen them do on the Ivory Coast. This is the age of art, which followed the age of emotion. In the sacred grove the boys will have relived these first two epochs of ancient times. There they will relive, above all, the third: that of the myth. They will be told how the king is linked through his lineage to the sacred Bull, himself the offspring of the god or goddess Moon. As Frobenius wrote: "Man first lives civilization and myth and is only later capable of expressing them"[8].

So the myth is firstly an account, a series of coherent images, by which a story is told. But it has to be revealed to the children, that is, 'ex-plicated' in the etymological sense of the word, because this story contains its sense within itself: in its symbolic images which up to then had only been danced, sculpted or painted, because in the obscure but expressive power of emotion and rhythm they were sufficient unto themselves. And Frobenius, supplementing the teaching of the masters of the initiation, teaches us to see in our myths both works of art and the values of the *Négritude:* of the *Negerheit,* which is ultimately nothing but *being Negro,* as my friend Janheinz Jahn said. Hence the title of Part III of the History: "Poetry".

"Emotion" and "intuitive reason", "art" and "poetry", "image" and "myth", these are words or concepts or synonyms which we confront when we are considering Negroes, and their study is pertinent. We shall connect the first two words with German words, such as *Einfühlung, Gefühl, Wesenheit* and *Weltanschauung,* for which corresponding expressions can be found in the Negro African languages and which interpret some of the fundamental values of the German *soul:* of *Germanité,* not to speak of the fascination which Africa has always exercised upon the Germans: the *nostalgia for Africa.* I need no further proof than the list of the great German Africanists, such as the one given by Booker W. Sadji, son of the Senegal writer, who is a teacher of German: Heinrich Barth, Adolph Overweg, Friedrich Hornemann, Edward Vogel, Gerhard Rohlfs, Gustav Nachtigal, Robert Flegel, Franz Thorbecke[9]. And this list is not complete, because we must add the ethnologists and linguists such as Sigismund Koelle, Diedrich Westermann and August Klingenhaben.

[8] History, p. 109.
[9] Cf. *Négritude et Germanité:* speech given on distribution of prizes at the Senegal General Competition (Dakar, 1972).

X

Nevertheless we had to wait for Leo Frobenius before the affinities between the "Ethiopian", that is the Negro African, and the German soul could be made manifest and before certain stubborn preconceptions of the 17th and 18th centuries could be removed. One of these preconceptions is that the development of every ethnic group, and of humanity itself, is linear, univocal, passing from the Stone Age to the age of steam and electricity and to the atomic age of today. In the *Destiny*, creating an "ethnic characterology" before his time, Frobenius tells us that, like individuals, ethnic groups are diverse, even opposed, like the Hamites and the Ethiopians, in their feelings and their ideas, their myths and their ideologies, their customs and their institutions; that each ethnic group, having its own *paideuma* – once again, its *soul* – reacts in its own peculiar way to the environment and develops autonomously; that, though they may be at different stages of development, Germans and "Ethiopians" belong to the same spiritual family. And he concludes: "The West created English realism and French rationalism. The East created German mysticism ... the agreement with the corresponding civilizations in Africa is complete. *The sense of fact in the French, English and Hamitic civilizations – the sense of the real in the German and Ethiopian civilizations!*" [10] This is confirmed today by the characterologists who class the Germans in the ethnic type of *introverts* and the Negroes among the *fluctuants*, the two being equally characterized by energy and depth of affectivity.

It is easy to guess the consequences of this discovery and the increased self-confidence which it gave us. Because, paradoxically, our French teachers had taught us to respect the German genius, in the wealth of its contrasts and even of its contradictions: the alternation of strict logic and visionary mysticism, angelic sweetness and brutal force, the alternation of scholars and poets, engineers and musicians, reduced to the narrow limits of a principality or expanded to the dimensions of the world – or even the universe.

It is by this road that Frobenius helped us to leave the ghetto of the first phase of Négritude, with which we had been all too content: to leave in order to attempt to realize the "conciliatory agreement". It was only this agreement which would enable us to realize ourselves, through an "integral humanism", to talk like Jacques Maritain.

Now that the African peoples have stepped on to the international stage, especially in the United Nations Organization, while colonial rule

[10] Destiny, p. 131.

has been abolished all over the continent, with one or two exceptions, the African States are moving towards association with the European Economic Community on the basis of the *Eurafrican* concept. And it was from Frobenius that we borrowed this most fruitful of all ideas, for the building of the Universal Civilization. By Eurafrica the German ethnologist meant a civilization developed round the Mediterranean, which was supposed to have spread during the Upper Palaeolithic and Neolithic eras, as adduced in Book 5 of the *History*, entitled "The most ancient Art of the Image". He returns to it in the *Destiny:* "The soil of Africa also supplies abundant documentation on the palaeolithic civilizations, especially in its mountainous regions. Many scholars believe that the Chelleans came from Africa, just like the Capsians who dominated Spain in the Neopalaeolithic era, up to the frontiers of the Franco-Cantabrian civilizations. This fact is of the greatest importance to "primitive history" and especially to its second, Neopalaeolithic period. In Europe all these civilizations disappeared towards the end of the melting of the glaciers in the middle of the Neolithic era (about 5000 B.C.); they were either absorbed or smothered." [11]

Eurafrica is now a concept familiar to us from the progress of prehistory. Moreover, since the Abbé Breuil and Père Teilhard de Chardin, almost every year brings fresh proof that it was in Africa that man emerged from the animal state. And the last congress of African prehistorians who met in December 1971 in the capital of Ethiopia put this date of emergence about 5,500,000 years back.

Here too, Frobenius was a precursor, whether we are discussing the emergence of man or the emergence of art. He writes: "At the beginning of this chapter we wondered whether the bone, stone and tooth sculptures of the first civilization of the middle Stone Age, found in Europe and not in Africa, might not represent transpositions, into the hard materials of the northern style, of the original materials of the equatorial pre-civilizations as they developed in the late phase of the Stone Age and as they were transformed in the South, for instance in the Capsian" [12].

*

Of course the situation of Africanism has evolved since Leo Frobenius and great discoveries and important progress have been made. We shall no longer carry his works with us like a Bible or the Koran when we

[11] Destiny, pp. 64 and 65.
[12] History, pp. 178 and 179.

journey. Nevertheless the two authoritative works are always in my library and I consult them often.

For although we have achieved political independence – which seems more nominal than real – we are still under the economic domination of *Euramerica,* and its ideologies, though mutually antagonistic, lay siege to Négritude.

I have been saying it for decades: the independence of the mind is an indispensable condition of all other independence. And it was Leo Frobenius who helped us to achieve it. Therefore he is still our Master.

Léopold Sédar Senghor.

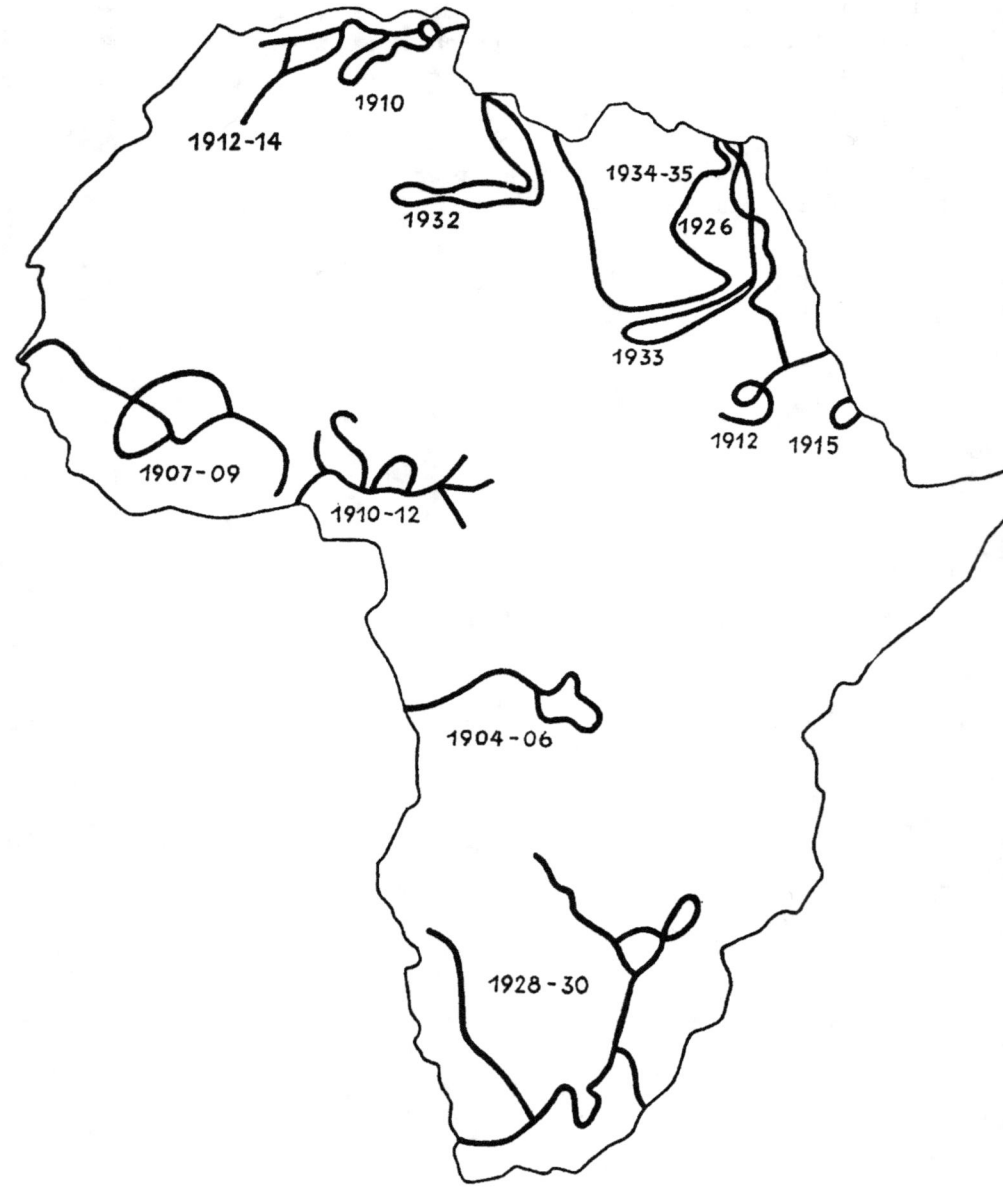

Fig. 1 Map of Frobenius' journeys through Africa on research

1. "The Atlas Africanus"*

When the research institute of cultural morphology (Forschungsinstitut für Kulturmorphologie) decided to publish, as the first major joint enterprise, the Atlas Africanus, or, in other words, a collection of maps symbolically representing the essence of the culture of an entire continent, its directors were completely aware of the fact that this project, which touched upon all sides of intellectual life, presupposed the formulation of an attitude to the fundamental problem of culture and of all academic disciplines concerned with culture. Just as there is only one human race, so there is only one culture (although there are many forms of culture), and a work as comprehensive as ours must start by providing information of equal significance to all forms of culture, whether the starting point chosen is America, Asia, Europe or Africa.

In addition to the fact that the project involved all disciplines, law no less than the sciences, comparative theology no less than philology, a work like ours, the first of its kind, exposed, as such, to all manner of error and misunderstanding, proposed to enter life on the watershed between two epochs, or centuries.

Reaching all the way back to Herodotus, there has been a succession of excellent historians of peoples, their cultural characteristics and differences. The centuries and millennia have provided such building materials in immense quantities, so that a man who like Adolf Bastian endeavoured to use them all in the building of a comprehensive structure merely, in so doing, manifested the impossibility of such a structure or the incapacity to produce it; whereas others, who decided to arrange analogies by groups (such as Tylor, Andree and other modern analogists or representatives of the theory of convergence) in their modest way renounced the possibility of a living doctrine. Even the man who merely investigates legal forms without taking account of the philosophy behind them, technical achievements in isolation from social organisation, or myths without reference to economic conditions, cuts something off from an as yet unknown totality and may move within the framework of dead facts without ever being able to penetrate to the living truth.

As recently as the beginning of the last century there flourished the collections of rare and curious objects made by princes and aristocrats in which were displayed the feather robe of Montezuma next to the rose of Jericho, an East-Asiatic Buddha next to the mummified remains of an

---

* From the introduction to "Atlas Africanus", 1929, p. 1–10.

erstwhile denizen of the depths of the sea, and the sword of an African "cannibal" next to a splinter from the cross of Christ. Collectors' mania was infectious and resulted in the growth of ethnographic museums to an extent such that their directors saw even the most palatial premises bursting at the seams and were unable to administer them "scientifically". The "rarities" turned into documents which increasingly shook off the rarity value and stimulated instead the call for completeness.

With unparalleled perversity and intensity, the last century examined the "past", looking at everything as something "finished" and not as something in a process of becoming. It created materialism and, to use a phrase of Viktor Hehn, unceremoniously banished metaphysics. This voluntary restriction to the physical world signified voluntary renunciation of all ultimate questions and resulted in a pursuit of the instrumental as an end in itself. – In this spirit, history and philology classified everything in systems of completed developments and turned aside from everything that was still evolving. Every part of the human race has tended, with the force of conviction, to consider its own ways the "right" ways, and to worship its own gods as the only gods, considering its own cultural eminence to be the highest peak of culture capable of attainment and applying to everything alien a scale of values evolved from within itself, but never has any form of culture or any cultural condition been able to carry its arrogance as far as "the modern age". There is no other explanation of the materialist onesidedness of this century, which increasingly, if tacitly, assumes the possibility of achieving "completeness", and an utopic scientific "doctrine of truth". It has had the impudence to designate as world history a mere segment of history extending from the Sumerians to the present day, to plumb the depths of nature by means of chemistry, physics, and experimentation, to classify human and cultural species in accordance with the shapes of skulls and languages. – There is no other explanation of this anti-metaphysical onesidedness except to ascribe it to monumental wilfulness and rigidity. This all-powerful age, acting always on the tacit assumption of the possibility of achieving "completeness" and "truth", without which it is inconceivable in its essence, arranged everything in orders and systems, animal and vegetable, weights and measures, time and space. Those objects which could not be subjected to such classification were considered to be unscientific and stowed away in the collections of freaks and curiosities.

The question that arises today in this introduction to a collection of maps devoted to the cultural forms and the civilisation of an entire continent is this: by what means is it possible to comprehend the essence of culture as such and to communicate such knowledge? This is the first question that must be asked and answered if the study of culture is to succeed in achieving a view of culture based on academic knowledge.

Let anyone enquire where he will about the raw materials of the study of culture: he will find that nowhere has the jurisprudent observed a standstill of the philosophy of law, the religious philosopher an inflexible ideology, the philologist a non-variable language. There was a time when Europe dreamed of a country whose civilisation had remained unchanged for millennia; this was China, considered to be the prototype of an invariable culture. Careful research has shown that this error could not have been more characteristic. The internal mobility of culture was also made manifest in external forms of expression to the anthropological collectors of the last century, so clearly that Felix von Luschan was moved to say: "There are no ethnographic duplicates". All investigations, the results obtained by all the sciences exploring the outlying provinces of culture, consequently showed that culture is eternally in motion.

Such mobility can be shown to exist more or less clearly in every object examined. The movement in itself may be dictated more or less by a direction, but the direction alone is never the decisive point. Movement can most easily be illustrated by the geographical distribution, the advance in various directions, the waves of outward propagation and, conversely, shrinkage and decay. Lastly, all organs of culture are in a process of constant mutual interaction. A change in textiles signifies a change in costume which in turn signifies a change in concepts of morality. A new kind of weapon results in new amulets, in a reformation of religion. The introduction of domestic animals and domestic plants affects economic, legal, traffic, philosophic forms. He who traces the finer ramifications of a culture realizes at the end that everything communicates in rhythm with everything else, that nothing is isolated, nothing is static, that in the last analysis no one thing can be understood without the other, without all the others.

No motion occurs in isolation. No motion is conceivable without another, which means that the problem of direction, considered in isolation, turns out to be wrongly formulated and superfluous to our comprehension of the total picture. However, all this means that culture as such will never become comprehensible if the forms in which it has found expression are subjected to systematic analysis according to 19th century views. It means that every line of research into one side or one motion, one subject or one line of development must without exception remain incomplete, even in the area of facts and, being isolated, can never penetrate to the truth, that the theorem of truths may be shattered by culture, and that the facts can achieve significance solely as the embodiment of a metaphysical reality.

Consequently, the study of culture as such could not provide results as valuable as those achieved by the other disciplines, and would be condemned to eternal fragmentation and chaos, if it were true that these other branches of science, with their assumption of possible "completeness" and "truth" in their forms of comprehension and presentation, in particular in graphical terms, corresponded to the nature of things and could thus reach their objective.

The question is whether this assumption in itself is or is not justified. From our point of view the decisive point is the performance of that branch of science which provides us, as map-makers, with the technical tools, i.e. geography and in particular cartography. In this context, we must represent actuality and reality to the point of banality.

The situation with regard to cartography is exactly the same as with all other so-called "exact" measurements and descriptions. Absolute accuracy is not relatively but absolutely impossible for all forms of measurement. Friedrich Ratzel rightly called the map a symbol. The use of the map as a symbol demands a clear answer from us to the question as to where it can be used as subject or as object of our task producing a cultural geographic atlas.

In the nineteenth century, geography increasingly chose geology as a basis, becoming a static science in the process. What exists is the starting point of life; what is evolving was relegated to the ancillary function of explaining what exists. To geography, a map became synonymous with writing; the map describes a continent, an ocean, an air current. Geography is a physical science; therefore facts as such are the objects of its activity.

We know what animals exist; a few hundred additional species may be "discovered", but the possibilities have been exhausted and from the knowledge gained science is in a position to say that by and large formation of species has been completed and that any surprises in the formation of new species of animals are becoming insignificant. The period of the formation of species has been followed by that of inactivity. – All in all, researchers investigating the ramifications of their specialities in the previous century were bound to be so impressed by the static principle in space that the kinematic principle, which though still undeveloped was nevertheless active in everything, became of secondary significance – which was necessary to the materialist view of the world in the nineteenth century.

Every observation of the study of cultures provide a marked contrast with the above. A walk through an East Prussian farm or an African village may deceive the eye for a moment: this hook used as a plough may appear to be ancient; a mortar hewn into the solid rock seems equally ancient; remnants now hidden under the ground from a civilisation thousands of years old reveal the same hut groundplan. At a closer view, this apparent permanence is, however, balanced by a revolutionary or evolutionary tendency of immense force. The hook, the mortar, the ground plan may long remain undisturbed, like a fossil. But, first, we know that the hook will make way tomorrow for the iron ploughshare, the mortar for the mill, the straw hut for the house of timber or corrugated sheet metal. Secondly, we know that the overall picture of the effect of civilisation consists of the cohesion of the forms of vitally and constantly changing "quirks" of costume and fashion, of the topping-up of the material stocks of an economy, of the transformation of social and religious life, – that every object, however conservatively it may be preserved, is subjected to the constantly changing *socialization of cultural material**.

Any attempt at a cartographic survey demonstrates the variability of the forms as such. For example, should I attempt to determine the distribution of a simple object such as the "double bell" I would be faced with a range of shapes, not all of which can be accommodated by the concept of the double bell. If the map is to be correct it would really require a differentiation which, strictly speaking, is impossible in most cases. An example of this is the dividing line between a pile bed and a pile dwelling, where no-one can say where the concept of the pile bed ends and that of the pile dwelling begins. All in all, all cultural objects, no matter how uniform they may appear to be externally, elude by their variability any attempt at a truly exact unforced classification of the kind that can be applied to the somewhat more static objects of geology, botany and zoology.

The kinematic element becomes even more striking if we remember that all cultural objects are subject to "socialization". The distribution of arrows is determined by the occurrence of certain types of bows, that of tuber cultivation by the appearance of types of cereal, that of the patriarchial dogma by the penetration of matriarchial customs. If arrows are

* "Constantly changing socialization of cultural materials" means that any given object(type) is embedded in a constantly changing spectrum of cultural materials. The function of the object or the type is influenced by the other cultural materials existing at the same time in the same culture.

entered on the map without reference to bows, fabrics without reference to costume, types of money without reference to economic systems, this constitutes an artificial isolation of facts, forcibly torn from the constantly moving context of reality.

Inadvertently, discussion of the material to be represented has led us by way of the description of the attempts at representation straight into the problem of the applicability of maps in the study of culture. That study can only be guided by kinematics, what is static can only be its object. Culture is a living reality which can only be comprehended by penetration of the facts. This means that the map can only circumscribe "culture" but not describe it; in the map as a symbol, the image must therefore only serve the purpose; the image must be nothing more than a means. The problem is to represent movement, which can only be done by deflecting attention constantly from the statically factual to the genuinely kinematic.

Distribution as such is meaningless. Whether a tribe lives in circular huts or in saddle-roof buildings is irrelevant in itself; it becomes essential only if it exhibits a movement, a change of style, if it shows that the change of style is due to an economic form, a legal situation, a social factor. The relationship between these factors and the style of building signifies meaning and motion. This answers the problem of geographical reproduction, i.e. I cannot express the influences at work by the representation of the distribution of a single fact: I require at least two facts for doing so; the essential point will not be represented by the two facts, but will have been symbolically suggested by the conceptual connection between the two, which the eye cannot see. Since culture is kinematographic, the map must become kinematographic. In recording the movement of culture in a series of maps we avoid hypotheses and render the invisible sensible to the searching eye as "map reading".

The kinematographic representation of a group of cultural forms ideally aims at summarizing all the essential characteristics of a culture. It is not a particular figure, nor any particular cultural relations, but a general relevance, in other words the full riches of life, which can intimate the meaning of the whole as an integral fabric to the reality of the human imagination, which is statically restricted by logic and abstractions. It is not the obvious, but only the multitude of living relationships, that should be allowed to decide the combination. The economic factor must throw its light on religion. The weapons must be linked with social organisation. Costume must be linked to the law of inheritance. Every individual factor must be shown in its relation to all others. Nothing must be isolated without motion and without reference, because this would be contrary to the nature of culture.

Naturally, this demands a substantial knowledge of factual material. As publication starts, the Institute possesses about 200 distribution diagrams and the base material for about twice this number. It is of course taken for granted that the existing maps and those to be published must contain all the material available. Any omissions are due to the shortcomings of the researchers, to the adventitious nature of existing research reports, and to the fact that the atlas is the first publication of its kind. We are certainly more conscious of these defects than previous authors of maps of primitive cultures.

The Atlas Africanus marks the conclusion of 25 years of preparatory work and the real beginning of classification of objects in the African study of culture irrespective of any errors and mistakes that may still mar its appearance. Culture itself speaks through these maps; learned and traditional hypotheses which have held cultural studies in thrall for too long are eliminated by the language of maps. The fact is that the static principle has proved to be a serviceable and reliable tool and working material has pushed back ancillary disciplines to their appropriate position in relation to the whole in a natural manner. The individual disciplines come together as equals: architecture and social building, technology and language, religion and economics. It is now apparent that the study of culture cannot be pursued from a single discipline and that philology in particular, which has long held up, by one-sided classification, the advance to a knowledge of the meaning of culture, will have to make do with fewer privileges.

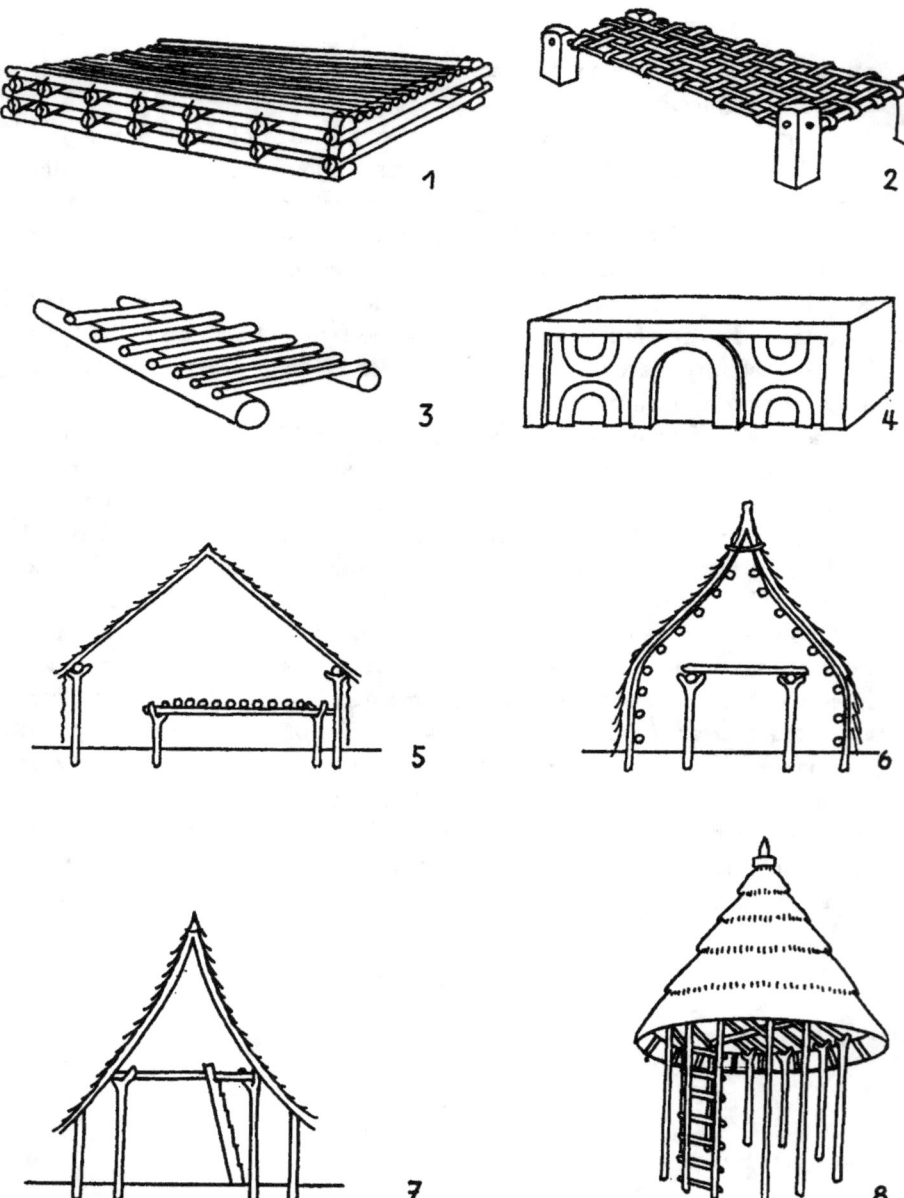

Fig. 2 From the Atlas Africanus: Bed and House
1. Kitanda from the West – 2. Angareb from the East – 3. Original kitanda –
4. Heated bed – 5. Pile-bed in the round house (Wolof) – 6. Pile-bed as inter-
mediate structure (Banziri) – 7. Pile-bed as upper floor (Sierra Leone) – 8. Pile-
bed as pile-building (Falémé)

An example from the "Atlas Africanus"*

Bed and House

Today, we Central Europeans look on the bed as a movable piece of furniture which can be put up anywhere in the house. Development has thus reached a certain centre line. The two ancient African forms of the bed by contrast represent extremes of what is possible.

The pile bed which still largely predominates today in equatorial Africa consists of four forked timbers rammed into the ground which support the two struts of the mattress frame. Its distribution extends as far as that of the Ethiopian** culture. By contrast with this, the other, evidently Hamitic bed probably consisted originally of nothing more than a simple leather coat which served as an article of clothing during the day and, at night, as a mattress and coverlet simultaneously. The "kaross" of the South Africans and the leather coat of the early Abyssinians and of the present-day Galla are used in this way. The bed itself is any place in the originally mobile hut; it is an earth bed. In the latter case, the hut determines the position of the bed; in the former (the pile bed) the bedstead determines the construction of the house, even tectonically.

In one sense, these two forms of bed are the expression of opposite economic systems: of the stable Ethiopian civilisation closely associated with agriculture, and the nomadic Hamitic culture which reverted time and again to cattle raising.

Apart from these two principal forms there are two mobile beds, i. e., in the West, the kitanda composed of palm leaf rods, and, in the East, the angareb which consists of a zinc-coated wooden frame and uses plaited cowhide for a mattress. The history of the kitanda appears to lead back to forms which have survived to this day, from the Zambesi to the Angola coast, as a primitive travelling bed of the porters. At night, the man places two logs corresponding to his height in parallel at a distance of about 75 cm on the ground and places a few rods transversely across them, on which the mat is spread. Among the Konde, this ancient form of bed has survived unchallenged to this day.

Finally, the last form to be considered is the clay bank bed from the West Sudan, the more highly developed forms of which, those which are found between Borgu and Schari, can even be heated.

This heatable bed leads to an investigation which shows that a wooden

* From "Atlas Africanus", 1929, No 1, sheet 2.
** cf. p. 30.

9

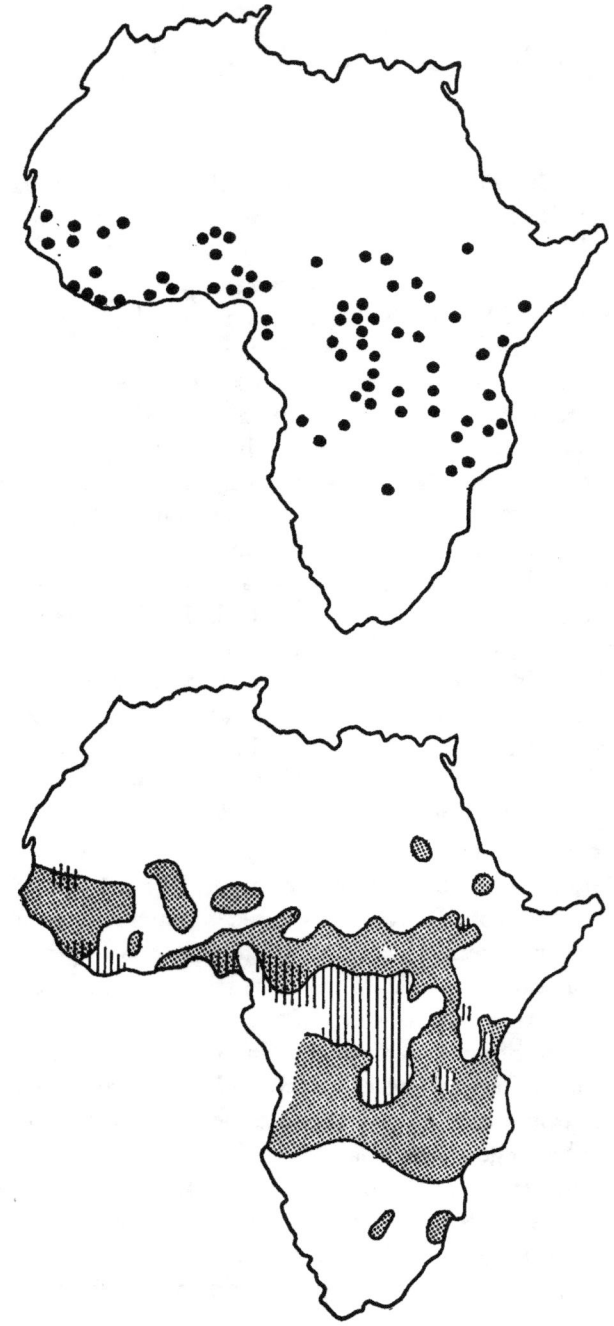

Fig. 3 From the Atlas Africanus: Bed and House
   top: Pile structure as living and sleeping area – bottom: Granary on pile framework

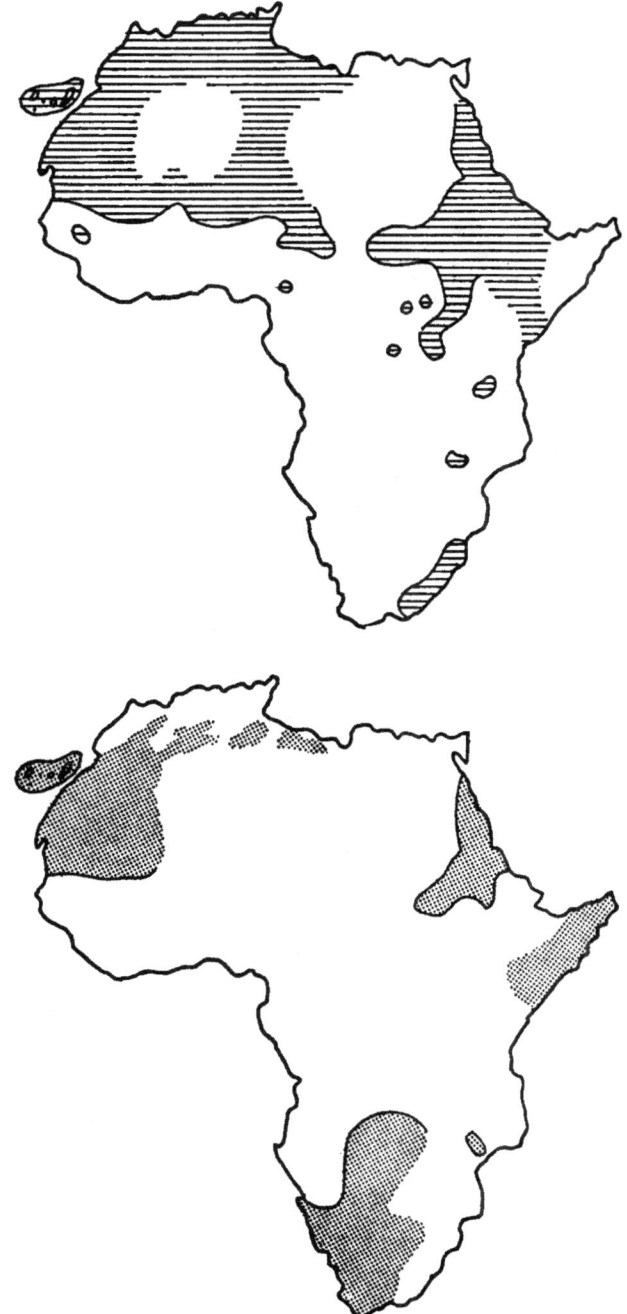

Fig. 4 From the Atlas Africanus: Bed and House
top: Silos (storage pits) – bottom: Underground baking

11

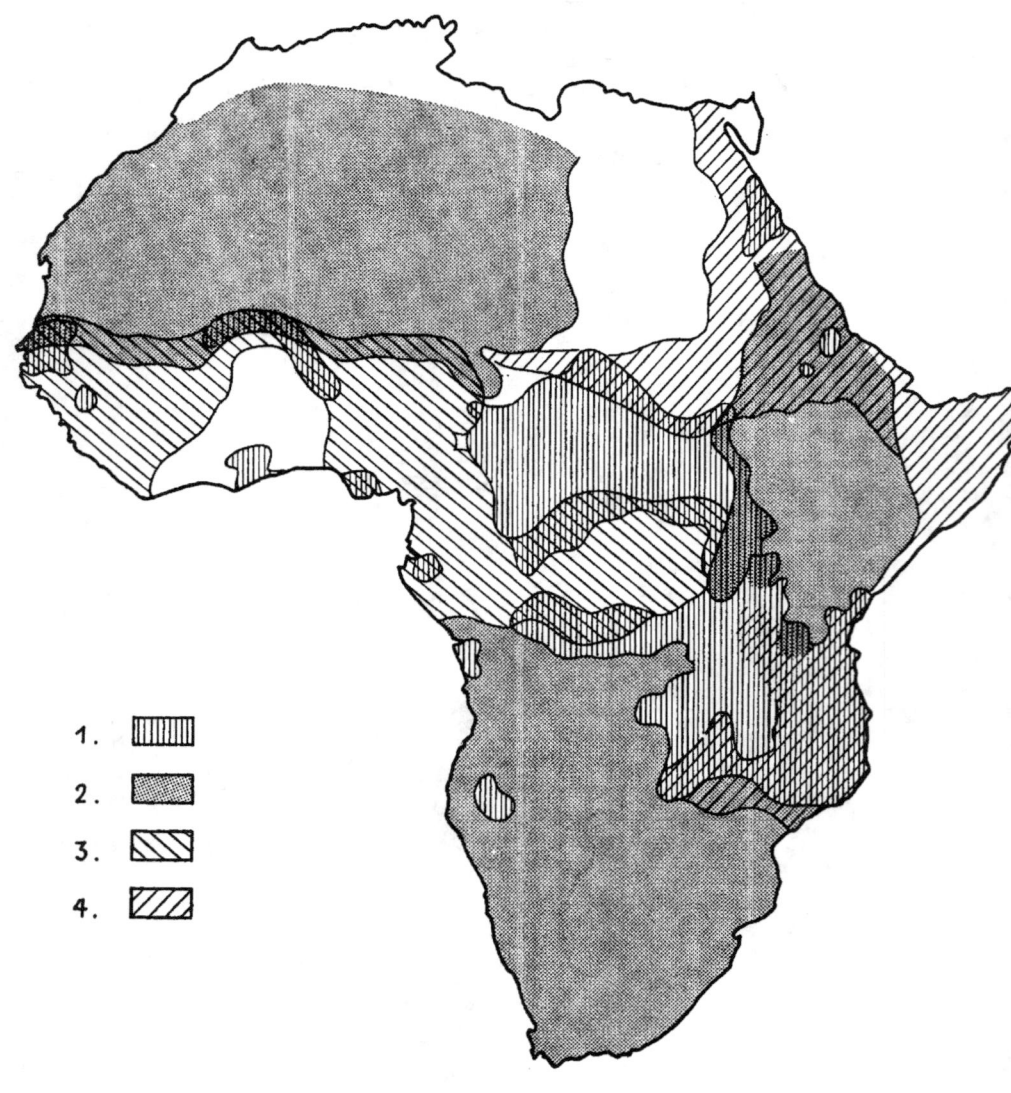

Fig. 5 From the Atlas Africanus: Bed and House
    1. Pile-bed – 2. Earth bed – 3. Kitanda of the West – 4. Angareb

12

internal structure or in other words a pile bed is involved, although it is covered by clay. This leads us to another observation, i. e. that on the Senegal river and on the Niger, on the Ubangi, among the Dualla and the population of the Nile valley, this pile bed is not infrequently placed at an elevated level so that a fire can burn under it which protects the sleeper from mosquitoes and warms him at night. Moreover, this entire group shows that the bed no longer deserves the name of a bed, since in many cases it already amounts to a pile dwelling.

Having been led along this path, we arrive, by way of examining other kinds of distribution, at the result that the Ethiopian civilisation in its relations with the earth everywhere prefers the pile grid. Storage containers are placed on pile grids. Pile grids are used for drying. The guards protecting cereals stand on pile grids. Large buildings on piles, like the Barla of the South Sea Islanders, are the places where the men assemble on the river Nile and in Senegambia. If we examine the distribution of pile dewellings in Africa which can still be detected today, we are surprised by the regular distribution of individual occurrences which can apparently only be explained as the gradual withering of a once flourishing phenomenon. The picture is one of typical decay and we are seriously driven to ask whether and to what extent we shall in subsequent studies of architecture have to consider as a fundamental feature this peculiar basic principle of Ethiopian life, which is exemplified by the pile grid of the bed and the pile grid of the house.

By contrast, and in connection with the earth bed, Hamitic civilisation always tends to burrow into the earth. On the maps that follow I indicate the distribution of silos, i. e. storage pits sunk in the ground, and of earthbaking, i. e. a roasting method performed in an earth oven. Just as the true Hamitic Hottentot moulds himself a bed in the earth whereas Ethiopian civilisation prepares a pile grid, Hamitic civilisation sinks its store rooms in the earth whereas the Ethiopian places them on a pile grid, and in the same way the Hamitic civilisation builds an earth oven and the Ethiopian a pile grid for food preparation.

In this there are clearly manifested many mutual relations between environmental factors such as climate and geography and the cultures connected with them, which in the end betray their vital meaning in the funeral customs and in relation to chthonic powers on the one hand and tellurian on the other. Everything in African cultures that rests in the earth is chthonic, everything that grows out of the earth towards the sky is tellurian.

2. Discussion of the Method of Cultural History*

The statistical part, which is used here [of the cultural-complex method rejected by Frobenius] proceeds as follows: in a particular patch of ground I find this, then this, and then this. The individual forms correspond and have the same distribution. On another patch of earth I find identical or similar forms with the same distribution. Now the various geographical regions of the earth are being explored and today it can already be said that there are more and more patches on the earth which can display identical forms, distributed over distinctly defined areas. *But,* when we ask if these identities of form are based on relationship, the statistical part of the method cannot supply the answer. We cannot proceed here as we do, for instance, in investigating the distribution of a species of monkey. A monkey species is a life-form; but a bow which we find somewhere, an arrow or a hut is simply one tiny cog in a whole organism. So then we have to try to assemble groups of similar distribution which possess an internal, organic, living connection. But what we have discussed up to now is merely statistical material, which has no force as evidence as regards the question of actual relationship and evolution – and it is the answer to this which must be the goal of such studies.

The greater question is this: is it really possible to produce biological evidence for the organic connection between cultural forms, for the development of forms? I think such evidence exists. But if we want to find it we will have to alter the current method a little. We must not be content to say: here we have *this* shape of shield, and here we have *this* shape of shield; we must look for the evolution of shield shapes, for the transitional forms. I believe that this second part of my method, the evolutionary historical method, is the more important. Thus, for instance, round huts may be absolutely identical externally, in various parts of the world. It is only the internal structure, the design and the evolution of the design along one path of distribution and on one level of distribution, that we have to know before we can make up our minds as to any organic connection.

* From the Discussion on the Lectures by F. Graebner: "Cultural Complexes and Cultural Strata in Oceania" and B. Ankermann: "Cultural Complexes and Cultural Strata in Africa". In: *Zeitschrift für Ethnologie* 37, 1905, p. 90.

3. On the Morphological Method of Studying Cultures*

Today, four branches of science and scholarship concern themselves with the history of human cultures; they are:

1. History, the archaeological arm of which reaches far back into the discovery of ancient monuments. It provides, among other things, the framework for placing events in time, i. e. chronology.

2. Prehistory, which, in conjunction with geological establishment of facts, classifies the documents relating to the development of prehistoric cultures according to periods. Archaeology today has already advanced into the earlier strata of prehistoric cultures.

3. Ethnography, which examines present-day cultures in so far as they are still alive outside the framework of verified history.

4. Cultural morphology, which endeavours to discover the meaning and the phenomena of culture as such. The data of the three other related disciplines provide its raw material and its aim is to discover the correlations of the building up of human culture as a unity, according to meaning, geographical distribution and chronological order.

Cultural morphology represents the common ground of all four disciplines. At present, it has a particularly important mission: to build a bridge between historical archaeology and comparative ethnography. So far there is a complete void here, mainly because no path has as yet been discovered that would lead from the facts of historical archaeology to those of ethnography.

Historical scholarship has given us Europeans a perspective which stretches back in space and time as far as ancient Egypt and Mesopotamia (Babylon arising from Sumerian civilisation). Even in their "primitive" forms in the fourth millennium both cultures already exhibit an inner maturity. The archaeological finds made on our side of the great cultural watershed in space and time between Egypt and Babylon do not disclose their sources. These sources must therefore be sought in the area on the far side of archaeological and historical monumental finds, or, in other words, in countries which have not as yet yielded archaeologically significant discoveries and have served as a field to be cultivated only by ethnography.

So the question which faces cultural morphology is whether the areas

* From "Erythräa", 1931, Appendix I, p. 347–349.

beyond the Egyptian-Babylonian civilisation are able to provide ethnographic material capable of contributing to our understanding of the development of Egyptian and Babylonian civilisation geographically, historically and philosophically.

When the knowledge of civilisation was still confined by the swaddling clothes of initial theorizing and the apron strings of academic Darwinism, a doctrine was born which was represented in Germany principally by Adolph Bastian and which started from the assumption that, to put it briefly, cultures were tied to individual peoples and must take parallel courses even if their bearers (peoples) lived without contact with others. In other words, according to this theory, each people must pass through the then dogmatically accepted sequence of hunting, nomadism and agriculture, accumulating at each level a harvest of inventions appropriate to each given stage of development.

This means that at a certain stage of development, each people must "discover" the bow for itself, at another the spear; at one stage, the idea of "fetishism", at another the idea of "pantheism", the family at one stage, the state at another, just as a plant produces first the cotyledon, then the branch structure and finally blossom and fruit.

This ethnographic doctrine took for its starting point the assumption that civilisations developed in isolation. This was disputed by Friedrich Ratzel but he did not succeed in discovering a method that would prove the opposite. Such a method was proposed in the form of the "cultural complex doctrine" at the end of the 90's and has since been accepted by all major ethnographic university departments in Germany (Berlin, Vienna, Cologne). The work done by this method has shown that the multitude of cultural relationships which we know to have existed in historical civilisations must be assumed to have existed also outside our western Asiatic-European group of civilisations, in the ethnographic world. No civilisation has accomplished its rise in total isolation: on the contrary, no civilisation can be understood unless relations with other civilisations are assumed to have existed. (There is no need for me to point out that work conducted according to the method postulating groups of civilisations is not done without considerable knowledge and without making use of all positive as well as negative material evidence, and that, of course, dreadful errors can result from neglect of the necessary knowledge, circumspection and accuracy.)

The development of the doctrine of cultural complexes was assisted by a considerable expansion of knowledge of prehistory. We can now see that there was a wealth of cultural relationships even during the earlier periods of the Stone Age. Nowadays, the study of prehistory takes this for granted.

Obviously, such far-reaching work can only be done by taking a comprehensive view of our knowledge of the facts of culture. Such vision and such knowledge must be required of anyone who sets out to pass judgement on such significant "ethnographic" facts as the temple of Zimbabwe, styles of rock painting, ore and metal mines, or the sacral state in South Africa. Unfortunately, the situation has so far been inauspicious, as the following example illustrates.

It is a fact that during excavations in the ruins of Southeast Africa, pottery with patterns and iron weapons were found whose style and shape were identical with those of implements used by the present-day inhabitants of this area. The favourite conclusion to be drawn from this has been: "This proves that the builders were negroes of the race that inhabits the country to this day". Further, it was concluded that "these ruins must therefore be very recent". What is the significance of such an assertion? Let us assume that somewhere along the Roman lines, a copy of the "Venus of Milo" or the "Zeus of Otricoli" is found during excavation of the ruins of an ancient villa. The archaeologist, having observed plaster casts of the Venus and the Zeus in many a front room of modern German houses, concludes that what he is excavating must be a German villa of recent date. The example may appear grotesque, but it is much less exaggerated than the reader may think.

The reader may indeed say: "Every schoolboy knows that the Venus of Milo and the Zeus of Otricoli were made in ancient times". Allright, this identifies the matter as a problem of education concerning a civilisation close to us. I would however still hold that anyone who goes to Africa for excavations must be at least as familiar with the fundamental roots of civilisation in that continent as the layman is with such problems at home. Should this not be the case, he must at least observe that the finds were made in the area of the ruins, so that the corresponding types of pottery and weapons could possibly have been brought into the country by the people who built the ruins. Quite generally it is an archaeological principle to start, in establishing the date of a discovery, from the older and only to postulate preservation to modern times as a second line of argument, and not to declare the old to be young because something continues to live as if it were young. Strictly speaking, scholarship is not entitled to draw any conclusions from this evidence as to the date. The "negroes" may have possessed these weapons and these pots several thousands of years ago.

The superficial processes by which some archaeologists arrived at the formulation of their views are illustrated by the fact that bronze objects have been found in the same excavations since Bent. The researcher must know that true bronze art in Africa is restricted to the area of the ruins and mines in South Africa and was about to die out when the Europeans arrived. In the same way, a certain kind of ceramic art is also found in this South Eastern region only.

Consequently, the question must be based on the following formulation: "Since bronze working and a certain kind of ceramic art can only be shown to have existed in the area of the old mines and ruins, we must first consider the possibility of a relation between these cultural characteristics and, should we find such a relation, we must, secondly, examine cultural relationships, and thirdly and lastly, the problem of dating."

Even this cannot be sufficient for the cultural morphologist in Africa. As a cultural soil, Africa is distinguished by an incomparable ability to keep tradition alive. What perished millennia ago in other continents survives to this day in Africa. This poses the further problem of examining what surviving monuments of a culture rooted in the mind may survive in the intellectual and political life. A foundation for the formulation of valid questions will only have been achieved when evidence has been obtained of exceptional intellectual life, of remnants of a socially preeminently typical cultural foundation, and of an organic relationship between these and the archaeological skeletal fragments.

4. The Nature of Culture*

"The world as a whole may progress, but
every young person must begin at the
beginning and live through the epochs of
world culture for himself." — Goethe.

Mechanistic and intuitive types of enquiry

There are two main ways of apprehending reality, which may be called
the mechanistic and the intuitive. The former seeks to establish laws as a
means of understanding the processes and phenomena of the external
world and of human consciousness. The strength of this method lies in
its power to elicit such laws; its weakness is that it cannot avoid setting
up an unnatural opposition between the norm and the abnormal, the
regular and the irregular, the rule and the exception. Whatever diverges
from the law is treated as second-class reality, so that the observer loses
his power of comprehensive and impartial judgement. The mechanistic
principle is, like a railroad track, the shortest means of reaching a given
end, but it prevents us from taking a broad survey of the country as we
pass through it.

The intuitive approach, on the other hand, is based on the conception
of structure. It is content to perceive the main phenomena and assign to
them, as sympathetically as possible, a place in the general structure. In
this way the intuitive observer can, with full understanding, enter into
all the vicissitudes of reality.

In the mechanistic view the world consists of a system of facts which
can be analysed into cause and effect, elements and combinations, and
from which it is possible to deduce relationships of universal validity.
It is a type of biological or psychological approach based on albumen
tests, laws of association, motives and impulses, ganglion cells and nerve
tissues, all duly classified and reduced to dry formulae. The intuitive
observer, by contrast, seeks to enter with his whole being into the lawless
profusion of spiritual activity, at the same time distinguishing the significant from the trivial, the expressive from the merely accidental. He
surrenders to the inner logic of growth, evolution and maturity, a realm
which system and experiment are powerless to unlock. Instead of petrified
laws and formulae, he discovers symbolic events and types of living,
breathing reality.

* From *"Paideuma – Umrisse einer Kultur- und Seelenlehre"*, 1921, pp. 7–125.

The mechanistic approach is nowadays very much in vogue, and the intuitive correspondingly rare. I am not here using these terms to denote philosophical doctrines. Both, in their way, are comprehensive, penetrating, almost compulsive modes of thought, with their own claim to interpret reality. Nor am I suggesting that there is anything especially new or superior about the intuitive method. As for novelty, Goethe himself took a thoroughly intuitive view of the world, though this was overlaid by the development of nineteenth-century specialization, so that he was not wrong in predicting that his work would never be popular – even though tags from *Faust* are on everybody's lips. As for superiority, every culture that we know of has oscillated between the two poles of mechanism and intuition. However, in advancing the theory that we are moving into a new cultural era, the advent of which can be felt rather than proved, I am bound to support the revival of an intuitive attitude.

It must also be stressed that there is no such thing as an absolutely mechanistic or an absolutely intuitive outlook. It is a question rather of the predominance of one or other of two tendencies which, in a sense to be explained in more detail, we may call the factual and the daemonic.

Since 1904, when I was introduced to the sphere of African cultures, my life has been crowded with experiences and impressions for which I can never be sufficiently grateful. I look back on periods of independence during which I was responsible for the lives and activities of comrades who helped me to gather a rich harvest of information and experience, and again on years of hard work between expeditions, studying and classifying the material we had brought home. Its wealth is such that I shall never be able to publish it all to the world, and this made it all the more important to put my collections and manuscripts in order, with the help of an increasing army of assistants in the field and in Germany. The scholar's den of 1894 turned into a research institute which it was my task to direct and animate, either on the spot or during my absence on expeditions. The fruits of my practical experience had to be compared with others' descriptions, with the relevant literature and with museum exhibits from elsewhere. The handful of ideas and theories with which I had started grew into hundreds; my staff of assistants increased steadily. Work which had been within the compass of a single individual demanded to be made accessible to a host of workers and enquirers, within the framework of a vast organization.

All this could not fail to affect the manner in which I had envisaged my task in 1895. At that time I was concerned with Africa and European prehistory in the light of a few broad concepts such as the geographical exploration of cultures and the "age of the sun god". But, on the one hand, the more I travelled about Africa and observed its different cultures, the more conscious I became of what was typical and organic rather than unique and individual; and, on the other, familiarity with the dark continent gave me a keener insight into the forms of modern European culture, which in many cases I beheld from a considerable distance of space and time.

Another change was that I came to distinguish more sharply between cultures and human beings. In Africa I made the acquaintance of obscure races with powerful cultural forms, while in Europe one might encounter advanced human beings with a vestigial culture, or vice versa. In the remotest corners of Africa one might find men and women of lofty views, deep religion and an exalted poetic sense, whereas Europe with all its achievements was not free from pettiness, envy and all the vices and distempers in Pandora's box. It is not a question of whether human beings are better in one continent or the other: they are in fact the same throughout, except for a few qualities which they imbibe as part of their cultural inheritance.

The following lines are not intended to depict one culture or another, but rather to help the reader to apprehend what I have called the "Paideuma", that is to say the spiritual essence of culture in general. What I have to say does not answer the question "This is how things are", but rather "This is how they are to be understood". My investigation is not concerned with modern psychology or physiology: it is obliged to pursue its own way, so as to remove from the path what would otherwise be gross and insurmountable obstacles. At the same time it is a modest enquiry, and in a sense an unscientific one. This may be perceived in the use of a special terminology and forms of language which are not readily intelligible, because their subject-matter is not. In particular, I have found it necessary for certain purposes to replace the word "culture" by the special term "Paideuma" as above defined.

The others and ourselves

Anyone who has noticed the increasing volume of recent ethnographical literature, especially monographs on particular races and peoples, will have realized that these works are the reflection of a kind of underlying impulse, and will also have been impressed by the constant improvement in observational techniques. Given the right previous training, it is now possible to give a fuller description of a primitive people after a few months spent in their midst than earlier scholars could have done after decades of study. The new method consists of observing in the greatest possible detail every aspect of life, including craftsmanship, social institutions, religious attitudes and customs. The result may fill many volumes and contain such a sensitive and complete description as to give an almost photographic picture of the lives of individuals and of their community.

We have reason to congratulate ourselves on this state of affairs. The rapid expansion of our own civilization is tending to destroy "primitive" forms of culture, but at the same time the latter's history is being enshrined by ethnologists in a priceless and permanent wealth of documentation. Nevertheless, I believe it is proper to ask how far this mass of knowledge will in fact meet the requirements of future ages. We should remember that in former days, when cultures were studied in no such detail, monographs were written which, while they may appear scrappy and clumsy to us, give a deeper and more penetrating idea of their subject-matter than many works of the present day. The latter are admirable in their technique and precision of observation, but they do not really show us peoples and cultures as they are, because their approach is superficial and more appropriate to an object than to a living body.

Another fact that springs to mind is that Latin and Germanic scholars approach this matter in different ways. The Latins and especially the French are more concerned with states of society, the Germans with historical description. The difference is an illustration of methods of work and intellectual habits in a materialistic age. This age, it should be noted, is now comig to its end and is giving place to a new philosophy that stresses the role of intuition. The comparative study of cultures, be it called ethnology, anthropology or anything else, will have as its tools the knowledge gained during the scientific era, but it will revert to the starting-point prescribed by Kant's conception of anthropology a hundred and fifty years ago.

The problem, then, is to determine what the future will think of our present monographs, what it will find wanting in them, and what it will regard as the essential aspects of a living culture.

Practically all the comprehensive monographs of modern times begin by describing material culture and proceed from that to the intellectual and spiritual. We find descriptions of clothing, huts and weapons, then political and legal customs, then general notions, myths and legends. We are told of spells and superstitions, ceremonies and ritual observances of all kinds. Attempts are made to single out characteristic features that distinguish one culture from another. A word or two may be said of priestly deceptions, but otherwise the description is at an end. It is excellent as far as it goes, but what it does is to depict the alien culture *as it appears to us*. If we compare descriptions of the same object by French and German scholars we find that they differ, and this is sufficient proof that they are subjective and at least partially distorted. Our mistrust will increase still further if we search these monographs for an account of the true nature or soul of the cultures in question. This, we must realize, is something that pervades their every manifestation. There is a psychological factor in the way a man handles the simplest weapon. The same is true of clothing, as we may see from the fact that discerning ethnologists no longer speak merely of a sense of physical shame but take into account the possibility of its displacement. The shape of a hut or other dwelling-place has a pronounced symbolic importance, as is shown by the relationship of the simplest architectural forms to other manifestations of cultural development and decline. Anyone who studies our own age from an extra-political point of view will recognize that the state itself is a symbol which, more often than not, transcends the utilitarian purposes of its subjects.

These examples suffice to show that culture in all its aspects is a product of the mind, working so to speak invisibly, and that its spiritual basis is more clearly expressed in objects of everyday life than in any conscious intellectual process. This is an essential fact which our present-day literature, from its method of approach, is scarcely capable of grasping. It may be added that we are able to take a more detached and perceptive view of alien cultures, especially what are called primitive ones, than of our own. The student and explorer is constantly coming across new manifestations of a people's inner life, in a variety of forms that we "superior" races have long ceased to enjoy. Primitive society displays in abundance features of a kind which, in Europe, have disappeared or been overlaid by the accumulation of knowledge and an excessive preoccupation with "scientific" fact.

We in Gemany, and in Europe as a whole, are exercised today by many questions which we seek to resolve in terms of our own speech and methods of investigation, practised on the most unsuitable of all objects, namely ourselves. The answers to these problems fill whole libraries and archives and are the subject of thousands of learned articles published every day. Yet they could be solved in a moment by anyone with eyes and ears and the requisite sensibility, if he were to go among "primitives" and observe what he finds there.

In the following pages I will try to show this by means of three examples. The questions to be asked in the first place are: what kind of poetry and fiction does a people have? at what level does the creative power of a culture reside? and what is the significance of knowledge within that culture?

Poetic composition

The work on mythology which I completed in 1894 led me to put the basic question regarding the origin of fables, myths, and poetry.

To us Northerners in our "scientific" superiority, the answer is usually clear enough: we use a facile term like "imagination" and consider ourselves dispensed from further thought. Let me recall here an episode that I described in *Schwarze Seelen*. On my visit to a certain part of Africa, an old missionary who had lived there for years told me that there were no folk-tales worth mentioning. A few weeks later I read him some stories of merit that I had collected: he was astonished and exclaimed: "They must have made them up for your benefit." We discussed the matter, and he admitted that Europeans, whether townsfolk or peasants, could certainly not have "invented" a body of well-constructed oral literature in so short a time. When I pressed the point he also agreed that the natives' myths, properly so called, were as limited in form and content as the world of their own experience, so that "imagination" could not be invoked to account for the stories. He was thus finally obliged to admit that they must have been handed down from distant times and places.

True fables, myths and fairy-tales present themselves to us in perfected form as an inheritance from remote ages. Hans Andersen and Hauff are men of letters, and their works have nothing in common with true folk-tales except an external similarity of language and subject-matter. No one will ever again be able to invent a story of the kind that peasant grandmothers, a hundred years ago, used to relate to a spellbound group of children; and, what is more, our own children will never feel that particular spell again, for nowadays they read stories from books instead of listening to them. They no longer cluster at the feet of an old dame who herself half-believes the story she is telling. If a kindly aunt or uncle "tells the children a story" they do so with detachment, not as a part of their ordinary life: the story is something they can vaguely remember or have come across in a book or magazine devoted to this sort of entertainment. I can speak of this from my own knowledge, for I remember as a child sitting in twilight at the feet of my old grandmother and sharing the magic experience of a story that enthralled us both. It is sad to reflect that one will not be able to impart this feeling to others. The Grimm brothers learnt stories in this fashion by word of mouth, and strictly speaking we no longer possess the stories – we can only read them or, still worse, hear them recited at literary evenings. We have lost the world of living magic, in which we absorbed and shared the experience of our ancestors. The old forms are no more than shadows on the horizon, whose fascination we can guess at but not feel.

So much for the disappearance of this type of experience – but what must have been the exhilaration of its beginning! This is what I went to seek for in Africa. I embarked on my first journey with high hopes, choosing an area in which different races lived in close proximity. At first, however, I was disappointed. The villages along the Kwilu river, west of the Kasai, were inhabited by cannibal tribes who were constantly fighting one another, and whose only common interests in the intellectual sphere were magic spells and lawsuits *(milonga)*. Old people were almost an unknown species. As soon as anyone's hair began to grey, he or she was arraigned for cannibalism in violation of law, was sentenced to ordeal by poison and, having succumbed to this, was eaten by the rest of the tribe. Clearly the Kwilu area was not one in which to explore the development of mental culture. All I was able to collect in the way of stories were a few remnants of fables, withered leaves from a long-dead tree, of which one could guess what they were but scarcely how they had come into being.

I had better luck 200 miles further east, in the middle reaches of the Kasai, a region inhabited by the gloomy, laconic Bakuba and the cheerful Baluba; the latter were given to trade and travelling and had some excellent stories to tell. I encouraged this propensity by making it known that I was prepared to reward story-tellers generously, and it was not long before I had assembled a whole company of them. In this way I learnt important things about the narrative art: for instance, while animal fables might be related in the daytime, other tales belonged to the twilight, the hearth or the camp-fire. Stories of all kinds were related word for word as they had been handed down, and if the narrator got a word wrong he was often corrected by his audience. Gesture and intonation were even more important than the text itself, and the best story-tellers laid great weight on "atmosphere". I realized this one day when I repeated a story I had just heard and the narrator denied that he had said any such thing. After much discussion it was explained to me that the gestures, intonation and so forth carried a separate and quite different meaning from the words themselves. A translation could not give the sense of the original, since it failed to reproduce its living soul.

It follows that while verbal transcriptions of native stories may be of great value to the linguist, and while literal translations are an aid to the study of form and subject-matter, including their historical development, neither of these forms of reproduction are sufficient to convey the paid-eumatic quality of the original. Translations reflect it in the same sort of degree as a sheet of music represents a song. As the spirit of a work of imagination is destroyed by literal translation, such a work can only be preserved by a different mode of communication which may be compared to a spiritual rebirth. This process begins in the narrator's consciousness, appeals to the intuition of the hearer and spectator, and reduces language to a kind of mechanical instrument.

A missionary in the Luluaburg district set about teaching the native children French. For this purpose he translated some of Aesop's fables and made the children learn them by heart, first the Baluba and then the French version. Some of the fables are very similar to Baluba ones, and one might have supposed that they would be readily assimilated to the native stock, but not at all. Many of the tribe became acquainted with the "white man's writings" *(mukanda na m'putu)*, and I had many opportunities of noticing that they aroused lively interest. But when I asked some intelligent people one day whether they thought our European stories *(tushimuni)* as good as their own, they asked in surprise "Have the Europeans got *tushimuni* too?" When I reminded them of the fables they laughed and said those were *mukanda*, not *tushimuni*. I tried to discover what the difference was, and received the following illuminating answer.

"In the *tushimuni* everything is alive – *gabuluku* (small antelopes), *ngulu* (wild boar), *kashiama* (leopard). When the tale is told, you can hear them all speak. But the *mukanda* only tells you what happened to them once upon a time. *Tushimuni* can happen today, tomorrow or yesterday; *mukanda* are things that happened once and for all, dead things." To make himself clearer, one of the men talking to me pointed to an elephant's skull in front of the hut and said: "That *nsevu* (elephant) is dead – he can't live again, and neither can the *mukanda*. But the *tushimuni* is just as much alive as the *nsevu* that comes every night and browses on our manioc fields. The *mukanda* are dead bones, the *tushimuni* are living flesh."

The sharp distinction made by these simple yet receptive tribesmen is of great importance, and it would be hard to express better the difference between written and oral tradition. In terms of the theory expounded in this book, writing and science belong to what may be called a "factual" world, divorced from living tradition and experience. Its opposite is the "daemonic" world of poetic or artistic rapture, as we may find it in a musician performing a Beethoven sonata or an old peasant woman telling children a fairy-story. Clearly the despised African is closer to a daemonic or intuitive apprehension of the core of his civilization than are we intellectualized Westerners, from whom the paideuma is hidden by an accumulation of soulless, objective facts.

Following this line of thought, we may come to understand better how fables come to be composed, though we have not yet penetrated to the roots of the process. A disconcerting factor which I next encountered was the variability of many tales, fables and legends: motifs and whole passages repeated themselves from one context to another, and whole stories could be and were made up from bits and pieces of others. This is true of German fairy-tales as well, but is more obvious when they are told than when they are read. In my later years in North and East Africa I came across mosaics of this sort, and observed their lack of organic life: in short, primitive story-telling contains both an organic and an inorganic element.

Resuming my travels in an easterly direction, I visited the Bena Lulua area. We camped one day at Kapulumba. After the evening meal I called for a boy, but none came. I walked to the nearby village of the Baqua Tembo and found everyone, including the boys of our own party, assembled in front of a hut. The reason turned out to be that a young man had died, the last son of old Kabamba, and the bereaved father was "telling" his grief. I advanced unobtrusively and saw him sitting beside the corpse. No one uttered a sound except the old man, weeping and bewailing his loss. He did not use the word "I", but spoke only of "Kabamba". His anguished lament, repeated over and over again, took the form of the following story:

The search for the dead

"There was a man named Kabamba: he had ten children, and they all died. Day after day he cried: "Where are my ten children?" Kakashi Kakullu heard him and said: "What is the matter?" Kabamba replied: "Where are my ten children?" Kakashi Kakullu said: "Go out into the middle of the road, and you will get your answer."

Kabamba left the village and stood in the middle of the road. He heard a man coming, The man's name was Evening. Kabamba said: "Where are my ten children?" The man replied: "I am Evening," and went his way.

Another man came: it was the Hour of Talk. Kabamba said: "Where are my ten children?" The man replied: "I am the Hour of Talk," and went his way.

Another man came: it was Sound Sleep. Kabamba said: "Where are my ten children?" The man replied: "I am Sound Sleep," and went his way.

Another man came: it was Unquiet Sleep. Kabamba said: "Where are my ten children?" The man replied: "I am Unquiet Sleep," and went his way.

Another man came: it was Dawn. Kabamba said: "Where are my ten children?" The man replied: "I am Dawn," and went his way.

Another man came: it was Morning. Kabamba said: "Where are my ten children?" The man replied: "I am Morning," and went his way.

Kabamba went back to the village and said to Kakashi Kakullu: "I asked them all where my ten children were, and none of them would tell me. Kakashi Kakullu answered: "It is your own fault. If you want people to answer, you must hold them fast. If you do not, none will reply to you when you say: 'I begat ten children, all of them died, where are my ten children?' See, everything passes away — Evening, the Hour of Talk, Sound Sleep, Unquiet Sleep, Dawn and Morning. Even thus have your children passed away."

Also in the Bena Lulua country, I once met an old woman picking fruit in the bush. The people said she was a bit cracked (*gulauka kakesse*). When I asked them why, they called her and she told her story. I learnt that she had hoped to marry a certain old man and end her days with him, but that this hope had been destroyed quite recently by malicious gossip. On the day she realized this she had burst into tears and composed a fable on the subject, which she repeated again and again until she lost her wits. The fable became well known to all and sundry, and I heard it on every hand when I returned to the Kasai territory from the east a few months later. It ran as follows:

The gossiping ghost

"A woman went out into the plains to look for locusts. She was an old woman, blind in one eye and toothless. A man came over the plain towards her: he had a penis, but no testicles. He said to her: "Where are you going?" She replied: "To my village over there. Where are you going?" He said: "To my village over there." They walked together for a while and came to a big tree. The man said: "I would like to marry you." She replied: "All right." He said: "Then let us meet again here tomorrow.

What will you bring with you?" The woman said: "Yes, let us meet to-morrow under this tree. I will bring some porridge and meat." The man said: "Very well, and I will bring two calabashes of palm-wine." So they parted.

Next day the man and woman were setting out to meet each other, but there was a gossiping ghost on the prowl. It went to the man and said: "The woman says she won't marry you, because you have no testicles." So the man stayed at home and did not go to the tree. Then the ghost went to the woman and said: "The man says he won't marry you, because you have only one eye and no teeth." So the woman did not go to the tree either. Both the man and the woman stayed at home, and they never married because of the gossiping ghost."

Among the eastern Bakuba, who have intermarried with the Bena Lulua, I mostly collected tribal legends, including one about a major quarrel between two families. This began with a dispute over hunting rights and ended with two villages breaking off relations: the road be-tween them was left to be overrun by the jungle. There was a *tushimuni* about this, people told me, and it was recited as follows:

The captive road

"A father and his son went into the forest to set snares. They came to a road that many people had passed along, and the son said: "I will set my snares here." The father said: "No, this is a place where people come." The son said: "I am going to all the same," and he set a trap there. Next day he found that his mother's brother had fallen into it. He called out: "Father! I have caught an animal." The father called back: "What sort of animal?" The son said: "My mother's brother." The father replied: "I told you what would happen. Now let your uncle go free, and don't set a trap there again."

But the son disobeyed. He set his trap again, and caught his father's father the next day and his mother the day after that.

On the fifth day he caught the road itself. His father said: "Let the road go free. If you don't, how can we get back to the village?" But the son paid no attention. He took hold of the road, rolled it up into a ball and put it into a sack which he carried on his back. Then, when he and his father wanted to go home, they could see nothing but bush around them. They wandered about and could not find the village. Finally the son threw down his sack; the road jumped out of it and ran to the village, the father and son following behind. When they got to the village, the son caught the road again. People said: "It belongs to him now, it was he who caught it." The son said: "Yes, it is my road and nobody shall pass along it." So from then on nobody used the road, and it grew so sad that it died."

At that time I collected and investigated tales told by the Kwilu tribes and many others: the Bakuba, Baluba, Bena Ki, Kalebue, Wakusu, Malela, Bena Mai, Bapende, Kanioka and Bena Lulua. All these had fables and fairy-tales of their own, but in almost every case they had been handed down from antiquity. Only the Bena Lulua and tribes that had mixed with them showed any ability to create new tales. This they were very apt to do after some noteworthy event – not as a conscious act of oral composition, but as the spontaneous expression of something in their inner life which reacted in this way to the stimulus of a particular occurrence.

Attitudes to life

The problem of identifying the basic factors in the historical develop-ment of a popular culture is a major one which is once again coming to the fore, together with the question of varying cultural forms as between one people and another. I propose to give an instance of differing his-torical development leading to a corresponding difference in cultural manifestations, in the hope of throwing some light on the problem and indicating the depths which must be probed in order to explain the indi-viduality of a culture and its historical evolution.

The western Sudan, between the lower waters of the Niger and Senegal rivers, is inhabited by three indigenous groups:

1. the Ethiopians*, who wear no clothes and consist of small tribes living in separate hamlets, a clan or family to each;

2. The Gurma peoples in the east, who rule the "primitive" peasants as feudal lords; and

3. the Mande or Mandingo, representing the fourteenth-century empire of Mali. These latter have absorbed the petty tribes that formerly lived on their territory; they have a caste system of their own and inhabit most of the western part of the area, dwelling in fortified townships surrounded by rural hamlets.

The Ethiopian peasantry are in course of disappearance: among the

---

* Frobenius uses "Ethiopian" in the classical sense of "black African", and "Sudan" in the sense of a belt of territory running east and west across the whole of Africa at about the latitude of Senegal (E. H.).

Gurma they are enslaved and deprived of their livelihood, while among the Mande they become serfs under the caste system. In the one case their culture is destroyed, in the other assimilated. On the other hand, the power and influence of the warlike Gurma is in a state of decline, whereas the Mande are increasing in numbers thanks to the absorption of the "primitives" and are steadily expanding by a process of peaceful colonization. But for the European colonial powers, with their disruptive effect on native cultures, the Mande would in a short time have extended their influence over the whole of the western and central Sudan. The process, as a rule, is a gentle and almost imperceptible one. Mande traders and craftsmen make their way amongst the primitive tribes, settle peaceably in their villages and teach them industrious and orderly habits. This is an impressive work of cultural penetration, whereby people who had no contact with the outside world are brought into a system of trade and communications, production and marketing.

The Mande are able to achieve this thanks to the elaborate organization of their society, which in turn reflects the peculiarity of their racial character. In the central part of their territory, i.e. within the borders of the old Mali empire, they were and are divided into five castes. The highest caste is that of the Horro or warriors, who mostly live in the townships with the Dialli or bards, whose task is to celebrate the feats of the warriors and their ancestors in epic poems declaimed to the accompaniment of a sort of guitar. The third caste, living in hamlets, are the Ulusu or serfs, who are Ethiopian by origin but have been assimilated: they are skilled at farming and also weaving. Like their forefathers, they are bound to the soil, but the tribute of work that they owe to the Horro is very limited. Then come the caste of the Numu, comprising smiths, magicians and soothsayers: they are respected as craftsmen and feared as the custodians of ancient spells, while the caste system keeps them apart from the rest of the tribe. The fifth caste are the house slaves, known as Djong.

The caste system is strictly observed and provides the basis for a healthy, straightforward communal life. The Ulusu are devoted to the land; the Numu have a respect for race; the Horro are proud, but are held to their social duties by the Dialli and certain elders; the Djong are resigned and may even be happy, since all they lack is an illusory freedom – they can own property, marry as their heart dictates and enjoy the friendship of their masters.

Thanks to this system inherited from the Mali empire, the Mande constitute the most valuable of France's colonial subjects. Mali, however, was itself only the heir of the still more powerful kingdom of Ghana, which flourished in the early centuries of our era in the northern part of the area watered by the Senegal and the Niger, on the border between the Sudan and the Sahara. The caste system must have prevailed in pre-Christian Ghana, as is confirmed by tribal lays, chronicles and the testimony of native sages. There are, however, two schools of thought as to its origin.

The priests of Islam, and the Moorish tribes of the Sahel north of Senegal, ascribe the caste system to Mohammed himself. To the objection that Ghana existed long before the Prophet, they reply that it must have been founded by ancestors of their own, tribes from southern Arabia who migrated to Africa centuries before the hegira. The rival opinion is that Ghana was founded by invaders known as the Gara, Garanke, Garassa or Garama, a people of high civilization who came into the land long before the Fulbe [Fulani]: they originated in the north-eastern Sahara, where their graves are still ransacked for semi-precious stones and copper artefacts, and settled in Faraka, the "Mesopotamia" between the upper Niger and the Bani. Before the time of the mythical Wagadu, the Gara are said to have founded their capital city of Wagana north-east of the Niger. They are regarded by those who hold this theory as warrior heroes and cultural pioneers, the founders of the Ghana kingdom and ancestors of the modern people of the same name. To them also are ascribed the pyramidal grave-mounds, brick-red in colour, which in so many places dominate the yellow sand and the green plains. They are believed to have composed many "books of heroes" and epic tales, of which I have collected a good many and published some. The Gara, in fact, are credited with having invented the whole system of bardic song and heroic epic.

The simplest way of deciding between these two views as to the origin of the Ghanaian culture is to discover whether any people at the present day exhibits a type of culture that resembles the inherited caste system of the Mande. I myself was convinced of the rightness of the second view on a day in July 1908 when my expedition, which was travelling by river, touched at Nyafunke on the Niger. What I saw there was enlightening not only as regards the origin of Ghana but also the wider question of cultural relationships in general.

We had landed and encamped on the riverside, and a mass of people assembled from the surrounding villages. I set up a work-table as my custom was, and began by asking the names of various funeral mounds that we had encountered during the day. One of the largest pyramids was, they told me, the tomb of Samba Gana. There was an ancient bardic song about him; none of the Diallis who knew it properly could be found, but a venerable member of the tribe told me its substance as follows.

"Annallya Tu-Bari was the clever and beautiful daughter of a prince at Wagana. Many Horro came to the city and sought her in marriage, but she demanded an exploit which none of them could perform. Her father had owned a single town and many farms. He quarrelled with the lord of a neighbouring town over a farm that they both claimed; defeated in battle, he lost the farm and died of wounded pride. Annallya inherited his town and lands, and she required of every suitor that he should not only win back the disputed farm but conquer another eighty towns and villages round about. The years passed, but no warrior dared to attempt such an exploit. The years passed, and Annallya was still unmarried. She became more and more beautiful, but lost all her gaiety. Day by day she became sadder and more beautiful, and in her country all the Horro, Dialli, Numu and Ulusu lost the power to laugh also.

There was a prince at Faraka named Gana, and he had a son, Samba Gana. When the son grew up he left his father's city, as the custom was, taking with him two Dialli and two grooms, to conquer a land of his own. He was young and merry and laughed as he set out; his teacher, who went with him, was the Dialli Tararafe. He came to a city and declared war on its prince. (He challenged him to single combat.) All the people of the city watched them fight. Samba Gana won. The prince begged for his life and offered Samba Gana his city, but he laughed and said: "Keep your city, I don't want it."

Samba Gana went on his way, defeating one prince after another, but every time he laughed and said: "Keep your city, I don't want it." Finally he defeated every prince in Faraka, but he still had no city or land of his own: he gave them all back and went on his way laughing.

One day he was lying on the bank of the Niger with Tararafe. The Dialli sang a song about Annallya Tu-Bari, how beautiful and sad and lonely she was. "No man can win her and make her laugh," he sang, "until he has conquered eighty cities." Samba Gana heard this, jumped up and cried: "Grooms, saddle the horses! We are off to Annallya Tu-Bari's country." He set out with all his company, they rode day and night, day after day, and they came to Annallya Tu-Bari's city. Samba Gana saw Annallya Tu-Bari, how beautiful she was and how she never laughed. He said: "Annallya Tu-Bari, show me the eighty cities." Then he set forth and said to Tararafe: "Stay with Annallya Tu-Bari, sing to her, beguile the time and make her laugh."

Tararafe stayed in Annallya's city and sang every day of the heroes and cities of Faraka and the serpent of Issa Beer, which can make the river ebb and flow so that one year there is plenty of rice and in the next the people starve. Annallya Tu-Bari listened to all these things. Meanwhile Samba Gana rode about, fighting one prince after another. He subdued eighty princes and said to each one: "Go to Annallya Tu-Bari and tell her that your city is now hers." All eighty princes and many Horros came to Annallya Tu-Bari's city and remained there. Her city grew larger and larger, and she ruled over the princes and warriors of the whole country round about.

Samba Gana came back to Annallya Tu-Bari and said: "Behold, everything you wanted is yours." She replied: "You have done as I commanded. Now take me." Samba Gana said: "Why do you not laugh? I will not marry you unless you laugh." Annallya Tu-Bari said: "Up till now I could not laugh because of my father's shame. Now I cannot laugh because I am hungry." Samba Gana said: "What will stay your hunger?" She replied: "You must tame the serpent of Issa Beer that brings plenty in one year and dearth in another." Samba Gana said: "No man has yet been able to do this, but I will finish the task."

He went off to Faraka and sought the serpent there. Then he sought further upstream at Koriume, then at Bamba and then further still. Finally he came upon the serpent and fought with it. The fight went this way and that. The Djolliba (Niger) flowed first one way and then another. The mountains collapsed and the earth gaped asunder. For eight years Samba Gana fought the snake, and in the end he conquered it. He had split eight hundred lances and broken eighty swords, and all that he had left was a blooded sword and a blooded lance. He gave the lance to Tararafe and said: "Go to Annallya Tu-Bari, give her the lance, tell her I have conquered the serpent, and see if she will laugh now."

Tararafe went to Annallya Tu-Bari and spoke as he was bidden. Annallya Tu-Bari said: "Go back to Samba Gana and tell him to bring the serpent here, to be my slave and to govern the river in my own land. When Annallya Tu-Bari sees Samba Gana with the serpent in his hands, then she will laugh."

Tararafe went back to Faraka and told Samba Gana the words of Annallya Tu-Bari. Samba Gana said: "It is too much." He took the blooded sword, drove it into his breast, laughed once and died. Tararafe took up the sword, rode to Annallya Tu-Bari's city and said to her: "Here is Samba Gana's sword; on it is the serpent's blood, and the blood of Samba Gana. Samba Gana has laughed for the last time."

Annallya Tu-Bari called together all the princes and warriors in her city. They all mounted their horses and rode eastward to Faraka. There Annallya Tu-Bari found the body of Samba Gana. She said: "This man was a greater hero than any before him. Build him a tomb that shall surpass the tombs of all kings and heroes." So they set to work. Eight times eight hundred men dug the foundations and built the underground chamber. Eight times eight hundred built the sacrificial hall above ground, packed earth and baked it and raised a lofty pyramid.

Every evening Annallya Tu-Bari climbed to the top of the funeral mound, accompanied by her princes, Horros and Diallis. Every evening the Diallis sang the hero's praises, and every evening Tararafe sang the song of Samba Gana. Every morning Annallya Tu-Bari rose from her bed and said: "The pyramid is not tall enough. Make it so high that I can see Wagana from it." Eight times eight hundred men brought earth and packed it and baked it, and for eight years the tomb grew higher and higher. At the end of the eighth year the sun rose, Tararafe looked about him and called out: "Annallya Tu-Bari, I can see Wagana." Annallya Tu-Bari looked westward and said: "Yes, I can see Wagana. Now Samba Gana's tomb is as great as his name deserves." Then she laughed and said: "Now, my princes and warriors, be off with you and show the whole world that you can be heroes as brave as Samba Gana was." She laughed once again, then she died and was buried in the chamber with Samba Gana. But the eight times eight hundred princes and warriors rode off, each one separately, and they fought and became great heroes."

Having heard the elder's story, I naturally asked questions about the families of the Ghana kingdom, its extent and the regions inhabited by its peoples. One of the gathering was a sheikh from the Mauritanian tribe of the Trarza, nomads living far to the west in the area north of the Senegal. He knew those parts well and gave me much useful information about them. Being a devout Moslem he insisted that Ghana must have been founded from southern Arabia, whereas the old man who had told the story of Samba Gana was convinced that the Gara-Gana had been on the scene long before the Arabs and Islam. The sheikh grew heated, after the manner of his people, and finally spluttered: "The whole earth belongs to the Arabs and Islam, as far as its uttermost boundary." To my question where that boundary was, he replied: "At the place where the sky touches the earth." The village elder broke in to say: "The sky does not touch the earth." This gave me the cue to ask their respective views on the structure of the universe, the earth, sky and stars. They answered as follows.

The Trarza believe that the earth is a flat expanse which the sky covers in the shape of a vault. The sun, moon and stars are attached to the underside of the vault and move about its surface "like a herd of grazing camels". There is nothing beyond the vault: God Himself dwells within it. If the vault were to collapse it would destroy Him together with all the heavenly bodies and angels and every living creature upon earth. Nobody knows whether such a thing could happen or not – if it did, it would be *kismet*.

The elder took a different view. The earth, he said, had no end and no boundaries (though he lacked a word for "infinite"). A man might roam about it for ever, either by land or by sea. There were places inhabited by winged serpents, others with birds that could talk, and others with trees that spoke and behaved like human beings. All these things were beyond that part of the earth that is known to us, but they were still on the earth, and a man might reach them if he travelled far enough. The sky did not touch the earth at any point: it was in fact not a tangible thing, only an effect of light and shade. The heavenly bodies moved, as God ordained, in the unbounded space above the earth; many thought, too, that there were "people" or creatures up there who could affect human destiny, though not so far as to prevent a man achieving ends that he desired and that were within his power. This was shown in olden times by the Gana race: those of them who were cowardly and incapable had met a miserable end, but those who displayed vigour and courage had become kings. If a truly great Gana were born today, he could drive all the Arabs and Europeans out of the land and restore the glory of the ancient kingdom.

In subsequent writings I have discussed the human tendency to form a world view in one of two basic ways, which may be called the spatial or extensive (*Weitengefühl*) and the enclosed or intensive (*Höhlengefühl*) respectively. I have also used the term "mental dimension" to express the difference between these. The Trarza view described above is clearly of the "enclosed" variety, while that of the elder reflects the aspiration towards infinite space. The first attitude is characterized by constraint, rigidity and fatalism, a permanent state of pressure relieved from time to time by fanatical outbursts. Opposed to it is a sense of yearning and infinity, an urge to create and to improve the world, and a delight in freedom. The dichotomy between these attitudes is not confined to the Sahel area: they coexist elsewhere in Africa as in Europe, where we have Frenchmen on the one hand, Englishmen and Frisians on the other.

A people whose attitude is of the "intensive" type may be dominated by another for centuries and remain unaware of the restricted nature of its existence, but it cannot itself rule other peoples without destroying them. Only a people of the "extensive" type can produce a sound caste organization, an organic culture with the power of expansion, a capacity for self-rewarding and creative work. It follows that the admirable social structure of the Mande people, their colonizing ability and urge to extend their boundaries can only have been derived from the mysterious Gana race from the north-west. Qualities like these could never have been instilled, preserved and developed by Arabs or other Semites from the east, whose psychological make-up is essentially of the "intensive" kind. If we consider epic tales like that of Samba Gana, Goroba Dike, Samba Kullung or Gossi, we find them imbued with spiritual greatness: the heroism and energy of the main characters is not diminished by any philosophy imposed from without, but is governed and directed by their own inner qualities.

"The eight times eight hundred princes and warriors rode off, each one separately, and they fought and became great heroes." That is the true spirit of the "extensive" culture. One may search for it in vain in the folklore of Oriental countries, where instead of spiritual energy we find miracles and magic, sensation and fatalism. The Oriental bedecks the vault above his head with costly ornament as an escape from the pressure and everlasting anxiety that weighs upon him.

Knowledge

In vast areas of Africa we still find variants of a culture that was known to the ancient world and respected in Homeric times for its distinctive quality. Already the Greeks spoke of the "blameless Ethiopians"*, and many centuries later the Moslems called the peoples in question "the trustworthy unbelievers". Gustav Nachtigal, the great nineteenth-century explorer, wrote that lying, theft and breach of one's given word were unknown among them. This, however, is not purely a moral judgement. The people belonging to this culture differ individually, no less than other men, in their characters and fortunes, their propensities for good and evil in whatever sense one uses these terms. What distinguishes them to the discerning eye is their culture as a whole, contemplated in every sense – broad and narrow, collective and personal. This culture has endured for at least 2,500 years and is so organic and visible a part of their lives as to give a unique insight, without parallel in any other part of the world known to me, into their innermost thoughts and feelings,

* s. p. 30.

so that we become aware of types of knowledge different and anterior to our own.

The Ethiopians are mainly peasants, and are no less industrious in Senegal than on the banks of the Nile. They are organized in patriarchal clans, with whole families living together on large farmsteads, often within fortifications. The oldest able-bodied man is the head of the community: his brothers, sons, nephews and grandchildren do as he tells them, and the old and infirm are under his care. He sees to the distribution of food and the use of resources of all kinds: profit, loss and enjoyment are regulated by him in accordance with ancient custom. The menfolk of this small unit take wives from outside the community.

The paterfamilias has authority over both material and spiritual life, and this he exercises according to a uniform pattern inherited from one generation to another. He oversees the sacrifice of seed and harvest, the order of burial and the cult of departed souls. He ordains feasts and ceremonies, above all those that mark the successive ages of man and the addition of new growth-rings to the family tree. The "ages" are distinguished with great precision in accordance with the laws of physical nature. Wherever Ethiopian culture has survived in its pure state and not fallen into decadence, a man's life is divided into four stages: (1) boyhood, up to the approach of puberty; (2) young men and the newly married; (3) married men with children, the most vigorous and experienced of those in the prime of life becoming the head of the family group; and (4) aged men, unable to work and losing their mental faculties, who are assigned a portion sufficient to keep them alive. This classification by age and physical status is applied automatically and is as fundamental to Ethiopian culture as the caste system is to that of the Mande.

However, the truly distinctive feature of Ethiopian culture, making it unique in the world as far as I know, is its purity of style, the harmonious interlocking and fusion of material, social and spiritual life. Every secular act is at the same time a religious one; every material instrument serves a purpose in the sphere of mind. To the Ethiopian, no contradiction exists between the daemonic and the factual. Such is the inner harmony of this "blameless" outlook that a high degree of morality prevails as a matter of course and is only threatened when the organic purity and unity of society is impaired by contact with foreign cultures.

Some aspects of the Ethiopian culture may strike us as ruthless. For instance, the death of an aged man is a signal for general jubilation, and if you ask why you will be told: "He was too old to work, he was no use on the farm any more." If, on the other hand, a young man without children dies, everyone is plunged into an ecstasy of grief, and the reason given is that: "He was still useful at farming, and as he left no children he cannot be born again: he has left nobody who can help him to re-enter this world."

The burial rites are significant. After an aged man has been laid in the earth and his body has decayed, the skull is removed from the funeral chamber to a consecrated place; here sacrifice is made to it at appropriate seasons, as at seed-time and harvest, and especially when a young member of the family takes a wife. On this occasion it is invoked by the youth's father as follows: "Grandfather, we beg you to return. You have been long gone from us, and we have all too few young people. My son has married this young wife: she is strong, well brought up and knows how to look after children, as I have seen her with her nephews and nieces. She has ample breasts and will give much milk. I beg you to return in this young woman, so that my son may beget strong children and he and I may soon cease to work in the fields." Before this prayer, it is a frequent custom to scatter seed-corn on the skull; then when the father has finished his invocation, the bride puts her lips to the skull and eats the corn. When she bears a child, it is deemed to be the resurrected grandfather.

The custom of swallowing the seed-corn is symbolic of the profound association between agriculture and social life. The element that unites the dead with the living is mother earth, in which the last remnants of life decay and its first germination takes place, so that birth and death are merged into a single act. As an African from the Gongola region explained to me: "When a young man dies, it is like a dry leaf that falls and rots on the ground; but an old man dying is like a ripe fruit that falls into the earth and grows up out of it again. A man is like a grain of sorghum. If you pluck it when it is unripe, dry it and then plant it in the next rainy season, it will rot; but if you do the same when it is ripe, it will put forth roots and leaves and bear fruit. The same is true of mankind. A young man cannot be born again, but an old man can."

Another remarkable custom is a major sacrifice which takes place every few years, the ritual murder or regicide of the chief man in the tribe, the high priest or "priest-king", as he is called in old writings. I met one of these men among the Kirri in the central Sudan. Like several other Dakka "princes" he was to undergo the sacrificial death in the following year; he spoke of it as something quite natural, with a calm that astonished us. "In the last few years", he explained, "the rains have been scanty and the harvest bad; once I am dead, the rains will be more plentiful." Later on he said: "I have a grandson of whom I am very fond. He will marry a woman of good stock, and when I come back from the forest I shall be reborn as his child." He said all this in a contented, matter-of-course way, as one might speak of a trip one had planned: many a European might have shown more agitation over moving house, especially if it were from one city to another.

At the same time, there are differentiations in this type of spiritual existence. Knowledge and experience are coterminous, but there are significant varieties of the latter, as the following example may show.

After the ritual murder of the high priest, the young men of the tribe undergo the first, initiatory stage of their life in the bush. First of all they are circumcised, the blood being regarded as a sacrificial offering to the dead king. The operation is performed by a priest wearing a token disguise as a leopard: he is painted with spots, wears a leopard-skin apron and carries his implements in a bag made from one of the animal's claws. Bearing in mind that the leopard is a sacred beast, the totem of the slaughtered kings and, in a sense, the spirit of the forest, we interpret the ceremony as follows. The king is sacrificed, and the blood of the circumcised offered up to him, in order that he may become a benevolent spirit of the bush. Those who are destined to make clearings for farmsteads, and thus wound his forest realm, are by this rite inflicting a wound on themselves in order to appease his displeasure. This, at all events, is a description in crude language of what is in fact a deeply religious sentiment.

Amongst the Kirri I spoke about the circumcision rite to some lads who had undergone it a few years before, and also to a group of older men. There was a subtle difference in their answers. The young men said: „We were circumcised by a leopard, and he was the former king." The others, however, said: "When the priest, as a leopard, circumcises the boys, he is the former king"; and in another Kirri village I was told: "It is the former king, as a leopard, who performs the circumcision." The interesting point here is not that the replies should be different: this may happen amongst any people whose actions are based on feeling, and we find plenty of contradictions in the fully mythologized cultures which come closest to the Ethiopian but are, so to speak, one degree beyond it in this respect. The important distinction to my mind, however, is that the boys describe the performer of the rite as a leopard, while the grown men describe him as a human being in the role of a leopard. This shows that, in the Ethiopian as in other cultures, the individual psyche undergoes a process of evolution. The change from a real leopard to something or somebody acting as one illustrates a difference of apperception from one age-group to another. This phenomenon may be called one of paideumatic variation, and is a basic characteristic of the creative period.

The stages of paideumatic evolution

When I was working on my study of the Masks and Secret Societies of Africa I noticed for the first time the importance of the age-class organization among many peoples of Africa and Oceania. Among simpler tribes and sometimes also among more developed ones, we find the custom that men of the same age (and occasionally women) form associations which, either for a time or permanently, lead a separate existence from the main body of society as regards methods of husbandry, the provision of food, dwelling-places and sexual relations. Frequently it is not just single groups that split off in this way, but the whole tribe is divided more or less sharply into different age-classes. The number of these appears at first sight to vary, but on the whole there seems to be an original or "natural" division into three. In many cases I noticed that a larger number of groups had developed from the basic three or resolved themselves into that number; and in tribes whose social organization was no longer founded on age-classes, it was possible to identify remnants of such groups that were always based on a threefold division.

The three classes consist of boys up to about the age of puberty, marriageable or newly married young men and the elders. In West Africa these classes provide the framework for the highly important institution of secret societies, which often represent the real power by contrast to the nominal authority of the chiefs, who may be compared to our village mayors. These societies attract attention, as far as externals are concerned, by masquerades, initiation and seasonal festivals, dances and "orgies" which have received much notice from explorers: they display an inner unity despite much variation of detail. The societies have their meeting-houses and sacred groves, their consecrated grounds and places of sacrifice, with an elaborate and strictly observed ritual. However, their activity is basically the same in simple communities as in those where local variations have blurred or complicated the original pattern. It may be described as follows.

Women and children do not belong to the secret society. They must not enter its holy places, and they must hide behind closed doors as soon as the masked men appear in the village street. When boys reach the age of puberty, they go through what is usually called an "initiation" ceremony. They are taken into the bush and live there for a longer or shorter time, during which they are made to witness various horrific

41

scenes. Then, before returning to their native village, they are tattooed or have their teeth filed or their hair cut in a special way, denoting that they have come to man's estate and are full members of their tribe. This rite often includes circumcision. Many natives believe that during this period the youths are actually sacrificed or devoured by the bush-spirit and then reborn. Travellers and missionaries have tried to find out what arts and mysteries are taught in the bush, on the assumption that there is a genuine initiation into tribal secrets. But this is not so: the ceremony is purely one of enrolment, conferring a right to take part in "palavers", i. e. the tribe's deliberations, negotiations and judicial proceedings.

The leaders of the societies are "elders", aged thirty-five and over – men of judgement and experience, with plenty of wives and with grown-up children, so that they no longer have to do much work at home or in the fields. These are the true "initiates": they have custody of the masks and ordain the times of sacrifice. They possess knowledge of old customs and traditions, and can be trusted to see that decisions are the fruit of reflection and not of impulse. It is sometimes said that they have the last word in matters of law and government and in deciding between peace and war. This is true in places where the societies take secret decisions which are binding on the community in a more or less dictatorial fashion; but this state of affairs only prevails in certain senile states and tribal communities in West Africa, just as in the West it is societies past their prime which evolve and tolerate the exercise of Caesarian power. By contrast, those communities in West Africa which still possess their youthful vigour are governed and administered by the decisions of a popular assembly. In that assembly the elders, it is true, have the principal say. But, looking back over the many tribal palavers that I have been allowed to witness, one fact stands out clearly. The elders, as already explained, are the depositaries of law and tradition; they have experience of events, they know the qualities and failings of their tribe and are skilled in unravelling complications, but in the normal course of events it is not they who possess the intellectual and political initiative. This belongs to the young men in their twenties or early thirties. Again and again I have seen how the elders, either from indolence or for their own advantage, stood up for "tradition", but were opposed by younger men advocating something unheard-of and unprecedented – and how often the young men were right and, albeit after a long wrangle, were admitted to be so.

In debates of this sort the age-classes played a manifest part, with conservative elders ranged against innovating youth, the champions of action and evolution against those of petrified form. At the same time, while the ideas may come from the younger generation, the elders carry them out in such a way as to preserve their own dignity and authority: the young are not permitted to exult in victory, and are prevented from fully realizing their own significance as a class.

Examples of this sort show the fundamental importance of the age-class system, which is by no means confined to primitive societies: it may be seen at work in all communities and periods of history, be it in modern times or among the ancient Romans and Egyptians. One does not have to look hard to perceive the importance of determining whether, in a particular state, the reins of true (not apparent) power are in the hands of an older or a younger generation, and it is also clear how profoundly the health of the body politic depends on the harmonious co-operation of the two groups in question.

The West African examples also show how the division into age-classes corresponds to the evolution, through life, of the human mind and character. The successive stages of mental development affect every aspect of life, be it concerned with work, family or possessions, with politics or with law. To belong to a particular age-class is not a conscious decision but a function of human growth, an inevitable process whereby individuals of similar status, "speaking the same language", tend to form a unity. This has happened more or less obviously in all cultures, at all times and places; and we are led to conclude that the human mind evolves according to regular laws which find their natural expression in the system of age-groups.

As I have argued elsewhere, cultural manifestations are to be regarded as expressions of an organic unity which is not something man-made so much as something that imposes itself on men. We call this "culture", but the term is too vague and hackneyed on the one hand and too specific on the other. For this reason, and to express something both broader and deeper, I adopted the term "Paideuma". This may be described as a substantive entity with its own laws of development, unfolding in three main stages: first "intuitively" in the daemonic world of childhood, then "idealistically" in the cultural and intellectual world of youth, and finally "mechanistically" in the active world of grown men. After these three organic stages comes the inorganic condition of senility.

The paideuma in the daemonic world of childhood

A scholar is writing at his desk; his four-year-old daughter is running about the room and, to give her something to do, he offers her three dead safety-matches and says "Play with these." The child christens them Hansel, Gretel and the Witch and plays happily on the floor while her father gets on with his work. Suddenly the child gives a cry of terror and runs to him saying: "Daddy, take the witch away, I'm frightened to touch her any more."

Many parents will be able to remember incidents of this kind, where a child has been absorbed in a private world and suddenly undergoes an emotional shock due to the workings of its own imagination. The match turns from a "pretend" witch into a real one; or, to put it another way, the notion of the witch shifts of its own accord from the plane of intellectual make-believe to that of sensation. The transition itself is invisible to the mind, which is only aware of the changed state of affairs. Yet the process of turning a matchstick into a witch is eminently a creative one.

The paideuma, in this instance, has a kind of spiritualizing quality, for which Goethe in *Wilhelm Meister* uses the word *vergeistert*. The child's consciousness is filled with something enigmatic and magical, a daemonic element reflecting the paideuma in its infantile phase. This phase may be called one of "becoming"; it is characterized by a process which escapes conscious thought (the mind being only aware of its result) and which may be regarded as belonging to the most primitive level of apperception.

The daemonic is not perceived by the intellect except through its effects. We observe this in adult human beings who are seized by religious ecstasy or the "daemon" of artistic creation, and who are unable afterwards to describe their condition. Yet it is of such significance that one would have expected much more attention to be given to it. The reason it has been neglected is no doubt firstly that it only occurs in children, primitives and geniuses, and secondly that, even in them, it only presents itself fully in a sporadic and spontaneous manner.

The importance of such daemonic moments is that they display a culture or paideuma in its creative aspect, with an elemental force that no adult can equal, be he the greatest artist or scholar in the world. Moreover the phenomenon as we see it in children is not merely an occasional one but a regular manifestation of the paideuma, whereas with an adult genius it occurs only by way of exception. If a child is given an elaborately made doll, carved and dressed to represent a human being as exactly as possible, and also a roughly hewn piece of wood with a rag by way of clothing, it will soon discard the first and lavish affection on the second. The natural child will have no truck with naturalism – it prefers a scrap of material, a ball of twine, a stone or a matchbox, for it is on these that the paideuma of infancy delights to exercise its creative power. A child's life in and with the daemonic – what we customarily refer to as the "play instinct" – is nothing less than essential creativity, and the paideuma of childhood can only exist and develop while the opportunities for such creativity are provided.

In the child's world, the daemonic and the factual exist in a particular relationship to each other. The facts and objects that are within the child's awareness are at once the raw material and the framework of its creative development. This, at all events, is true in the natural state; in the cultivated paideuma, on the other hand, as I shall show, the daemonic element is increasingly stifled by a plethora of intellectual objects introduced from without. Cultivation of this sort is in fact the enemy of the daemonic and, by the same token, very often of genius as well. In the natural world of infancy, the daemonic power dominates impressions of the external world and uses them as the subject-matter of creation. Then, as the individual reaches maturity, what were previously isolated and sporadic moments of divination merge into a unity of self-awareness and a system of ideas which, by their permanence, coherence and effectiveness, represent the culmination of paideumatic development.

However, in adult life no less than in that of children, true creativity springs from the impulses of genius. Philosophers and musicians, painters and sculptors have time and again been inspired to their greatest work by some overwhelming sorrow. Many folk-tales, and hundreds of works of literature, bear witness to this theme. The daemon or genius, call it which we will, requires to be awakened by a natural shock, either from within a man's mind or from without. The more creative an individual is, the more his nature demands a life full of change and incident, to provide the impulses which transform intellect into direct awareness.

It is, however, a superficial view to regard emotion as creative in itself. The powers of genius in which the paideuma finds expression were already in being when the emotional shock was received; the latter's function was only to transfer them from one plane to another. Thus the manifestations of genius in advanced years are similar to those in childhood. In the first, naively daemonic stage it displays itself in a random and spontaneous manner; then, as awareness of self develops, this sporadic quality disappears. But genius preserves its spontaneity in every age, though less obviously so in later life.

The daemonic, as opposed to intellectual apprehension, is the vital element in the paideuma, the expression of its first development, while ideas and facts represent ensuing stages. From this point of view, the paideuma signifies life and fulfilment and is the antithesis of knowledge.

It can, of course, be transposed into logical and communicable terms, but its ultimate essence is private to the individual and cannot be imparted to anyone else.

The paideuma in the "ideal" world of early manhood

As compared with the child's paideuma which creates a witch out of a matchstick, we find that in young men the creative faculty is expressed in a relationship to the world of fact as apprehended by the intellect: what was daemonic is now idealistic; i. e. formulated in terms of ideas. These are no longer spontaneous, sporadic and incoherent, but are logically consistent elements of a conception of the world which may still be intuitive but obeys the laws of causality.

The daemonic is in itself a thing of the mind; at this stage, however, it may seize upon the objects of sense and present itself as a specific daemon, or *numen* as the Romans would have said, divorced from conscious awareness and possessing a tangible reality of its own. This, however, is not the main point. As we saw, the child's daemon is essentially spontaneous and sporadic, subject to constant change unhampered by the judgement of the senses, and the significance of its activity lies in detachment from the objects of sense as a means to the formation of paideumatic elements. These do not at first join into a coherent whole, but they develop into ideals in so far as the mental faculty interpenetrates the world of reality. In other words, the human being becomes aware of his own self as a separate entity, the "I" of the paideuma over against the external world. This dualistic perception, the second phase of the paideuma, may be termed that of individuality.

We may see from this why the ancient Greeks regarded themselves as the only people in the full sense of the term, all the rest being "barbarians"; and, by the same token, why we in the West talk about "world history" when we mean the origins and development of our own culture, ignoring all others. In the same way, an adolescent in a state of turmoil is incapable of recognizing any destiny but his own and defies the authority of parents, friends and teachers whom up now he has treated with veneration.

The ideas of early manhood are thus similar in origin to the daemonic impulses of the child, but differ in so far as they represent a conscious, permanent and logical association of the mind with external reality. They begin with the individual's awareness of his ego, which itself constitutes the first of his ideas.

The possession of ideas is synonymous with the ability to develop a culture, provided they are such as to transform the external world, considered as an organic whole, into an equally organic paideuma. This is a creative and inspirational act, and the term "style" may properly be used of its consequences.

Ideas as we have defined them belong to a specific and fairly short period in the lives of individuals and peoples. In the cultures known to us they are confined to the period of development that corresponds to adolescence in human beings; but as far as individuals are concerned, one can think of many geniuses whose lives continued to be informed by seminal ideas at an advanced age. Ideas remain alive as long as they encompass reality in a harmonious manner. What causes them to wither and die is the proliferation of intellectual knowledge, experience and pragmatic decisions which is summed up nowadays under the heading of "intelligence".

The paideuma of facts in the world of maturity

As impetuous youths turn into level-headed men, so ideas turn into facts. Ideas, as we saw, arise from the self-identification of the ego, the opposition and fruitful interaction of the self and the outside world. The ego creates a universe for itself, making a spiritual abode out of a physical location. Ideas are their own justification: they arise from the joyful, springlike consciousness of the self, oblivious of time, delighting in the present moment with no thought of the past. Daemonic intuition, unpredictable as lightning, knows nothing of time or space. Ideas, by contrast, have a spatial though not a temporal existence: they are an expression of consciousness but not of the reasoning faculty. They stand in a continuous relationship to the external world and undergo its effects; this world, however, is a kaleidoscope or growth, existence and decay. Ideas represent, first and foremost, the awareness of existent things, but transience is not far from their horizon. Once at their zenith they are bound, being conscious, to feel the onset of a decline. Concern for survival sets in; the outside world becomes more obtrusive; anxiety and self-preservation lead to the analysis of experience and the adjustment of means to ends, in short the use of practical reason.

The autumnal concern for the preservation of the self introduces the element of rational causality, the austerity of the intellect and the full development of "facts". Whereas ideas were an end in themselves, facts are harnessed to material purposes. They arise in and from the mind, so that this phenomenon of causality is incomparably easier to recognize, both in its origin and in its manifold effects, than that of daemonic creativity or the individuality of personal ideas. The dominant feature is a restriction of the conception of the self, which ceases to be an ideal counterpart to the factual world and instead, in its intellectual aspect, becomes merely a part thereof. This process is accompanied by a dissolution of the harmony of which we spoke earlier.

Whereas in the adolescent stage the paideumatic self stands over against the factual world, in the adult stage the sense of self evolves in the direction of causal incorporation in it, by way of the systematic accumulation of experience. This produces a mechanistic view of the world, with intuition giving place to knowledge and reflection.

Whereas ideas comprehended the whole vast field of reality as a counterpart to the self, the factual approach concentrates on details of the world mechanism and weighs them against the self in particular instances. Out of these details the intellect creates a pitiful structure which it presumptuously calls the "natural world" and which it regards as the only ultimate reality, thus rejecting whatever stands outside the cause-and-effect nexus. Oblivious of the titanic grandeur of a world illuminated by ideas, the intellect ascribes value only to phenomena which can be proved by science and put to practical use. The word "value" suggests the process whereby the individual learns to say "for me" instead of "I". The self of the ideal world was a power; the self of the factual world is no more than a measuring device. Instead of contemplating facts it is itself one of them, a central standard by which everything, including space, time and power is measured and evaluated. The organic sense of power is replaced by awareness of mechanical forces which can be put to practical account. Geometrical calculation acts as a substitute for the sense of space, and clock-time for the awareness of life and destiny.

Finally, the factual approach is characterized above all by anxiety and the intellectual preoccupation with causes. It is a mistake to talk here of "necessity" which, as we are so often told, is the stimulus of all progress towards civilization. Certainly necessity is an imperious force among primitive peoples, but in the paideumatic context it gives rise to anxiety only at the factual stage of evolution, in association with the dawning notion of transience and causality. It is only the intellectual apprehension of causality and purpose that enables anxiety to become a rational and effective force. Cultural progress, on the other hand, is typically the product of the adolescent phase, that of ideas.

To illustrate what I mean I will give some examples from the history of hoeing and ploughing. Until recently it was supposed that both these techniques were consciously invented by mankind under the pressure of necessity.

Among a people in the northern Cameroons – a Chamba tribe which had been driven from the low country to the hills – I found that it was their custom to go down to the plains in autumn and harvest the corn that was growing wild on their former fields. Then in spring the people would come back with wooden implements and plant the seeds here and there as a sacrifice to mother earth. When the corn sprang up they used it to make dumplings which were shared equally between the women of the tribe and the ancestral spirits. In this way the women were supposed to be prepared for the rebirth of the tribe's forefathers, who were closely associated with the fruits of the earth. At the same time, the tribe also harvested the corn which had grown of its own accord on the fields in question, but this had no sacramental character and was eaten by everybody.

This example allows us to perceive the origin of hoe culture. The first stage was evidently to harvest the wild-growing corn. This was then "idealized" into the custom whereby, as an expression of gratitude to mother earth and reparation for the wound inflicted on her, seeds were re-inserted into her bosom, but the fruit of this sacrificial planting was kept separate from profane uses. It was not until a later period that hoe culture became a secular and rational pursuit.

The paideuma of peoples: forms and periods

The area between the Niger and the Nile is inhabited by hundreds of different tribes, but if they are studied from the paideumatic point of view they will be found at once to fall into two main groups. This applies especially to those in the Hausa region, with which we are here mainly concerned.

Tribes of the first group live in small communities and have no market economy; their language often differs from one village to the next, and their social system has hardly evolved beyond the clan or extended family. Those of the second group, on the other hand, are town-dwellers, and their language extends over a wide area; they have an advanced political and economic system, with organized professions, guilds, large markets and active trade relations. I distinguish these basically different types of culture as "horizontal" and "vertical" respectively.

Those who belong to the horizontal culture are generally laconic. In converse with them one soon realizes that they regard every human being as an individual type. They "feel" the characters of others, whether acquaintances or strangers, and behave towards them with friendliness or aversion. They have a well organized mental universe in which – and this is true both paideumatically and symbolically – every set of household possessions has its own appointed role, every tree and stone is different from every other, every value is fixed and immutable: everything, in fact, has its own unchangeable and unmistakable existence. People of this culture share a collective destiny from which all questioning is excluded and in which no one dreams of the possibility that things may appear differently to different people.

Members of the vertical culture, on the other hand, no sooner meet a person than they attempt to place him in some category. They are less interested in the individual than in the class to which he belongs and by which they judge him. They are always ready to trade or negotiate, enjoy conversation and are eager to explore new opinions which may affect their lives.

People of these two groups see life in synthetic and analytic terms respectively. To the first group fate is something general, to the second something particular. The former inhabit a daemonic universe which is alike for all; among the latter, each has his separate view of reality. The paideuma of the first is almost wholly barbaric in character, while that of the second is chiefly mechanistic.

The two types of culture live in close physical proximity but affect each other very little. The horizontal culture usually begins a mile or two from the city wall. What we are concerned with here is the course of paideumatic evolution, and the significant point is that in the Hausa area I found that every political formation of the vertical cultures went hand in hand with a change of geographical location and also a change from one paideumatic stage to another. Each state was originally founded by one of the "horizontal" peoples, but it never enjoyed a second period of vigour under the rule of its founders. The formation of a state was accompanied by the development of language, a specific variety of decorative art and probably also poetry (the creation of legends). This evolution, however, came to an end as political life assumed a rigid form. The process may in fact be described as follows: (1) the paideuma of the horizontal culture is of the childlike or daemonic kind; (2) the formation of states, accompanied by a geographical shift, represents the short heyday of the youthful idea; and (3) the period of vertical culture in cities is marked by the almost complete domination of the factual viewpoint of mature manhood. Barbarism bears fruit for a short time in culture before declining into mechanicism. This may go far to explain a simple and frequent experience. When horizontal peoples suddenly evolve political forms in this way, it is not only the leaders but the whole tribe that changes its location. Having conquered the new territory, they build fortified cities to protect themselves and the "facts" of their environment against the indigenous horizontal culture and its daemonic elements.

This state of affairs may be compared with the corresponding forms observable in nations of advanced culture and the Mande tribes as distinguished from the Hausa peoples.

We in Europe also have both extremes, with horizontal cultures in the countryside and vertical ones in the cities. The peasantry and townsfolk exist on different levels, but the distinguishing fact in Europe is that both classes belong to the same nation, race and speech. They interact upon each other, to a degree that is still perceptible even though modern life is reducing it more and more. There are cultivated country-dwellers as well as cultivated town-dwellers, and quite often they have more in common with each other – especially in countries where there are large landowners – than they do with the less educated members of their respective cultures.

Among the Hausa peoples we found a horizontal culture imbued with daemonic feeling, and a vertical one distinguished by factual sense, in complete isolation from each other. In European societies the two are similarly opposed but are in a state of constant interplay, as differences of education cut across those of geography, especially where small towns are concerned.

This, however, is not true only in the West. An example is provided in Africa by the Faraka-Mande area in the western Sudan. Here we find a network of vertical culture, consisting of small fortified market-towns connected by busy roads, superimposed on a horizontal culture covering the whole area. Owing to the influx of a northern people the population of town and country is uniform in both race and language, and the barriers between them are slight. The vertical culture is not self-contained. In the small townships, for example, anything which is about to give birth, a woman, a horse, a she-dog, is brought to the countryside to give birth on a soil which provides healthy foodstuffs and where work is healthy. At the same time, the population is strictly divided according to learning and occupation. The Horro (warriors and rulers) and the Dialli (bards), the smiths with their stores of legends and fancies, the Ulusu (peasants) all live alongside one another, and their interaction enriches the paideuma of the individual as well as of the community.

The Horro and Dialli on the one hand, the smiths and Ulusu on the other, represent two different cultural stages. To the second group belong fairy-tales and fables, which are highly popular, the traditional mask societies and shamanism; while the former have produced sublime bardic songs, richly adorned costumes, imposing monuments and ancient palaces.

If we compare the works of imagination produced by the two groups, we find that the fables and so on are universally current, impersonal in their themes and not subject to alteration. The bardic lays, on the other hand, tell of individual feats and destinies and are the work of conscious artists whose creative gifts have been improved by training in professional guilds.

A division of this kind into two groups is the mark of all civilized as opposed to primitive peoples, from ancient Egypt to our own day. The Egyptians lived in mud huts alongside rock-hewn temples; the Greeks and Romans had their myths as well as their dramas and schools of philosophy, and in modern times we have the folk-song as well as the fugue.

The paideuma of an earlier day lives on at the lower level and continues to exercise a daemonic influence on the higher, in which ideas find their place as a monument to the creative self. The daemonic spiritual forces at work on the lower level constitute the roots of the paideuma, be it that of a people or of an individual. We may see this by contemplating the decline and fall of any culture, however monumental it may be; naturally enough, for the creation and perfection of a city, as the abode of pure actuality, means an end to daemonic influences.

Thus the development of the paideuma can be clearly marked off into periods. The first stage, which I call the creative period, is typically preserved in the Ethiopian culture of the Hausa region: it is tectonic in character, that is to say it establishes the broad outline or ground plan of a culture on the basis of essential spiritual data. The Mande-Faraka culture, on the other hand, is a two-level one and belongs to what I call the formative period, the origins of which may be dated from the time of Babylon and Egypt.

The formative period witnesses the appearance of an upper layer of society which allows play to the individual paideuma and, in supreme cases, to individual genius. During the creative period the individual soul was only a microcosm of the community. The communal soul, as we have seen it reflected in the horizontal cultures of the Hausa peoples, develops in the formative period into a national paideuma such as we find amongst the Mande.

It will be clear from what we have said that the wealth of these forms is less easily appreciated by those who regard the primitive environment as purely chaotic, and who deny any distinctive features to the paideuma of humanity in such conditions. Moreover, this attitude prevents a full understanding of the infinite ramifications of paideumatic development. As we have seen, the spiritual life of every individual passes through phases that can be defined as barbarism, culturism and mechanicism, and the same is true of the development of a community or a nation. The creative and formative periods express themselves in forms corresponding to the paideuma of childhood and youth respectively; and as the formative period evolves into mechanicism, it gives place to a third and final stage which we may call the period of fulfilment.

This can also be looked at from another point of view. If we consider the rapid extension of modern civilization with its means of communication and transport and the demands of commerce and finance, the ever-encroaching empire of books and newspapers, the telephone and telegraph, we may well imagine how short a time it will be before the entire habitable globe is enveloped by these manifestations of a pragmatic and mechanistic age. No community on earth will any longer enjoy the isolation and seclusion which is necessary for the ideas of a national paideuma to take shape and develop into a culture. The unbridled urge for expansion, the triumph of will and factual purpose over daemonism, and the resulting impossibility of separate national cultures – all this means that the formative period is evolving towards a state of affairs in which new monumental forms can no longer be created, that is to say a state of absolute decline. What happens then?

In the creative period, the paideuma found expression chiefly on the plane of feeling; society was undifferentiated, and the individual was inseparable from the community. In the formative period society consists of two levels, the individual is emancipated and the paideuma develops on the plane of intellect. In the period of fulfilment, when every national or local paideuma is merged in a world-wide one, the geographical difference between horizontal and vertical cultures will lose importance as compared with the community of culture at different levels of education. We may expect to see three levels instead of two, characterized respectively by feeling, intellect and reason – a threefold division corresponding to those of the daemonic (childlike), the ideal (adolescent) and the factual (pertaining to manhood), or again to the sequence of barbarism, culturism and mechanicism.

In the undifferentiated type of society, the individual was inseparable from the communal soul and this fact was expressed by the institution of age-classes. The daemonic element displayed itself in the community undisturbed by any individual action. Humanity at this period had no history, since the community as an undivided whole had not developed the sense of time. Permanence appeared to be in the nature of things; the dominant sense was that of the here and now.

With the development of the self and of ideas came the dichotomy between "myself and the world" and that between "my own time and the time before me". The transience of the ideal was expressed more and more clearly in the rapid transformation of ideas into facts, lending this period an essentially episodic character.

The third and last period, however, will be marked by a harmonious blend of the daemonic, the ideal and the actual, i. e. the typical phenomena of all three stages – the creativity of daemonic genius, individual idealism and intellectual purpose. At this "phenomenalistic" stage, what is episodic will be done away with and the sense of time will evolve into that of the supertemporal.

Conclusion

These general principles serve to explain the nature and task of cultural morphology, which uses as its starting point the date of ethnographic research.

Although many valuable accounts of primitive cultures have been published, they are not comprehensive enough to throw any systematic light on the basic problems here described. A planned survey will be necessary to display to the public the nature of African cultures and their importance in world history.

This will involve in particular an extended study of the history of western and central Africa. These areas, which were not part of the Roman empire, have ideas and achievements to their credit which go back more than two thousand years. Furthermore, the African past is intimately related to the prehistoric monuments of the cave-dwellers of southern France and Spain, to the Etruscan problem and the dawn of Egyptian culture, and this points a new way to the study of the most fundamental questions of human history. Whatever we can learn today of African religions and social institutions, art forms and poetry, is of immense importance for our knowledge of mankind and may radically alter our understanding of the past.

Another lesson that we may learn from African studies is that of the organic character of primitive cultures, which unite tectonic with monumental features, ideas with practical effect and facts with a conceptual content. As a result, we receive flashes of enlightenment which continue to inspire the mind and will gradually obliterate the differences of method that are still customary in approaching "primitive" and "historic" cultures respectively. This means that it will be possible to make a scientific study *of the whole of human culture* from its first beginnings, *as an organic unity.*

For this purpose, the ethnographical study of the key areas of African culture is an essential starting-point. These areas, and they alone, beckon the voyager who seeks for a tangible counterpart to the monumental culture of Europe and the lands adjoining it. Our task is to build a bridge across the intervening waters, and thus to gain an insight into both worlds and the life that flows eternally between them.

5. Reflections on African Art*

What does Africa mean to us, as people living in the middle of the 20th century?

This is not a very difficult question to answer compared with the question as to what Asia means to us – Asia, with its infinitely rich structure as a continent, the cradle of so many cultures and of all religions and even – so many people think – of mankind itself. Asia, with its yellow, brown, black and white races, with its eternal winter in the north, eternal summer in the south!

Beside it Africa looks like a shapeless, uncouth giant. A flat cake without a form, vast and amorphous. Deserts to north and south, plains and jungles in the centre. The people of the central regions blackish, to the south brown, to the north brown and sunburned white. What has this continent ever given to humanity? The Egyptian civilization? Well, that miraculous flower-garden is so self-contained, cut off from the rest of the continent, so closely associated with Asia that it is difficult to count it as part of "our Africa", even today.

May this Egyptian civilization not have originated in neighbouring western Asia? Are we not constantly discovering more and more clues to indicate that the Babylonian and Sumerian culture of Mesopotamia is much older than anything born in the Nile valley? A stream of Asiatic inspirations, capable of penetrating as far as neighbouring Egypt (but no further into the monstrous body of boorish Africa), and fertilizing it! There is much evidence to show that this was what happened. From western Asia came the Phoenicans who settled in Africa Minor, the kernel of the greatness of Carthage. From western Asia came the Arabs and Islam which, over-running North Africa, awakened in Egypt a new golden age with a new life-style and new nations in the Mediterranean countries. Legend also had it that the great empires and spreading cities of the Sudan were also the offspring of these Arabs and of Islam.

All this has been swallowed credulously and without opposition and has hitherto not really been called in doubt. For what sort of culture could ever have been produced by the immeasurably vast wastes of North Africa? These deserts, whether they be called the Sahara, the Libyan or the Nubian Desert, are entirely "dead" lands, oceans of sand, stone, rock, a limitless basin, filled with the life-destroying blaze of the African sun. After all, these northern and north-eastern countries of Africa are even

* From "Die Kunst Afrikas" in: Der Erdball, 1931, p. 86–114.

today so constituted that their only response to culture is to behave like a constantly absorbent and constantly dehydrated sponge! So much for the North African desert and the margin of Africa, in as much as it lies in close proximity to the great historical cradle of civilization (western Asia and the Mediterranean). But what is our traditional attitude to the great, black Africa of the south?

A steel-grey sky over a vast expanse of plain – red earth, dark grass, grass, grass. Here and there an acacia – now and then a miserable native village, round huts with straw roofs like truncated cones – a few chocolate-coloured natives clad in rags, loin-cloths or skins and armed with bows and arrows – a few women rhythmically pounding their pestles while their slack breasts flop up and down; a few miserable chickens, goats and half-starved dogs; the theme of a film scenario, an endlessly repetitive sequence of images. Day in, day out, week in, week out, constantly the same, constantly repeated – the same experience, the same dull impressions, fatiguing to the point of exhaustion. Now and again the passage of a waterway in an unsteady canoe, a meeting with a group of wild animals, a herd of game or cattle, or an encounter with a crowd excited by too much beer, and the variety provided by such encounters. This was roughly the picture which the majority of Europeans had formed only a generation ago of the general pattern of a journey from Senegal to Abyssinia, or from Abyssinia to the Cape.

And then, the jungle! Trees 50, 60, 70 metres high, dark green and threaded with lianas above a red-brown swamp – a flowerless roof of leaves and sticky, lightless air – here and there a village of square, mat huts, very savage natives with cannibalistic tendencies, here and there some banana groves – an unchanging monotony until it is interrupted by a river of legendary dimensions filled with hippopotamus, sandbanks covered with elephants, serried ranks of rhino – all these belong to the same collection of generalized ideas about the wide forests of the west and the great Congo basin. Whenever carvings, figures, animals, masks were found among the natives of these western lands they were dimissed as "fetish" or "the barbaric art of the devil".

We must not forget that only a generation ago in the minds of Europeans of average education Africa was a desperate land, a continent of fever and sickness, fit only for adventurers and missionaries. And its indigenous inhabitants were semi-animal barbarians, a slave race, a people whose crude depravity was capable only of producing this brand of fetishism and nothing more.

Any conversational mention at that time of the great cities of the Sudan with their hundreds of thousands of well-dressed and well-trained artisans would be greeted with a shrug: "The Arabs passed that down to these fellows!"

That was the view of Europe in the previous century, a period in which a heroic band of defiant warriors set out, and in the teeth of disregard, fever and cannibalism broke through the shell encapsulating the heart of the continent and with admirable courage exposed the external picture of the continent.

These men knew that the popular image was wrong. They gained an insight into astounding splendours. Unimagined glory was unveiled for them. But another generation passed before the whole of Europe was prepared to receive this knowledge.

Let us not forget that the first European seafarers of the late Middle Ages had already made highly reputable observations of a similar nature. When they arrived in the Bay of Guinea and went ashore near Weida those captains of old were greatly surprised. Well laid-out streets, running for miles without interruption, lined with planted trees; for days' journeying, nothing but a countryside covered with fine fields, people in splendid robes made from hand-woven fabrics. Further to the south, in the kingdom of the Congo, masses of people clothed in "silks and velvets", an order which extended into the minutest details of large, well-organized states, mighty rulers, flourishing industries, culture in the very marrow of the people! The same conditions were found in the countries on the eastern seaboard, for instance the Mozambique Coast.

From the reports of voyagers from the 15th to the 17th century it is quite clear that black Africa, stretching from the Sahara desert belt towards the south, was at that time still experiencing the highest flowering of a harmoniously civilized culture. A "flower" which the European conquistadors destroyed wherever they were able to penetrate. For the new land of America needed slaves, Africa had slaves to offer. Slaves by the hundred, slaves by the thousand, shiploads of slaves! But traffic in human beings has never been an easy business to answer for. It demanded justification. So the Negro was transformed into a semi-animal, an article of trade. So the term fetish (= feticeiro, a Portuguese word) was invented as the symbol of an African religion. A European trade mark! I myself have not found any signs of fetish-worship among Negroes in any part of black Africa.

The concept of the "barbaric Negro" is a European creation, which had its effects on Europe as late as the beginning of this century.

The things that these ancient captains and commanders – men such as

58

d'Elbée, de Marchais, Pigafetta, and all the rest – reported were demonstrably true. In the old Royal Chamber of Art in Dresden, in the Weydmann Collection in Ulm and other "curiosity cabinets" of Europe we still find collections from the West Africa of that time. Fine, rich velvets, deep as plush, manufactured from the most delicate layers of leaf from a particular strain of banana. Fabrics soft and supple, shining and delicate as silk, woven from the expertly processed fibres of a raffia palm. Mighty spears of state, their blades most delicately inlaid with copper. A bow so graceful and so covered with decorative patterns that it would be an ornament to any armoury. Tastefully decorated calabashes. Seriously and stylishly executed ivory and wood-carvings.

All this, from African peripheral territories which subsequently fell victim to the slave trade and in which the visitor now finds only European rubbish, degenerate 'trouser-niggers' and parasitic Negro clerks.

But when the pioneers of the last century broke through this zone of "European civilization" and the protective wall which had by now arisen round the untouched lands, they found everywhere the same splendours as the captains had found on the coast in the 16th century.

Yes, even in 1906 I saw villages in the Kassai Sankurru region whose main streets were lined for miles with rows of palm trees four deep on either side, whose huts were, each and every one, works of art exhibiting the most fascinating weaving and carving. Not a man without his lordly iron and copper weapons, with their inlaid blades and snake-skin covered handles. Velvets and silks on all sides. Every beaker, every pipe, every spoon a work of art, worthy to hold its own with the creations of the Romanic style in Europe.

Yet all this was no more than the delicate and softly-glowing bloom on a fine, ripe fruit: the gestures, the bearing, the customs of the entire people, from the smallest child to the oldest man, displayed a natural reserve, dignity and grace; no more among the princely and wealthy families than among those of their retainers and slaves.

I know of no people in the North whom I could compare with these "primitives", given equality of education.

Meanwhile, even these last "Islands of the Blessed" have now been overwhelmed by the tidal waves of European civilization, which have swept away their peaceful loveliness.

I am far from being the only person to have had this experience. Explorers coming from the belligerent, savage heights of the east, south and north and descending to the lowlands of the Congo, Lake Victoria and the Ubangi, men such as Speke and Grant, Livingstone, Cameron, Stanley,

Schweinfurth, Junker, de Brazza – they all had the same experience. They came from countries in which the rigid laws of the African war-god prevailed and discovered lands of peace, where the decorative and the beautiful were appreciated. Countries with ancient cultures, cultures in the ancient mode, the mode of well-balanced minds.

Were things any different in the great Sudan? Not in the least! But in the last century the superstition about the origin of all the higher culture of Africa coming from Islam still persisted. Since then we have learned a lot and now we know that the exquisite garments of the Sudanese people were already indigenous to Africa before Mohammed was born, or any Arab of much education had set foot in Central Africa. Since then we have learned that the extraordinary organization of the Sudan States existed long before Islam, that all these arts of expert agriculture, careful education, the maintenance of civil order and the crafts of black Africa are many thousands of years older than those of our own Central Europe!

So the Sudan, too, had its own ancient, truly African, warm-blooded civilization. We venture to claim that Europe found the ancient cultures prevalent and alive in Equatorial Africa wherever Arab superiority, Hamitic blood or European civilization had not washed the powder off the once beautiful wings of the dark butterfly.

And wherever we can still find evidence of this ancient culture it bears the same stamp. If we walk through the great museums of Europe, the Trocadero, the British Museum, the museums of Belgium, Italy, Holland and Germany – in all of them we encounter the same "spirit", the same character, the same nature. From whatever part of this continent the various articles may have come, they always unite to speak the same language. If the onlooker wants to find an expression for this he need only compare the images offered to him with those which form the neighbouring collections of Asia: the splendour of soft and supple fabrics; the fantastically delicate lines of pictures and sculpture, the enchanting beauty of bejewelled weapons, ornaments, clothes (which even from air-tight cupboards seem to pour out the perfume of ambergris and attar of roses); collections bearing silent witness to fairy-tales from the Thousand and One Nights, Chinese romances, Indian philosophies, magic formulae, and multitudinous variety in every shape and form!

By comparison with such spirituality the expression of "African-ness" is easily and quickly defined: every material falling into hard folds, every decoration unpretentious, every weapon simple and functional (even the many forms of the throwing-knife, which lends itself readily to imaginative treatment), every line of carving austere and stern. There is nothing here which makes the slightest attempt to beguile by expressing a yielding softness. Everything exudes the same odour of smoking hut fires, sweating, grease-soaked skins and animal glands. Everything is practical, austere, stern, tectonic.

This is the character of the African style. Anyone who has come close to a real understanding of it will recognize that it prevails throughout Africa as the expression of the African essence. It expresses itself in the movements of all Negro peoples as much as in their plastic art, it is uttered in their dances and in their masks, in their religious sense as much as in the tendencies of their lives, national constitutions and racial destiny. It lives in their fables, fairy-tales, sagas, myths.

What if we also make a comparison with "Egyptian-ness", once we have reached this realization? Does the formula discovered for Negro Africa also apply to the essence of this special area? Does not pre-Islamic Egypt express itself in the austere, stern, functional, grave style?

The peoples of Africa are merry, voluble, vivacious. But the style of their spiritual expressiveness is grave and austere now, as it was in ages past. This style must have originated somewhere, come to birth at some time, and then crystallized into its particular character. It contains the enchantment of an enigmatically far-off birth. Is it possible to come any closer to the spiritual reality of such a distant event?

Here I must turn back to the statements I made at the beginning: the image of the character of the North African desert belt, which stretches from the Atlantic Ocean to the Red Sea; that belt which, to judge by its present nature, can never have been the home or birth-place of a civilization, assuming that its nature was always the same as it is now. But this is not in accordance with the facts. Therefore our image is shown to be a false one. Because in the period when Europe froze in the harsh climate of the last Ice Age, North Africa, Africa Minor and the Sahara were going through a rainy period, when the fruitful rain was pouring down on the now arid surface of the earth. This region was the homeland of huge numbers of people. This is not simply a theory. The soil of many Saharan valleys, now hopelessly barren, is covered with countless stone tools corresponding to the types whose age we know from the geological levels of Western Europe which have been so accurately researched and chronologically determined. We know now that the whole deep cleft of the Nile Valley was filled with water at that time, forming a lake on whose banks vast animal herds grazed.

This is not only proved by the layers of stone tools in their chronologically established forms. The men of that time left other and clearer signs of the nature of their environment. The rocks of the Sahara and of the Saharan Atlas, and those of the Nubian and Libyan deserts are decorated with their paintings. Even those of Africa Minor and Fezzan, the old country of the Garamantes, are great in their fashion and grand in conception, great achievements of an important past.

In a place which now shows nothing for many days' journey but steppe and desert, with here and there an salt-lake, we found paintings of the wild bull, rhinoceros and ibis, animals which cannot exist without swamps and fresh, grassy lowlands. A monument which speaks with unmistakeable clarity of climatic change.

Many of these rock paintings in the Saharan Atlas and the Fezzan are of enormous size. In one place the battle of a pair of wild bulls has been painted. Each of the two monsters measures almost three metres in length. Then there is an elephant shielding its young with its trunk against an approaching leopard. A bull before which a man stands with raised hands, praying; a ram with a disc on its head, again with men in the attitude of prayer. Elsewhere, however, the representation of animals is so predominant that the few human figures almost vanish beside them. But what do these few inclusions of men have to tell us about the meaning of the paintings? Once and once only in the course of my many years in Africa did I experience something which may explain the significance of all these paintings. In 1905, in the primeval forest between Kassai and Luebo, I came upon representatives of that race of hunters who were driven off the plateau into refuges in the Congo jungle and have become so well known to us as Pygmies. A few of the people, three men and one woman, accompanied the expedition for about a week. One day – it was towards evening and we were already great friends – the kitchen was once again very short of food and I asked the three men to kill another antelope for us, a simple thing for them as hunters. The people gazed at me in obvious astonishment and one then burst out with the reply that, yes, of course they would be glad to, but it would naturally be quite impossible today, since no preparations had been made. The end of the very long negotiations was that the hunters were prepared to make their preparations at sunrise next morning. At that we parted. The three men went about, examining the surrounding terrain and found a high place on a neighbouring hill.

As I was very keen to see what the men's preparations consisted of, I got up before sunrise and slipped among the bushes, close to the open place they had chosen for their rites the evening before. In the grey light of dawn the men came, but not alone; the woman was with them. The men crouched on the ground, cleared a small space and swept it smooth. Then one of the men squatted and drew something in the sand with his finger. Meanwhile the men and the woman murmured formulas and prayers. An expectant silence followed. The sun appeared on the horizon. One of the men, his bow drawn, approached the bared patch. A few more minutes passed and the rays of the sun fell on the drawing on the ground. At the same instant, and like lightning, the woman raised her hands with a clutching gesture to the sun and cried out some sounds incomprehensible to me; the man shot the arrow; the woman called out again; then the men ran into the bush with their weapons. The woman remained there for a few minutes and then returned to the camp. When she had gone I stepped out of the bush and saw that the drawing on the smoothed ground was of an antelope measuring about four spans, with the arrow now firmly planted in its throat.

While the men were away I wanted to return to the spot to take a photograph of the drawing. The woman, who had stayed near me, stopped me and implored me to desist. That afternoon the hunters returned with a pretty bush-buck. It had been killed by an arrow in the throat. The people handed over their booty and then went off with some tufts of hair and a bowl of antelope blood to their place on the hill. They did not overtake us again until the second day, and that evening, over a foaming brew of palm wine, I ventured to mention the affair to the one of the three men with whom I was most intimate. The oldest man told me that they had gone back to smear the picture of the antelope with hair and blood, to withdraw the arrow and then to wipe out the picture. I could discover nothing about the meaning of the words used. But he did say that the blood of the antelope would destroy them if they did not do this. The wiping out must also take place at sunrise. He begged me insistently not to tell the woman that he had talked to me about these things. He seemed to be terrified of the possible consequences of his chatter, for next day the people left us without saying goodbye, not questioning his command, because he was the leader of the little company.

In the rock-paintings of France and especially in the Trois Frères Cave in Ariège wild buffalo are depicted with an arrowhead on their bodies. There is one such picture of an elephant, its heart painted in within the outlines. Surely this must indicate a connection with the ideas with which the Pygmies were familiar in their magic rites?

There is another group of rock-paintings which might well be claimed as evidence of kinship between the phenomena of palaeolithic rock-painting in South Eastern Europe and North West Africa. In the art of the

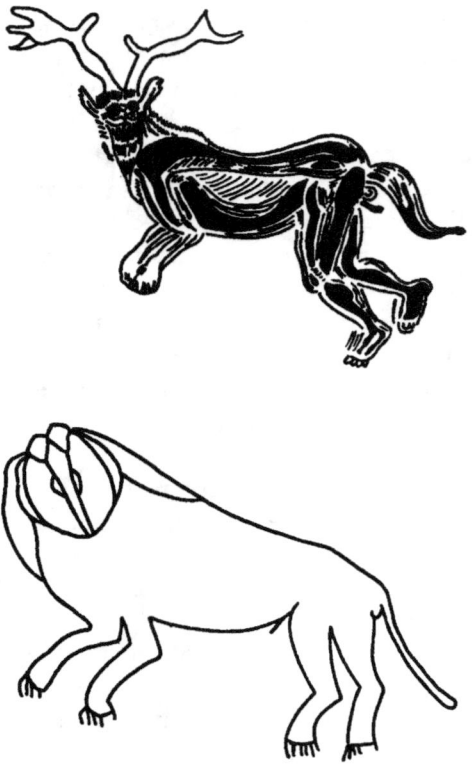

Fig. 6 Sorcerer (Trois Frères) and Lion (Saharan Atlas)

Saharan Atlas all the animals are depicted completely in profile (there is a unique group in which the head is looking back). Only the great cats (lion and leopard) are mostly (seven times out of ten) shown with the body and limbs in profile but the head turned *en face*, so that the gaze of the round eyes is directed at the onlooker. And a lion painted in just this way was discovered by Count Béguin in the Trois Frères Cave in Ariège. He presides in majestic might over the procession through a main hall; here there are many buffalo with arrowheads, but above them, with striking originality, the "magician" is portrayed. Here he has a position of dominance over the animals, like an imposing lion above the animal ranks of the Yashu Plateau in Morocco. I show the two pictures here, one above the other (Fig. 6). The reader can decide for himself whether or not there is a relationship. Suppose we unmask the sorceror, take away his horns and his tail. Then of course there will be a pair of human legs left, but also an image which can very easily be compared with a lion figure such as the one on the Yashu Plateau: the round eyes of the cat family, the genitals, the beard in place of the mane, the front legs with the clawed paws. Here too, in the caves of Ariège, it is apparently only the sorceror and the lion over the entrance who turn their full faces to the viewer, just as in Africa it is also only the lions and the leopards whose portraits gaze at the viewer in this way.

The idea of going in search of further clues to kinships of form in this area is temptingly attractive. We shall have to disregard it if we are not to lose our thread. Let us not forget that the task we have undertaken here is to "penetrate the African mind and style", and in this context historical associations with non-African art are significant only in terms of chronology.

But if we look round on African soil for the inner meaning of these pictures of staring lions above the animals of the Yashu Plateau we shall find a rewarding answer. All kinds of Sudanese traditions, customs, memories and usages of the past can be recorded and will be referred to in outline in the paragraphs below.

As the Sahara dried out, peoples and cultures trickled away towards the south. These refugees still live on today in the memory of the Sudanese. The Sudanese have had all sorts of stories handed down from them which are completely original and full of archaistic ideas about the relationship with game, showing them, indeed, in a highly organized form.

It is "Lord Buffalo" who appears most often amongst these. He bestowed on the favoured hunter the right to kill animals from specific herds. We often hear about a "lord of the animals" who rules the congregation of all animals, as their highest embodiment. Sometimes a hunter sits in a tree-top in whose shade the gathering is taking place. He is discovered and forced to explain himself. When the hunter declares his occupation, however, the lord of the animals is not angered. On the contrary, he gives him certain hunting rights. Only in future he must fulfil one requirement. The lord of the animals breaks a horn off one of the antelopes and hands it to the hunter. In future he must allow some drops of blood to run into this horn from every animal he kills. The horn of blood recurs in all these legends. It is also known to the Kabyles, who preserve remnants of the civilization of the past and who live in the Atlas, that is north of the Sahara, and was in use among the Pygmies who wander the primeval forest. This horn of blood is a survival of the days when human beings pictured themselves praying before the image of the great buffalo. It is a symbol of a predominantly *magical culture*.

But we can also show other traces of this magical culture in the Sudan and along the whole line from the Atlantic Ocean to the Red Sea. We can find them in the actual significance which the lions and leopards possess for the hunter. Over and over again we find the legend that the blow of a wild beast's paw plays a decisive role in the man's sexual maturity. There are still peoples whose initiation ceremonies for young men culminate in the operation being performed by a priest, disguised as a leopard, at the moment of extreme ecstacy. These ceremonies are fearful. In some the boy has to walk through underground passages. From round a corner the terrifying figure of the beast of prey leaps to confront him. The paw blow and the gaze of the eyes are vital to those who wish to become hunters. The full-faced paintings of the lion with his gaze resting on the viewer can easily be interpreted in this light.

Gaze, blood, sex are the three themes of the inner structure of this "Mahalbi" culture. Once, when the horn of blood was upset by a woman, the "lord of the animals" threw it at her, since when women have menstruated. The leopard paw bestows maturity on the hunter. A glance from the dying eyes of the slaughtered antelope, falling on the hunter's sexual organs, robs him of the power of procreation. Blood, gaze, image!

Monuments to the magical Mahalbi culture have been preserved for us in the rock-paintings of African palaeolithic art.

The Pygmy of the Central African forests who shot his arrow into the picture and then into the body of the antelope – the first at the very moment when the eye of day cast its first glance upon the picture – who then mixed the blood from the horn with his picture – was releasing himself from the curse of blood. An attitude to life which has become quite alien to us is being expressed here. Completely alien, and yet it still prevails among large groups of African peoples and has a determining effect on their culture. This attitude to life was the cause of the "spiritualization of matter". It implies no recognition of anything which cannot be apprehended by the senses, thus no concept of the soul. This must be discussed.

When a man belonging to this culture dies, whether in the North, East or South of Africa, his body is taken as quickly as possible from the place of death to a barren place. Agatharchides has described such a funeral to us. The corpse is bound with skins and cords. Stones are piled on it until it lies under a weight which the "force" still present in it cannot shake off. Every passer-by adds another stone. In a similar manner mothers are released from the bodies of their children, children from those of their parents, husbands from those of the beloved. The human being does not want to have anything to do with the matter which has now become sinister. The man who believes in magic will never transcend the idea of ghosts.

To this attitude everything becomes spiritualized matter: the name, the glance, the blood. The seat of life is not in the blood, but the blood is life. The name is not a sound, it is matter and as such a part of its bearer. The glance is matter, its effect is material. Hence the constant fear of the evil eye. And accordingly the image of an object, a man, an animal is also part of the thing portrayed and the influence it exerts on the image extends to the living exemplar, the object portrayed itself.

The effects of this magical attitude to life can be found even in the most trivial customs. If the hunter comes upon a tree on which an elephant has recently been scratching, leaving a few hairs in the bark, he has only to fix these hairs to the tree-trunk in order to bind it to the spot in which it is then standing. The action performed with an animal's leavings extends to their originator. In order to destroy a man it is enough to procure a tuft of his hair, or some finger or toe nail cuttings. When these hairs or nails are burned, the man to whom they belong will fall sick. The part stands for the whole.

This is the philosophy of the ancient hunter civilization. But to understand it from the inside it is necessary to be able to imagine the life-style of this ancient life form, born of the impoverished steppes. For this is country which offers little or no vegetable food to the man who is ignorant of agriculture and who is therefore obliged to pursue the fleeing game. All the more so in the desert, where this outlook has persisted to the present day. The man who lives in such poverty has to confront nature. To be or not to be! Nature forces him, quite directly, to invent weapons. Weapons of the mind, which are followed by weapons of the hand. But the principal weapons of the mind are the sense organs and among them by far the most important is the eye. The ability to see develops into something astonishing; sharpness of vision leads to speed of decision. Passions rise, to give way, when action has been completed, to a corresponding relaxation. Thus the outlook of the huntsman of the desert and plain is characterized by intoxication with life. However, just as intoxication is followed by sobriety, here too jubilation alternates with gravity; the development of the sensory weapons of attack also releases the defensive tendencies of the spirit and the emotional life. The predominance of the one-sidedly disciplined capacities of the senses develops a contrasting mistrust and rebellion in the excluded spirit, which being excluded from the realm of creative life, now exhausts itself in the development of measures of defence, rejection, dissolution and negation.

Of course all this can only emerge in its true significance when the contrasting movement has been described. But even here it must be quite clear when I say: the hunter *kills!* His occupation calls for the constantly repeated act of extermination. Ecstacy recurs in blood-lust. He is constantly subject to passion. This is why blood for him is the allegory of life, and the bloodless is inimical to life. For this reason, all the peoples who have this attitude to life have developed the spirit of heroism to its fullest extent. But in place of religious feeling there is only fanaticism; in representative art the extreme of verism and naturalism where the representation of animal life is concerned, but never the depiction of a plant.

Far back on the path of the evolution of human civilization lies the step in the huntsman's culture which signified the creative period of the great rock-art galleries. Since then, agriculture and cattle rearing have become decisive factors and it is only in the barren and remote areas, despised by the more demanding, that the spirit of the ancient age lives on, and with it the rock-painting, in a degenerate and impoverished form. It is in this way that we may be able to understand the fact that wretchedly poor bushmen still eke out their existence today in miserable regions of South Africa in the spirit of the ancient attitude to life.

But in proximity to the ever more richly and fruitfully evolving landscape between the Mediterranean countries, the Nile and the Sudan, a new state of affairs arose among the peoples with the magic-oriented attitude, among the Tuareg and Teda, the Ababde and Hadendoa. They became cattle farmers. Hunting lands turned into pasturage. Many things changed now in the external conditions of life, but the thought behind the animal pictures remained the same. The senses, directed towards the observation of everything physical, the evolutionary tendencies built up on physical sense values, called hitherto unknown human virtues into life. Racial instincts strengthened.

This outlook on life, always striving to carve out a section of the environment for itself and possess it, celebrated new triumphs. First the only object was the game animal. Then the herd animal was added. Freedom had previously been restricted only by the sharp definition of hunting territories and hunting rights. Now hunting rights were followed by the right of plunder; for to these men, educated in the struggle for existence to the enjoyment of extremes of muscular and nervous tension, the rise of cattle-rearing and ownership of herds offered a new field of intense activity. Cattle raids! Not in the form of a brutal and despicable crime, but as a manly activity, kept within bounds by specific rules. This has so often been misunderstood. This manly activity did not depend on a large group of men falling upon a smaller group and, having defeated them, appropriating their cattle. That would have been an unmanly deed, according to the unwritten laws of their civilization. No, this was an artistic procedure which presupposed all sorts of skills. Having explored the possibilities, the people would drive the strange cattle off, at night if possible, in such a way that the previous owners would find the trail obliterated. The victim would, of course, become aware of his loss next morning. He would look for his beasts. If he found tracks and caught up with the raiders by swift pursuit they were forced to halt and answer to him and here again the result would not simply be a savage onslaught in which the superior numbers of the raiders wiped out their pursuers, or vice versa. That would be criminal. On the contrary, a struggle would begin which had to proceed according to distinct rules: a series of hand-to-hand encounters, man against man. Everything was prescribed, the weapon, shield and defence. During the battle butter was heated in a stone pot in the background. If a hand was chopped off the stump was dipped in the pot. If a man had his stomach slit open the wound was treated with hot butter and sewn up. Duel followed duel until one of the parties lost his nerve and conceded victory and possession of the herd by flight.

Under the constant refinement of a compelling morality this philosophy of the "spiritualization of matter" gave birth to a new concept, that of honour. For the people of this civilization honour was all. Under the influence of this idea everything was turned into a great game: hunting, raiding, courtship. And so we come to the most recent area, in which the evolution of this attitude led to organizations.

Everyone who has attempted to record the inner nature of these Hamitic northern peoples has found that a characteristic female peculiarity goes hand in hand with this concept of honour, this male intoxication with blood. The women are so deeply attached to their blood relations, their fathers and brothers, that their husbands are of significance to them only in periods of ardour and at moments of passionate abandon. The family structure is that of the matriarchal clan society. The woman does not find her happiness in the enchantment of blessed motherhood. From birth she has been the beloved, remains the beloved, and will always be the courted beloved. To the reckless lover who steals into her tent at night and demands to possess her – whether her husband is sleeping next to her or not – she can deny nothing. So in addition to cattle-raiding, love became the goal of masculine deeds of valour.

The manliness born of the struggle for existence led to ambition as an attitude to life. The fame of the victor was celebrated. The heroic saga and the love epic were born. Only such an attitude, based on such a spiritualization of matter, can explain this group of works of art in Africa, which betray the same spirit in all traditions.

This is one of the two currents which were decisive in the evolution of African culture. From the region of the peoples of this civilization, the Berbers, the Tuareg, the Fulbe, the Libyans, the Bedouin, arose the mighty rulers, the intellectual-physical powers of the African nations, and the great epics of chivalry.

Negro Africa itself, Africa beyond the desert belt, has, as long as man has existed, always been tropical – an area in which the luxuriant growth of the plant world always afforded everything a man needed for his bodily needs and nourishment: fruit, tubers, roots, fungus in plenty and also the honey of the bees, the birds' eggs and the small creatures such as larvae and termites. Nor did he have to worry, anywhere or at any time, about his drink.

There can be no doubt that mankind was already in existence in these countries when the north was still living in the grip of recurrent ice ages. But at no time was the style of tropical existence akin to the rigours of the northern regions. Another world, another outlook. The northern philosophy expressed in animal pictures was matched by the southern sensitivity to the plant world. The northern experience of frenzy and the oscillation between high tension and deep relaxation is matched here by a twilight existence, a dream state; here a surrender to life, there a life subservient to the will.

I met with this outlook in the primeval forests and on the rich plains. I met it among the smaller tribes who live between the great nations of the Sudan. This outlook makes itself felt here in a touching structure of custom. These people live side by side in patriarchal family groups, all the men of the same descent in one farm area. The women are brought in from outside. The eldest is the leader. He administers all the supplies, distributes corn for meal and beer and the Sunday raiment for feast days. When the elder dies, having had to drag himself painfully through his last years, the whole world rejoices. At the death of a young man who is still childless there is no end to the mourning. Why? The corpse of the old man is laid in a hollow and allowed to decompose. At the right time the skull is taken from the grave and placed in a chamber with the skulls of the other ancients. There he shares symbolically in the first beer vintage and the first harvest. But if a son of the family decides to marry, the new elder of the family presents the bride before the assembly of family skulls. He makes a speech, lays a few seeds on the skull of the ancient. The girl takes the seeds from the skull with her lips. The body now being blessed, no one will ever speak of the descent of the young family. Not one! Yet the great mystery is incorporated as purely and clearly in such customs as can possibly be conceived. That is why everyone weeps and laments if a man dies leaving no children behind him. A barren fruit.

It is the intimate attachment to plant life, whether through root, grain or juice, which works on the culture and gives it its shape. The outlook which arises from the hunting life, the battle for blood and death, culminates in intoxication and in a sensually-based magic. But the creative spirit arising from plant life sheds its dream over the mystery of life. This explains the principles which enable one to understand the difference between the two art forms of Africa.

The way in which the evolution of the magical attitude to life led to a spiritualization of matter has been referred to already. The rock-painting of the palaeolithic era and the epic poetry of the heroic sagas are both art forms which bear witness to an astonishing authority in this line of creative artists. In contrast to this stands everything which has produced in Africa the art of the men adhering to the other outlook, that of mysticism and the problematical. It is to this attitude that the continent owes its imaginative art.

South Africa possesses works of art in both modes. I would like to use the works found there to illustrate the line of argument I have been elaborating.

The southern part of the continent, from the Zambezi to the Cape, from the Drakensberg Mountains in the east to the rocky landscapes of the west coast, is like one great picture-book. In every district which affords suitable rock faces or stone walls we find rock-paintings, or remnants of them. For thousands of years men have striven to express this abundance. Naturally by far the greater part of this work has not stood up to the exigencies of the climate and other destructive forces. Today most of it is but a pale shadow of its former state. But those fragments which have been well preserved are enough to illuminate the main point, if you are sufficiently observant. The main point is that all this was produced, not by one people, one time, or one period. It is not difficult to distinguish several completely independent styles which obviously correspond to several periods of work and as many independent creative forces. There are at least three of them.

1. First we are struck by engraved pictures. On the smooth surface of hard stones such as basalt and diorite or dolerite surfaces have been

hammered out with fine points. The pictures, hammered or punched out, represent animals, and all the older and particularly beautiful works represent *only* animals and no human beings. The singular geometrical figures, such as concentric circles and pictures drawn in straight lines, also seem to belong to an earlier period. The ancient, true art of this type produced animal pictures of incomparable naturalism. Elephant, rhinoceros, giraffe, hippopotamus, zebra, antelope. Animals are always portrayed singly; only once do two giraffes overlap in an engraving. Composition is unknown to this art. Apart from the naturalism of the pictures, one is struck by the extraordinary skill of the artists. The folds in a rhinoceros' skin, the draughtsmanship of the zebra's coat are so delicately and pregnantly executed that any onlooker must be captivated by the refinement of this, in fact, very primitive technique. But what captivates him is its naturalism and extraordinary virtuosity. The art itself is cold.

2. The next group contains a large number of paintings. The great antelopes and elands must be classified as the oldest works. According to the observations of early travellers the oldest pictures of the south continue to represent only animals. Man does not seem to have become a motif of this art until the later periods. But it is very difficult to pick out the earliest art under its covering of many later over-paintings and even today we do not know if composition was familiar to them or if they were satisfied by the representation of details, in other words if their art was based on a certain one-sidedness, as in the first style mentioned above. At any rate this second artistic group is distinguished from the first by the fact that it did not bloom once in an extreme form and then die out in unsuccessful imitations. This second group contains an enormous number of variants and must have lasted a very long time, even into modern times, being constantly renewed. The last painters of this style were the little bushmen and so these paintings have all erroneously come to be described as bushman paintings.

The "bushman paintings" which have been preserved to this day probably originate from widely varying periods. Yet they all represent a single style. They are all painted in flat areas and in this way are related to the first group of engravings. They are polychrome and a high degree of skill has been developed in the smudging or blending of the different colours. Most of the paintings which have been preserved are compositions and the predominant motifs are animal herds, hunts, dances, processions, battles, gatherings of people. Remarkable are a great many mixed representations: people with antelope, rabbit and goat heads. Then there is an elephant which walks like a man and is armed like a man, and men with antelope heads, carrying home slaughtered antelope as booty (cf. pl. 2, fig. 20–23).

But even if the compositions here display a rich abundance of combinations, this art produced nothing which transcended the reality of observed detail. Much has been distorted in deliberate caricature. But this too is only the result of sharp observation and technical skill. Nowhere can we distinguish a movement of the creative spirit.

This art, too, is cold, just as the first one described was, and like all the rock-paintings of the palaeolithic age and of North Africa.

3. We come to something totally different in the art we find between the Central Transvaal and the Zambesi, in other words in a rather more northern South African country. Even a fleeting observation will enable certain basic differences to be recognized: the art we have just discussed above is polychrome and always painted on sandstone; this one is always executed on granite walls and always in only one colour, red (even if the transformation of the colour under the varied influence of water and air has led to a lively range, from yellow through to purple). The paintings in the first group were painted in flat areas of colour, by smudging. These are produced by a kind of draughtsmanship; strokes between two and four millimetres in width are placed side by side until the area is filled. Thus even the technique is completely different in each and every one of them.

Of the first, the southern art, we can say that nature alone was teacher and creator, the nature of the environment supplying the motif, the nature of man supplying the receptivity. Therefore the animals and men depicted hold a thousand different positions and aspects; therefore the tendency to produce stereotypes is relatively slight. And therefore, too, this art can express itself in an entertaining host of caricatures. Art remains a cold game here, dependent on the capacity of sensory perceptions.

The "Rhodesian" art is quite different. There is no doubt that the technical capacity of its creators in its golden age was in no way inferior to that of the artists of the more southern works. For instance, among these pictures we find representations of antelopes which bear witness to an astounding delicacy of outline and in the depiction of fine detail such as joints, ears, muzzles, withers. This delicacy is evidence of technical ability as well as of good observation. And yet every figure and every line is subservient to an artistic canon. The finished picture of the antelope is not simply the reflection of what nature offered, but of what was selected by the observer's eye and sense of style. This fact, which can be observed in individual paintings, is common to the essence of this style.

What I am saying becomes most apparent in the representations of the human figure. The body is given a broad chest and narrow hips and is therefore wedge-shaped. It is almost always full-face, with the limbs in profile. The limbs show a tendency to form sharp angles.

Everything which has been said here refers to the works from the golden age of this art. It must be emphasized that we found these great works in two relatively small areas and that all the pictures found outside these central areas display a diminution and decadence in style. All the later works show neglect of the originally strict artistic canon, loose limbs and body, with spindly lines and diagrammatic designs. They turn into rather uninspiring pictures, which are worthy of notice only as proof of the continued existence of an unmistakeable virtuosity. But we are not going to discuss these decadent forms.

The art of this classical cuneiform style of South Africa is further distinguished by a content of meaning which is displayed by no other rock-painting art, no style in palaeolithic Europe, in the Sahara, the Libyan or Nubian deserts, or even in South Africa. The mere fact that trees, rocks, lakes and even whole landscapes appear is conclusive. The variety of the trees is astonishing. The depiction of rocks evolves, by a process of progressive transformation, into the essence of mathematical profiles. The landscapes serve as a background to various scenes of human life (cf. fig. 28–34).

Beside these landscapes, the pictures of animals produce a striking effect. I have already mentioned one characteristic of their representation: that the animal of nature is not as important in this context as its appreciation by the human senses. This had to be expressed in the creation of forms and images alien to nature: animals with double heads, giant birds with crocodile bills, elephants with crenellated backs, etc. Here we can see a riotous imagination at work.

The human element in the masterpieces of this art is not displayed in scenes of hunting, dancing or battle. This type of motif, preferred in the art of the south, was unknown in the golden age here. The most significant and most familiar motif seems to me to be one which we have classified as the "pieta". A number of people sit, stand and mourn round a corpse. Often a tree towers overhead. It is these works, which do not actually portray any action, which seem to me the most characteristic. The meaning inherent in them points to an inner relationship with death. This also explains the fact that they were applied on stone walls above or beside caves which even today hold the relics of plundered graves (cf. fig. 35–37).

74

The most outstanding, among all those found to date, are the great paintings of a singular nature which must be portraits of dead kings. In one case we see the elevation of a young king on one side, while on the other we see his corpse wrapped in mummy cloths, the rock cave which is to receive it, the row of sacrifices and the trees from whose fruit the mummifying oil has been pressed. On another occasion the royal body in its winding cloth is at rest; the face is covered with a horned mask; on one crooked knee sits a small bird; one hand supports the head, but the other reaches towards an oval object in the sky. To the right below is another figure covered with indeterminate shapes; a few smaller figures, possibly grave-diggers, are running away. Among all these a few dividing lines, a sort of sketchy frame, surrounding baskets and sacks, no doubt sacrificial offerings, together with people and animals; a confusing medley which all the more characteristically contrasts with the peace of the great figure in the upper part of the painting (cf. pl. 1, fig. 39).

In yet another picture a procession of ghostly figures, led by a female being, climb out of a space, also framed in parallel lines, filled with all sorts of phantom figures. The female figure leads her train to the king's camp, behind which, among wind-blown trees, a mass of stone blocks stand out, arranged in the shape of a full-blown rose.

These pictures are filled with such a warm sense of pregnant emotion that we can understand them without an intellectual comprehension of each detail. The symbols of wordless suffering and the close of life are so explicit that they need no commentary. Though much may be strange to us, that is only because they were created by an attitude infinitely remote from our own. But no one would claim that these pictures have any connection with the mentality which culminates in the spiritualization of matter. On the contrary, these pictures are the fruit of an imaginative outlook on life. What is portrayed does not exist in the living environment of its creators, but is the reflection of the phenomena of the inner life, born of their philosophy. Their art stemmed from a highly-developed theory which in turn could only have emerged from a surrender to life and a mystical outlook.

The difference between the two art forms, the first prehistoric, palaeolithic, and the second belonging to ancient history, is so great and so significant that we should spare no pains to make it as distinct as possible. So here is yet one more attempt at interpretation. The pictures and images of the magical culture flow from the need to create reasoned allegories of the existing: they originate in concepts. The works of the southern Rhodesian culture, however, were born as symbols of the inner life and represent embodiments of emotions.

There can be no doubt that our judgment of Africa is being reversed. In whatever country I happened to be speaking about the discovery of the soul of this continent, sympathy has radiated towards me from every individual. Every audience has been pleasurably stirred by the thought that this Africa, so long despised and assumed to lack soul, is filled with creative life.

True, this life does not create in soft lines, flattering folds, intellectual philosophies, intoxicating fragrance. This Africa affords none of the beguiling magic of the Asiatic orient. The destiny of this continent is a harsh and solemn one. The cliché of the luxuriant splendour of the tropics does not fit, and in particular it does not apply to the African. His destiny is labour, earnest, arduous labour. From the cornucopia of painlessly acquired abundance not one drop has fallen to his lot.

What has been created through suffering and toil can only be austere and serious. But, as such, what is achieved has its own status. This is the only way in which we can understand the fact that we found those cultures which died in the motherland of Asia thousands of years ago still alive in Africa today – that the art which vanished in one ice age in Europe is still practised by the bushmen of South Africa.

It is ancient and austere, this soul of Africa. But its forms are full of dignity. Africa still has much to give us.

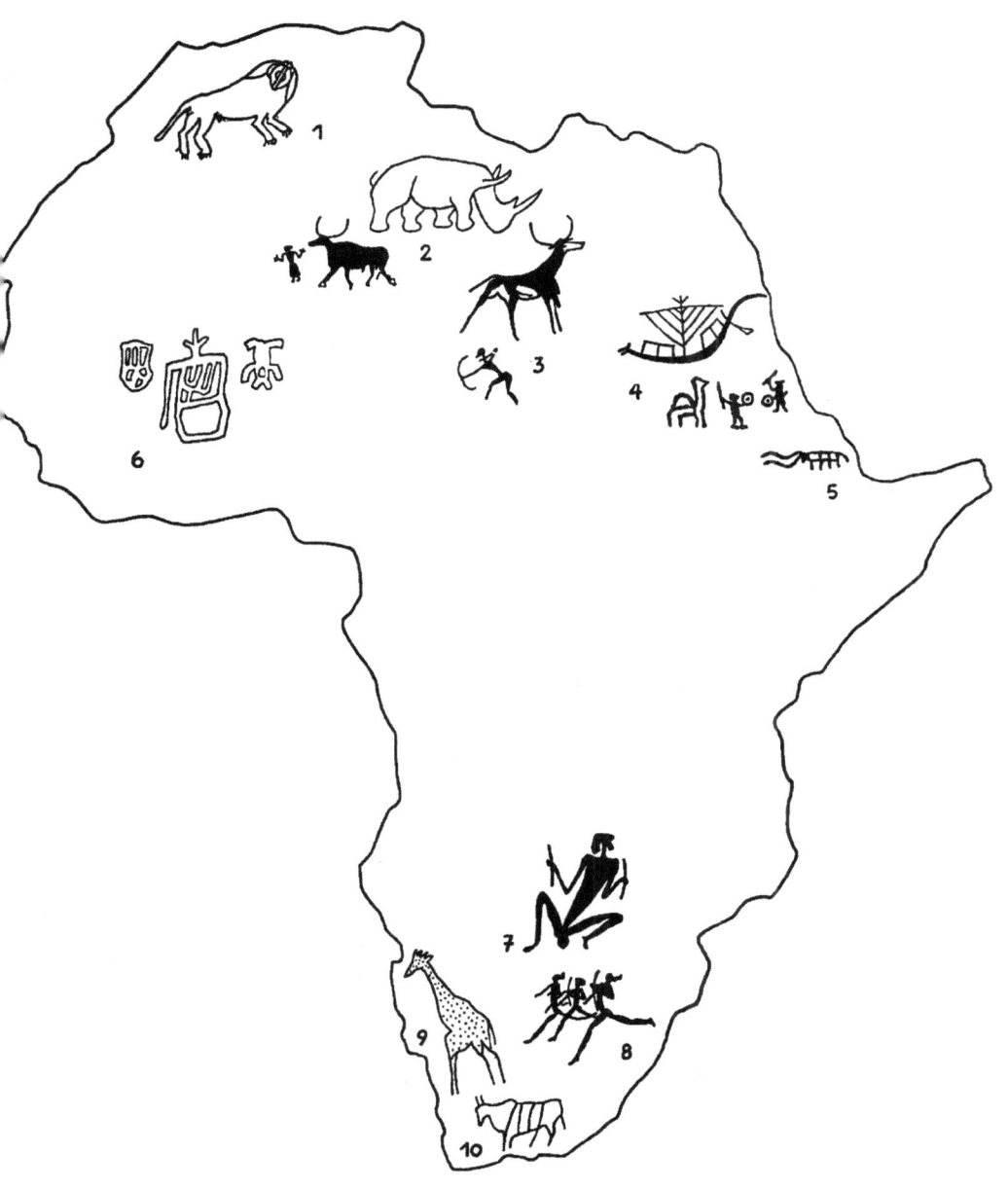

Fig. 7 Map of rock art recorded by Frobenius in Africa:
1. Saharan Atlas – 2. Fezzan and Tassili – 3. Libyan desert – 4. Nubian desert –
5. North Ethiopia – 6. Mali – 7. Zimbabwe (Rhodesia) – 8. Lesoto – 9. Namibia –
10. Cape Province

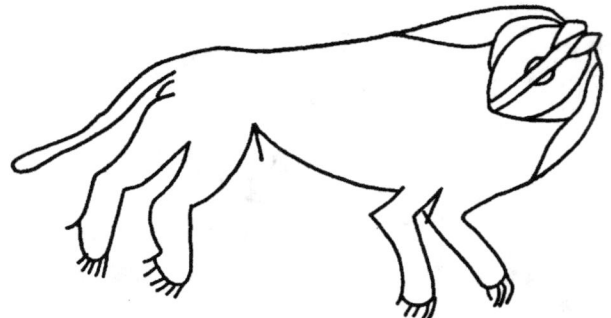

Fig. 8 Lion (rock engraving, Saharan Atlas)

6. Rock Art of the Saharan Atlas*

The aim of our expedition [1910] was not only to photograph and make a fresh study of known rock engravings, but also to find hitherto undiscovered material. Obviously the works situated on well-trodden routes have come to light more quickly than those decorating the rock walls in places which are remote and little frequented today. I and my colleagues therefore made a point of visiting the more remote areas. We not only travelled through the valleys, but also went up into the mountains and explored the Hammada, the plateaus and the peaks. It is highly significant that although we discovered many new sites, we were not able to find a single one outside the valley regions. I was also able to gain some information which throws some light on this question. The Berber peoples whom we find in the valleys and oases of the Saharan Atlas have today been converted to Islam. However, they are still rich in super-stitions which have nothing to do with the Islamic religion, and seem more like relics and remembrances of ancient religious attitudes and rituals. Although these Berbers tend to be reticent about their ancient beliefs, it is not too difficult for a skilled and experienced researcher to obtain concrete information without the native resenting the intrusion. Thus shortly after my arrival in Figuig, the nomads and Berbers told me very readily where they carried out their sacrifices, and this resulted in the discovery of the engravings on the Yashu rock-face (Fig. 8). The natives themselves were mostly unaware that there were rock engravings here. We met one leopard hunter who knew that there were lines cut in the rocks. But there was not

* From "Hadschra Maktuba – Urzeitliche Felsbilder Kleinafrikas", 1925, pp. 19–23.

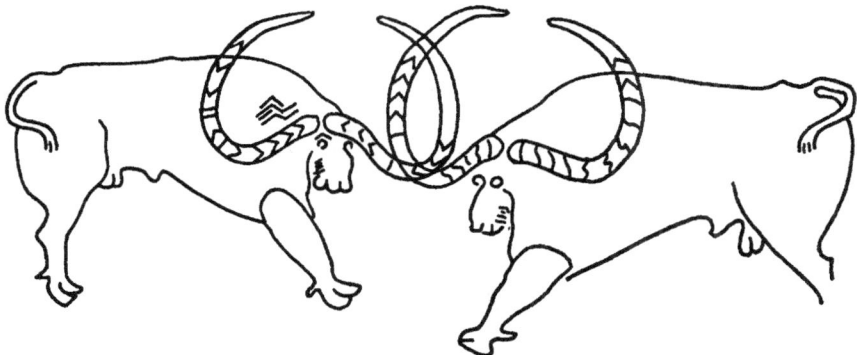

Fig. 9 Fighting buffaloes (rock engraving, Saharan Atlas)

a single person who had recognised the lion or the elephants, which seemed clearly enough drawn to our eyes, and which emerged quite distinctly on the photographic plates. The people were ignorant not only of the rock engravings but also of the Stone Age tumuli, which were very small and plainly formed here. In their search for copper, the treasure-hunters of the area only recognise formally built graves and not simple mounds. People laughed when we began to investigate these graves, and were greatly astonished when the stone coffers appeared once the inside had been uncovered. The native inhabitants were also completely ignorant and unskilled in recognizing external indications. And yet it was here that they carried out the holy sheep sacrifice of Muslim ritual. In former times the ceremony had mostly been carried out at the foot of the picture of the lion, and had only been neglected after the abandonment of the Yashu oasis. Thus the investigation of the places of sacrifice led us to discover a whole series of rock art sites, and gave us a means of checking whether we had found all the existing sites in the area. And the results of these investigations were always the same: not a single rock picture and not a single place of sacrifice was to be found outside the valleys and the lower mountain slopes. Even the nomads of the high stone plateaus descend into the valleys for their sacrificial ceremonies. It was some people from the Tafilelt region who mentioned the south Taghit site to me as a place where they carried out a religious ceremony each year. They too knew nothing of the presence of rock engravings at this place, and only told me that the rock face had once collapsed here, burying a holy man underneath. That proved to be an important moment for the cultural significance of the rock engravings.

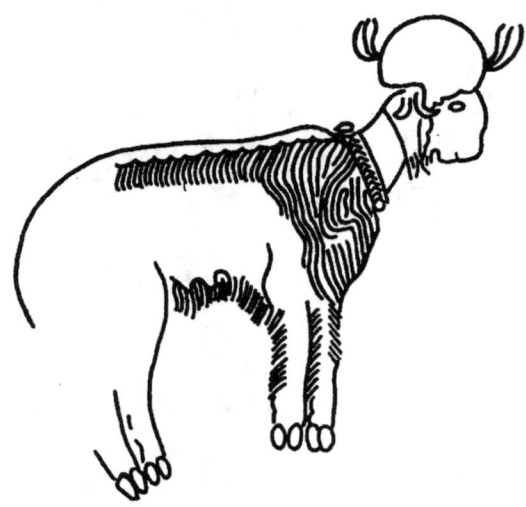

Fig. 10 Ram with sun disk (rock engraving, Saharan Atlas)

Let us now consider the rock art found both in our region and in others in relation to the vegetation, which must have changed over the course of the centuries; let us take a brief look at the history of the oases.

The representation of particular animals in individual places – the giant *Bubalus* buffalo (Fig. 9), rhinoceros, ibis, etc. – indicates in itself that at the time when these engravings originated the land harboured a native fauna which would be unable to exist under present-day conditions of climate and vegetation. They are animals which need marsh and bog alternating with savannah. This agrees with our observations that the valley floors are wide and meandering, with a gently sloping surface and no sharply cut water courses. Nor could the wind have softened the edges of sharply defined channels in the stone, any more than it has been able to obliterate the sharp grooves of the rock engravings. The region must therefore have once been a landscape of swamps covered with luxuriant vegetation and with numerous obstructions to the free flow of water. The present-day oases are carefully preserved relics of what was once the natural vegetation, with man-made plantations replacing the original woodland, swamp and bush. This means that the men of that time must have executed their rock engravings amid a luxuriant natural vegetation which had hardly been influenced by human cultivation.

It would furthermore seem possible to draw some conclusions as to the meaning of the rock pictures. In numerous different places, they show a ram

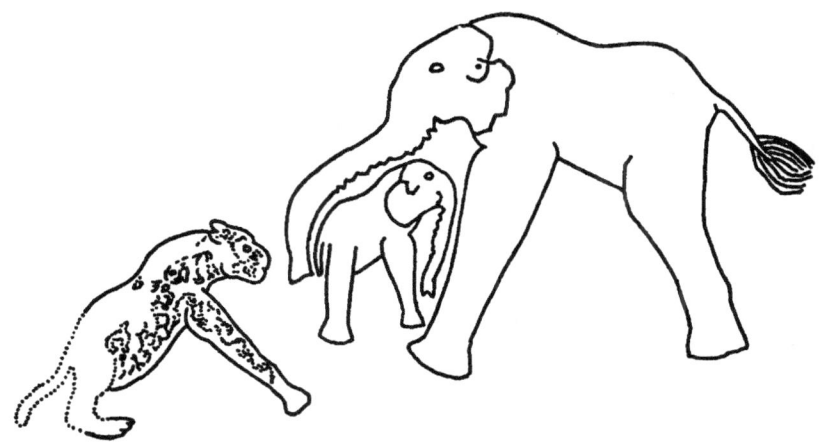

Fig. 11 Elephant defending its young against a leopard (rock engraving, Saharan Atlas)

with a disc on its head and a man in an attitude of prayer in front of it (Fig. 10). We found an explanation of this among the distant inhabitants of Kabylia. There is also the fact that even today the Berber tribes tell of the holy ram, and the present-day inhabitants still carry out their sacrifices at these rock art sites, even though they do not know what these monuments mean. At a whole series of sites we could also demonstrate easily that the orientation of the rock engravings was quite definitely related to the incidence of the rising sun. The Zenaga rock face is situated outside the valley containing the Zenaga-Figuig oasis. In the Goursifa valley, the light of the rising sun falls first on the Yashu lion. South Taghtania receives the dawning day right across its face. Furthermore, the rock art monuments almost everywhere stand in the middle of, or in front of, or behind the burial grounds, and it seemed to us that many of the skeletons in these lay with their skulls pointing in an easterly direction, although we may have been mistaken in this.

The features of different artistic periods are easily identifiable among the rock engravings. All of them seem at first to have been marked out by lines of chip marks in the stone. At a relatively early stage these broken lines were then hollowed out into continuous grooves. In many cases the surface of the figure itself was smoothed, no doubt to take colour. It is highly probable, however, that this treatment only took place at a later stage of Stone Age art. There was apparently a middle period in which the pictures were only chipped, or very slightly hollowed out. This period is characterized by smaller pictures. In a quite late period, the pictures were

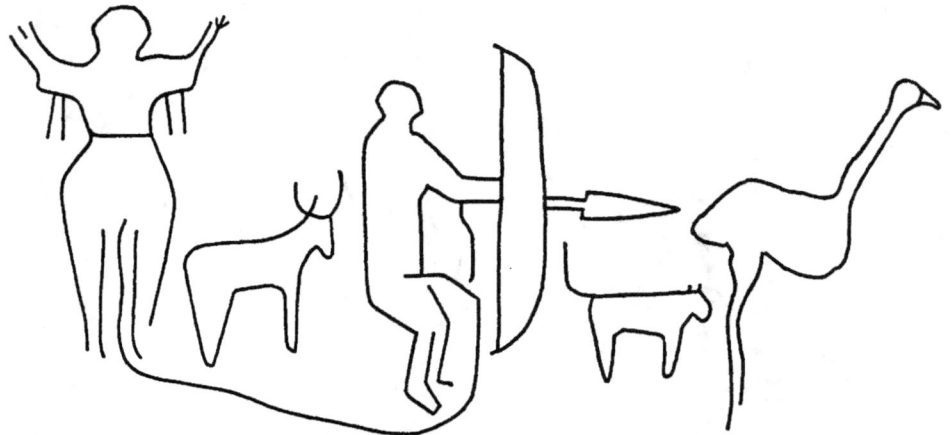

Fig. 12 Ostrich hunt (rock engraving, Saharan Atlas)

chipped once again; they were remarkably small and clumsy, with little or no development of the surface.

The oldest period features animals almost exclusively; the human form appears relatively seldom, and human implements such as shields and boomerangs are represented only exceptionally. Large compositions appear as well as representations of individual animals: an elephant cow defends her young against a springing leopard (Fig. 11); a leopard follows a herd of antelope; a man goes ostrich hunting with a hunting leopard, while his wife stands praying at home with a small cow (Fig. 12), etc. The art of this period is remarkably realistic. The second, middle period, turns to smaller pictures, abandoning large compositions, and has lost the power to give life to its subjects with a continuous outline; instead the latter is filled with a wild but symmetrical confusion of letters, swastikas, circles etc. A large number of figures could be recognised as representing the plough. Many of the ornaments can be found in the tattoos of the present-day Berbers. The fact that I saw similar drawings in the great water conduits poses the question whether this middle period of Stone Age art coincides with the construction of the great underground vaults. The latest period, which features representations of camels, is of little significance.

7. Rock Art of the Fezzan*

We must start by emphasizing that Libya, insofar as it contains Tripoli and the Fezzan, perhaps with the exception of the Hammada el Hamra and the dune belt, was for a long time the homeland of the ancient art of rock engraving. By the end of 1933 old monuments of this kind had been discovered in the regions of Hizda, Brach, Ghat, Djerma, Tel Issaghen etc., and also in the Tibesti mountains. No doubt a thorough survey of the country will bring to light many other valuable finds in other places. Unfortunately we cannot hope to find another region in which the richness of the galleries and the excellence and state of preservation of the works approaches that in the valleys of the so-called "plateau of Murzuk". It is a simple matter of geological predisposition. For the types of stone in the north are calcareous and also exposed to the salt sea air, and therefore unable to offer much resistance to climatic conditions. In the Tibesti mountains there are no long or even formerly fertile valleys which could have offered a home to a relatively advanced culture. The caves on French soil beyond the marl mountains of Ghat contain coloured paintings with their own distinctive style in which there are only a few traces of the archetypal scale which is so strikingly characteristic of the rock art of the Fezzan.

The main centre of monumental rock art in the Fezzan lies at the tip of the sandstone tongue which runs slightly south-west of the Sebha-Murzuk axis, with a length of about 450 km and a breadth of 60 km. This sandstone tongue is surrounded to north and south by mighty masses of the Erg or Edeyin – the yellow desert sand-dunes. To the west lies a deep Serir of grey sand with Auwenat in its centre. The tongue is a somewhat tilted slab of sandstone, with an old river valley running parallel to each of its two edges – Wadi Adjal in the north and Wadi Berjush in the south. Wadi Adjal, which runs along the convex side of the tongue, arises out of a many-branched network of channels in the Serir of Auwenat. Wadi Berjush, which runs along the concave side, on the other hand, stems from valleys cut into the tip of the tongue. The northern Adjal valley is bordered in the north by sand dunes and has on its right the sloping stone face of the plateau of Murzuk, which varies between 80 and 120 metres in height. As late as Roman times, this valley was probably still a luxuriant oasis landscape with palms and tamarind trees, extending about 20 km westwards past present-day Ubari. The southern Berdjush valley is bordered by sand-dunes on the south side of its middle section and runs

---

* From "Ekade Ektab – Die Felsbilder Fezzans", 1937, pp. 13–20.

along the lower slope of the tilted Murzuk plateau, from which it emerges at Elauen. Towards the east it is blocked by a bar of sand-dunes and flows into a depression which has the name of Sharaba. This depression contains many signs of earlier fertility, including both palms and tamarind trees, and above all the ruins of an early town stretching over some 2.5 km. In its central and main sections, however, the Berdjush valley consists of an expanse of scrub between 1 and 3 km wide and lacking all signs of earlier flowers, trees and oasis cultivation. The upper course of the Adjal valley is formed from the network of channels in the Serir of Auwenat; the upper course of the Berdjush valley, on the other hand, stems from a number of deeply cut gorges in the widest part of the tip of the Murzuk plateau. As far as Elauen, while it is still cut into the sandstone plateau, the valley is not called Wadi Berdjush but In Habeter; the three shallowest gorges of the In Habeter are named Aramas, Tel Issaghen and El Gamaud.

The pattern of vegetation in these areas is very unusual. Running from west to east, the Adjal and Berjush valleys enclose a narrow sandstone plateau some 60 km wide and 450 km long. From its origins in the north-west African plateau, the latter runs between the sand-dunes towards the north-east African plain. If one draws a line across this narrow plateau from Ubari to Sharafa, the resulting eastern sector contains valleys in which tamarind and palm trees are found growing wild or still under cultivation, while to the west of this line such valleys are completely lacking. Neither Wadi Berdjush nor the upper part of Wadi Adjal west of Ubari show the slightest remnant of earlier palm or tamarind plantations, and can never have been anything more than pasture or rice fields. I observed rice plants growing wild on a number of different occasions. The resulting division is particularly noteworthy since it also marks a sharp cultural and tribal division which has lasted into modern times. Thus to the west of this line the tribes build domed or beehive-shaped huts, while to the east they build barrel-vaulted huts and mud stalls, or half-sunken barrel-vaulted structures. This line also marks the border between the Tuaregs, who originally lived towards the west, and the Teda, who are natives of the eastern part.

The rock picture galleries invariably lie in the valleys at places where there is still water today. Altogether five large galleries became known to us: Tel Issaghen I, Tel Issaghen II, In Habeter I, In Habeter II and In Habeter III (Pls. 7–9, Figs. 13–19). There are also the pictures of oxen which Heinrich Barth saw in 1850 at the Amman Sememis water hole – which we unfortunately rode past owing to the inattention of our Tuareg guide. And we found some old, though less important pictures of giraffes

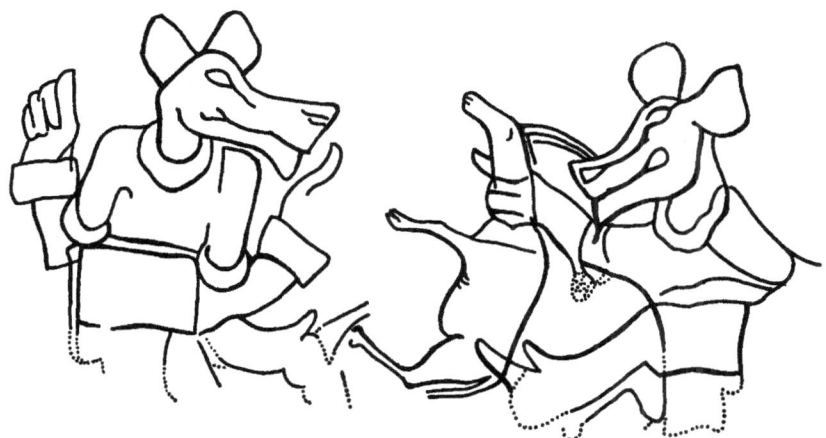

Fig. 13   Jackal-headed demons with slaughtered antelope (rock engraving, Fezzan)

at the water hole between In Habeter I and In Habeter II. The fact that these galleries always seem to lie in places where there is still water today is of decisive importance on the one hand in showing the pattern according to which the land has dried out and turned to desert, and on the other in all questions concerning the age and natural conditions of the period in which the rock engravings were made. A second, equally important fact is that there is evidence of a radical change in the water conditions. The situation seems to be everywhere the same: the galleries are cut into more or less vertical rock walls, and in front of these walls is a flat tongue of land on which people lived in the time of the rock art culture. It was a period of human history in which stone tools were used. These stone tools and the chips left by their manufacture are to be found lying on the ground, and their distribution indicates exactly the limits of the settlement.

The expert in such matters, who also knows that the distribution of pieces washed away by heavy rains is different from their original positions, can make allowances for this blurring of the limits and establish exactly where the old water level came to. In fact the general picture was the same everywhere, but emerged most clearly at In Habeter III: between the village and the rock wall there was a lake, whose surface lay some 5 to 10 metres above the present-day wadi bottom. If one considers the fact that the latter must have risen since through the accumulation of sand, partly washed in by heavy rains and partly blown by the wind, then these lakes must have been extraordinarily deep in the rainy season. Among the animals known to the artists were large crocodiles. These beasts would hardly

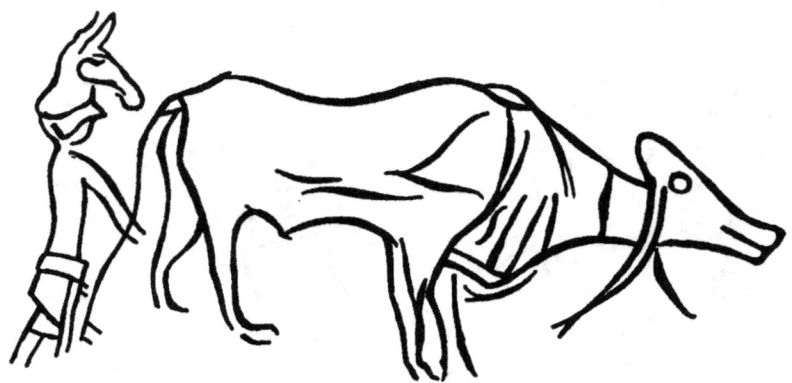

Fig. 14 Masked man with wild ox (rock engraving, Fezzan)

have lived in the lakes between the villages and the rock face, but in the "backwaters" of Wadi Berdjush. Thus we can see that the landscape was particularly rich in water at that time.

Apart from Tel Issaghen I, the general character and appearance of the rock picture galleries is more or less the same; they consist of a near-vertical wall some 50 to 100 metres high and stretching in a slight curve for 100 to 400 metres. The rock face is by no means smooth and regular, however, and reveals the cross-section of a series of sandstone strata of different thicknesses. Sections several metres thick alternate with others of a few decimetres; hard stone strata with soft; coarse grained (even conglomerate-like) with fine. The colour of the stone itself varies between yellow and reddish, changing at the seams, but this is of little importance since the whole is covered with an even, brownish-black patina. The variation of the stone in grain, hardness and thickness naturally makes for a great irregularity in the strata. Some are great solid blocks of stone, others have been clearly worn away by the effects of the weather, temperature changes and sandstorms. Thus there are whole areas which seem made specifically for the creation of rock engravings while in others a favourable surface is hardly to be found.

The best example of the rock pricture galleries is perhaps that of In Habeter III. Among the numerous strata making up the rock face, one at the bottom, another particularly deep one in the middle, and a section on the left of the topmost layer all offered a good area for decoration. The bottom stratum has a giraffe with some men hanging onto its tail; the central one has 1) a group with the animal-headed rhinoceros hunters (Fig. 15), 2) a group of wheel symbols, 3) a giraffe with wheel symbols

86

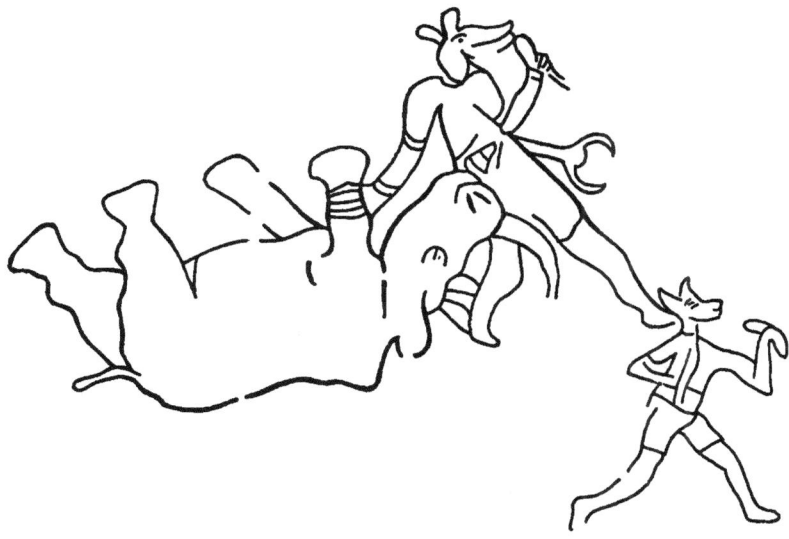

Fig. 15 Animal-headed rhinoceros hunters (rock engraving, Fezzan)

(Fig. 16), 4) a man 'catching' a pair of giraffes, 5) a large composition with
two giraffes and an elephant (Pl. 11), 6) a lion ready to spring (Pl. 13),
7) a giraffe with pointed legs; and a good section of the top stratum has
a group of long-tailed monkeys. The whole arrangement gives the impression of a carefully worked out ensemble. The careful exploitation of the
usable surfaces is matched by the overall arrangement of the site. Here
the rock face does not rise directly out of the floor of the water course,
but is slightly concave and grows partly out of a flat slab at the bottom,
which is large enough for 100 to 200 men to stand or move about on
comfortably. The slab has been cleared of accumulated rock debris and
walled off on both sides – except for a narrow entrance – with stones
laid side by side or on top of one another. As a result it has altogether the
appearance of a closed stage, with the rock wall rising up behind it. A
further artificial addition is a rock staircase on either side which leads
up to a 1 to 3 metre wide platform in front of the central (second) rock
art group. The steps have been made by using the horizontal seams in the
stone, but are of different heights, following the natural thickness of the
strata. The former inhabitants of these rock art sites adjusted the irregu-
larities by placing slabs of half the thickness on the natural steps which
were too high. At In Habeter III, these artificially finished stairways
run at the side of the main picture face. At In Habeter II, however, they

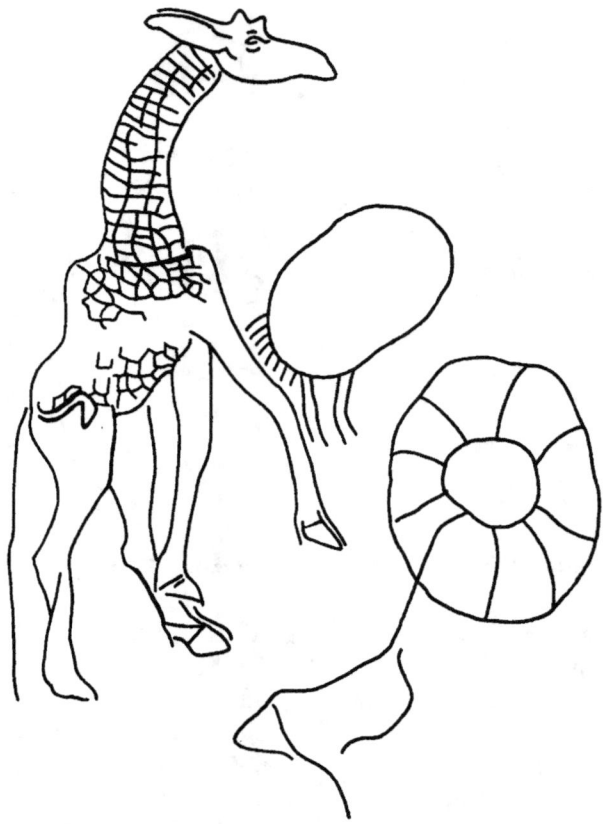

Fig. 16 Giraffe with wheel symbols (rock engraving, Fezzan)

run in a gully at the side (to the left of the rock picture face) through which a path led to a place where stone tools were manufactured on the edge of the plateau, and also right in the middle of the wall itself, past the "landscape" to the main highland track.

In Habeter III is perhaps the best example of a meaningful overall design in which the rock engravings emerge as part of a natural ensemble. We did not find another site with this carefully arranged stage and approaches to the galleries. Many other important pictures, such as the big front-view elephant at In Habeter II (Fig. 17), the big slanting slab at In Habeter I, the moufflon, dancing – and hunting – ceremonies at Tel Issaghen II, etc., are situated at the back of recesses which look as though they must have been used for religious rituals. Generally speaking, with

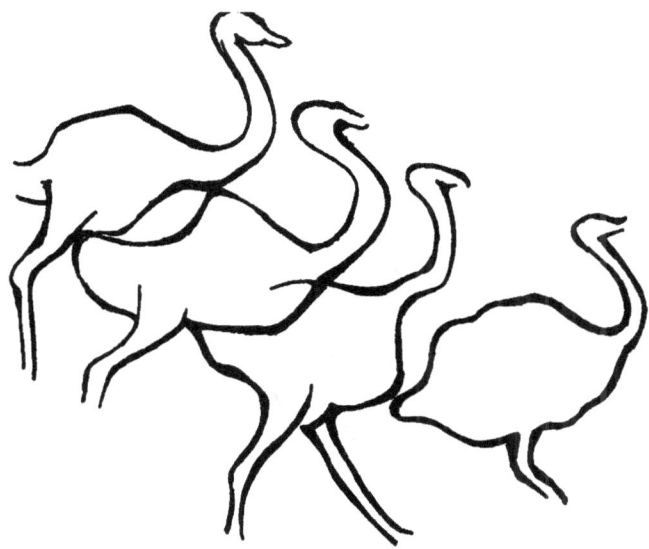

Fig. 17   Ostriches (rock engraving, Fezzan)

one single exception, all these galleries or consecrated places are condemned to a certain unimaginative uniformity by the simple, natural fact of the rock wall.

The one exception is Tel Issaghen I, which was first seen and surveyed by Heinrich Barth in 1850. Here the "holy of holies" does not consist of a steep wall facing the flat tongue on which the village stood. The rock face was ruptured in an early geological age, and the settlement is faced by a knoll only 25 metres high, which slopes away gently towards the back. Here the sanctuary is marked by the engraving of the two men with horned masks fighting over a cow, already sketched by Heinrich Barth. However, the engraving does not stand vertically, but is carved on a large, almost horizontal slab, which is flooded by the first rays of the morning sun. Around this main picture are curious lines and figures chipped and cut in the slab, which Heinrich Barth was unable to decipher. On closer inspection they appear as copulating human couples; the motif is then repeated on the front and vertical faces of the knoll. A little way away from this unusual but clearly recognisable place of worship, was erected a large circle of monolithic stone slabs. One of the sandstone slabs carries a picture of a kneeling male figure with a horned mask. But what is more, if one climbs up to the knoll from the left, one comes to several strikingly large and exposed, visually isolated blocks. These carry the fine

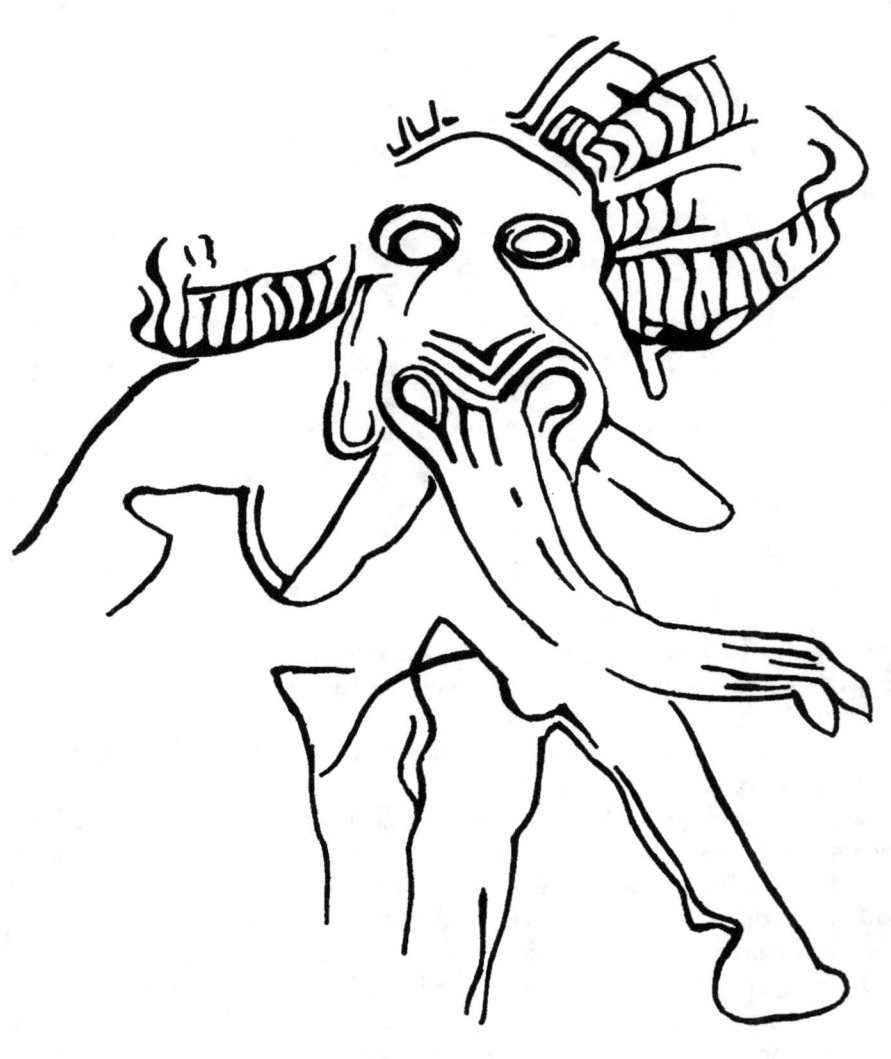

Fig. 18   Demonic elephant-being (rock engraving, Fezzan)

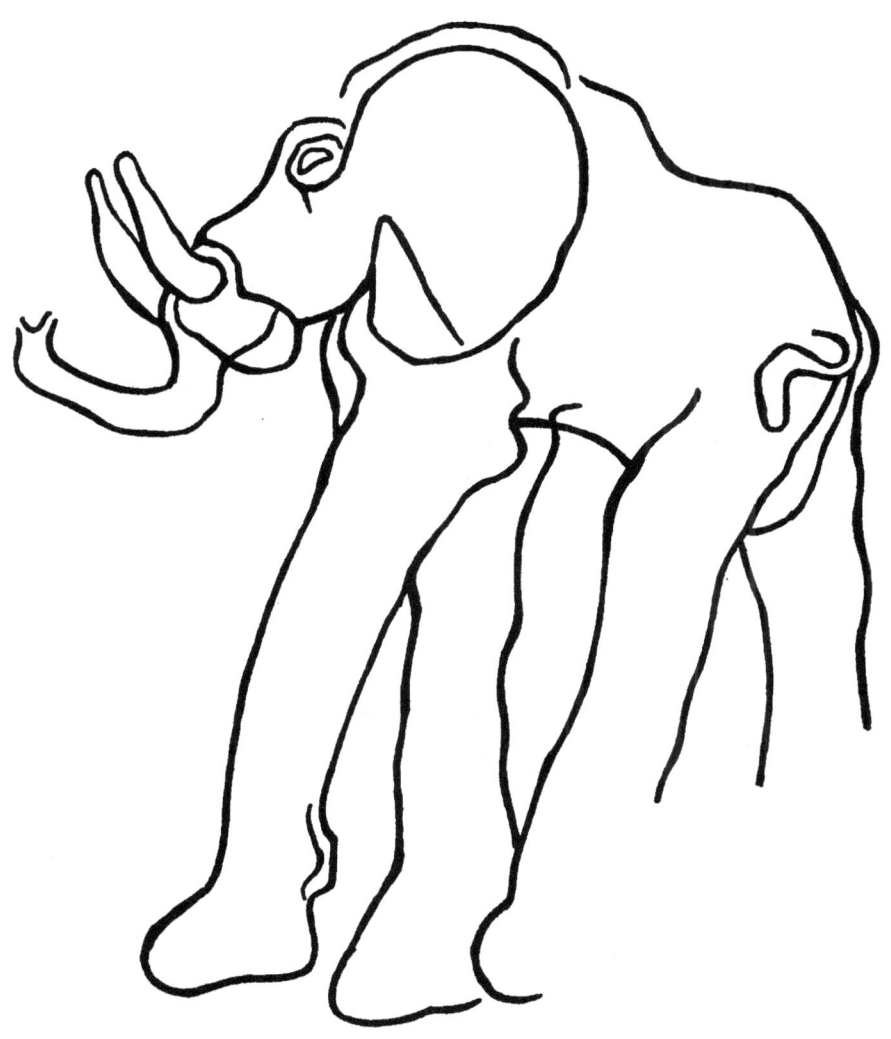

Fig. 19   Elephant (rock engraving, Fezzan)

Bubalus buffalo in half relief and the large head of another horned animal, which escaped Heinrich Barth's notice, and which cannot be regarded as anything but an essential component of an enclosed "temple precinct". These engravings of horned animals by the stairway at the foot, the "holy image" with the scene of worship on the knoll itself, and the large stone circle, in the centre of which the remains of smashed human skulls were excavated – all these elements point to a deliberately planned ensemble.

This impression arises not only from the many relationships which become increasingly clear with observation, but is also given by each individual work and by an overall view of the whole. Moreover not one of the engravings from ancient times shows the slightest trace of frivolity. The lines were carefully hammered and then hollowed out in the hard cliff walls, to a width of 1 to 2.5 centimetres and half that in depth. The procedure must have been extremely laborious. By their noble dimensions alone, these works tower over the few small and miserable figures which the men who introduced the camel felt obliged to "scratch" or "pick out" between them. The difference between the many prehistoric archaeological pictures and the few from historical times is so great that there is no possibility of confusion.

The technique of the old engravings is always the same: the outlines are roughed out first with a dotted line, then hollowed out into grooves. The oldest engravings show a simple rounded depression, while those of the later, most accomplished period, show a triangular cut. Relief outlines are found relatively frequently among the older works. Scraped surfaces are rare; more often one finds a light sculptural effect produced by the smoothing off of outlines. On the other hand some kind of surface treatment must have been carried out for the application of colour, since the remains of several giraffes done in the old style in the cave entrance at Tel Issaghen II show clear signs of having been painted. A little red and rather more white could be recognised. Naturally such traces could only have remained on the protected walls of a cave. On the exterior rock walls, all traces of colour or of a fine surface treatment would have been destroyed over the millennia by sandstorms.

We must not forget that these are the fragmentary remains of a monumental art of the past. Hundreds of engravings must have been lost as the rock face crumbled, and most of those which remain today are no more than the "shadows of former perfection".

8. Rock Art of South Africa*

The words "rock art" remind us of many works which have enabled us, during the past few decades, to draw closer to the cultural life of past ages. Most famous of these are the monuments of rock art in the Franco-Cantabrian style which have been discovered in caves in southern France and north-west Spain, and which belong to the Palaeolithic age (Solutrian, Aurignacian and Magdalenian). The rock paintings of eastern Spain also belong in this group, and are now generally linked in origin with the Capsian in Africa, which would mean that they were roughly contemporary with those of the Aurignacian period. The rock art of north-west Africa and the Sahara is in many strata, of which some are perhaps near in time to the oldest in Europe. But there is no doubt that the representations did not come to an end with the early Stone Ages. The older works are often covered with later paintings, and it can easily be established that at a period when writing was known and even at a time when the camel appeared, examples were produced which are at any rate sketches based on the monumental creations of the past.

In addition, the Nubian and Libyan deserts and the Nile Valley between, were the home of ancient rock art (Pls. 3, 4, 14, 15, 18). Here there is a similarity with the art of north-west Africa (Figs. 8–12), although there are no great monumental works among the paintings. It can clearly be seen here, too, that the rock walls were decorated during a wide range of periods. The older style ended with the Egyptian temple wall paintings and only died out after the Semitic immigration.

The artistic output in these two African centres of rock painting did not, in contrast to the European centres, die out with the Stone Age, but this applies still more to the third African region concerned, South Africa (Pls. 1, 16; Figs. 20–41). It has been established beyond doubt that many of the paintings there were produced in our time, that is, after the arrival of the first Europeans. It is said that at the time when general hostilities against the small, "thieving robber" bushmen in the mountainous country of the south and east had not yet led to their total extinction, many of the early immigrants considered them to be the originators of these paintings. It is even said that they were seen painting them. It is noteworthy, however, that no one who has expressed this view has been able to answer the next obvious question, as to the tools used for the pictures.

---

* From "Mitteilungen des Forschungsinstituts für Kulturmorphologie", 1930, pp. 88–93, and "Erythräa", 1931, pp. 304–316.

From the sum of the known facts it may be concluded that the "bushmen" did in fact still practise the art of painting, but that they were only the creators of the final, most recent layer of paintings, since these great galleries of rock paintings, the greatest in the world, with their succession of countless styles, can only be explained by the fact that they were executed during different periods. One of the northern styles, for example, is similar in technique to the paintings on the walls of the old Mashona huts, and died out at an early date. The term "bushman art", still frequently used today, is incorrect and unscientific, as it gives a totally wrong idea.

The South African rock paintings are the richest in the world, both as regards style and individual or groups of paintings. Unfortunately one must add that this may possibly soon be a thing of the past; most of the paintings are in great danger, for a variety of reasons. Where they are on the sharply overhanging walls of "caves" or in cave-like niches, these are frequently used today to shelter cattle from the rain, for hours or days at a time. In several places the animals' backs and horns have rubbed the paintings away and completely destroyed them. Elsewhere the damage has been done by smoke from fires, which has corroded the paintings even more seriously. Then again there are places where the thoughtless herdboys have used them as targets in their stonethrowing games. And it must also be admitted that these "bushmen's caves" are favourite places for excursions and picnics, and that the sightseers love carving their names over the old paintings. Finally, in the north, some of the paintings have been scratched and rinsed off, to make powerful remedies from the solution.

However, there are in general two more serious sources of danger, which are very hard to fight. The first is that there is a strange feeling among the natives that these paintings, which they cannot themselves understand, but which they hold in awe (in Rhodesia they are held to be the embodiment of departed spirits), should not be visited by Europeans. So that the Mashona and Basuto, for example, have intentionally destroyed paintings. The second danger is the climate. It is quite clear that many rock paintings which thirty years ago were still brilliantly fresh are today faded or have crumbled away. Many people hold that this deterioration is a sign that the paintings are of recent origin, but as there are walls which have three or four overlaid layers from different periods which are peeling off, this theory does not seem to hold water. Another point is even more important. Reports agree that – especially in the south – all the rock paintings have undergone a surface change during a single generation, and are more crumbling in one place, more brittle in another. I would certainly relate this to another fact, the undeniable change in the climate, which must have affected the water content of the air. The difference between the dryness of the cold season and the dampness of the hot season must have increased. It is therefore understandable that even the millennia old rock paintings with carved contours of North-West Africa and the Sahara are today peeling off and have only retained small patches of their coloured decoration.

If we consider the rock art as such, the same questions as regards style and difference in age must be asked. A consideration of the techniques is revealing here. Two completely different and independent methods can be distinguished: firstly, pictures made by chiselling, in other words relief work, and secondly, colour work, drawing and painting.

The first group of "engravings" are in a completely individual style. They are not worked in the monumental style of the Atlas mountains in the Sahara, cut and with polished surfaces, but picked out in the style used universally in the Nubian desert. One can find clumsy and finely executed examples. The engravings never appear to have been made on "vaults", overhanging rocks or cave walls, but always on flat or sloping blocks of stone which were lying about. They show two different motifs: animals, and incomprehensible geometric designs. The former are without doubt the most artistic, the latter more carelessly worked. There is no feeling for composition. All the animals are represented singly. Two giraffes standing beside each other are the nearest approach to a composition. Human figures are hardly ever shown, and when they are, one cannot escape the impression that they are "more recent" work.

The better South African engravings are really fine works of art. The surface textures of the antelopes, hippopotamuses, rhinoceroses and so on are so finely embossed, the folds of hide or skin so skilfully tooled, that they look as though they are coloured; especially as only those works have survived which are engraved on hard stones such as basalt, diabase and diorite. Here the colour of the tooling and the flat surfaces is the same throughout. This indicates a very early date, because for the coloured effect of the freshly cut surface to be dulled by the patina of age takes a very long time, many centuries in fact, on these types of stone. These rock engravings belong in technique to the style of the Nubian desert and to the oldest and most recent of the Saharan Atlas engravings but their accomplished style places them among the very first. In Klerksdorp and by the Orange River stone tools have been dug up near these fine engravings, which are typically Capsian. There is no connection between the style of these engravings and the paintings discussed below. The two styles are diametrically opposed. Quite often engravings are found underneath paintings.

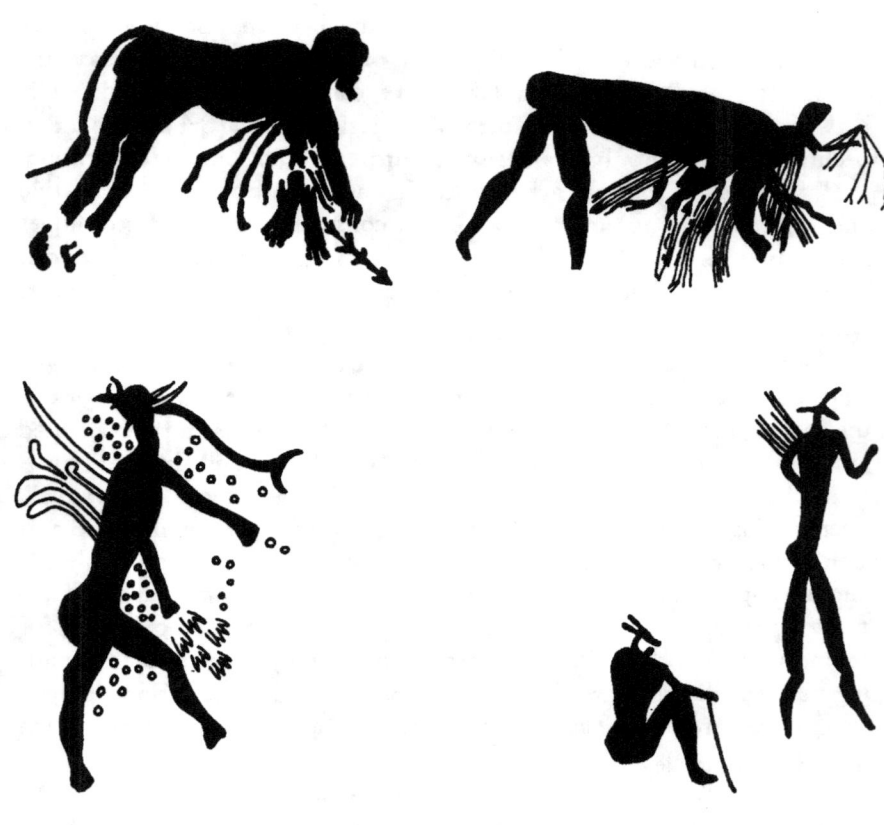

Fig. 20 Man in animal disguise (rock painting, Cape Province)
Fig. 21 Man in animal disguise (rock painting, Cape Province)
Fig. 22 Striding man with elephant head (rock painting, Natal)
Fig. 23 Two men with animal heads (rock painting, Lesotho)

Among the South African paintings two very different major styles can be seen – styles which seem originally to have been completely unrelated, but which have both influenced later works.

The southern style (Figs. 20–24, 26) is so called because these works are prevalent in the south from Cape Town to the southern and eastern Transvaal; and beyond the Transvaal Great Escarpment from the Limpopo northwards while in Bechuanaland they are only found in rare instances. This style has a tendency towards the polychromatic, and towards a highly polished treatment of the surface. It is a painterly style. In contrast to the engravings, the works have a strong feeling for composition. Dancing, processions, council meetings, hunts alternate in lively succession. It is striking how many paintings in this style show human bodies with animal heads (Figs. 20–23). At times one is inclined to think that these are hunting masks. But when one sees an elephant with its natural limbs or a ram-man walking next to a vulture-man, one relinquishes this idea. Here too, the most artistic and scrupulously executed works appear to be the oldest.

In distinguishing the style of the northern group, (Pls. 1, 16, 17; Figs. 25, 27–41), which are mainly found in Southern Rhodesia, the main characteristics are, firstly, the almost exclusive use of ferric oxide colouring, i. e. red. It is a monochrome, silhouette style, to which the only detailed treatment is added by white colouring or stippling. It is difficult to say how general this detailed work was, because the white additions have only withstood the weather in a few places. Secondly, the representation always starts with a contour; the surface is then filled in with closely hatched lines, and never polished as in the southern style. Finally, the authentic, clear paintings of this northern style group are so different from those of the true South African style, that a skilled eye can recognize them at once.

The character and style are also reflected in the forms and nature of the motifs used; this can be seen in the simple human figures and their gestures. The southern style has more rounded forms, cylindrical bodies, with extravagant movement, the northern a tendency to angularity, cuneiform bodies and measured gestures; in the profile representations hands, feet and head are clearly shown in profile pointing one way, with body facing forwards. In seated figures which are stylistically pure the same trends are evident. The sitting position is quite different in the southern paintings and the northern.

Whereas the southern style is content to portray limited scenes such as dances, processions, gatherings, and herds as single scenes, and – if there is more room available – several of these one above the other, the northern paintings delight in covering a surface with a single design. Particularly

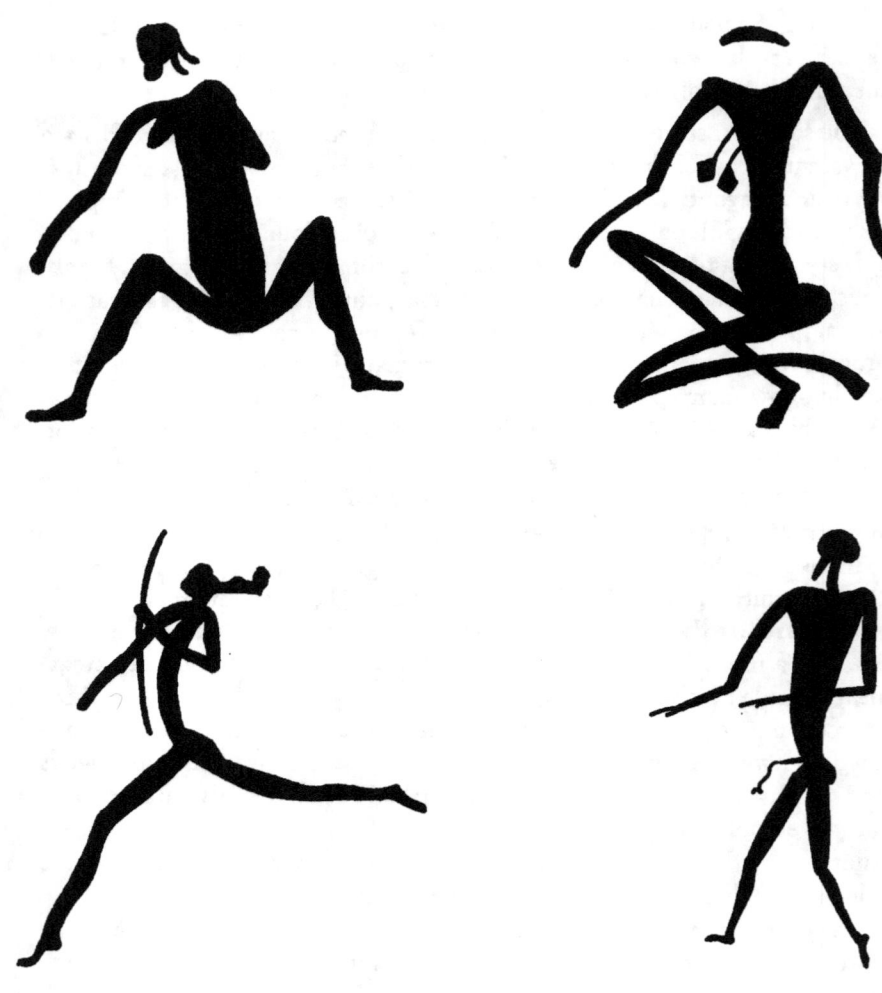

Fig. 24 Seated woman (rock painting, Cape Province)
Fig. 25 Seated woman (rock painting, Rhodesia)
Fig. 26 Running man (rock painting, Lesotho)
Fig. 27 Striding man (rock painting, Rhodesia)

98

typical of this are the great spreads in the Inoro Cave, and hunting scenes.

Like the southern area, the northern naturally includes many individual paintings of animals and human figures (Pl. 17, Figs. 25, 27, 41). Yet the quantities of compositions which remain today must be described as very large. Here too there are many representations of hunts, processions and battle scenes, but they are not the most stylistically important, even as regards the composition. Group paintings are more significant (Pl. 1, 16, Figs. 28–40). In the great Inoro Cave, which was certainly used in several instances as a burial chamber, tragedies and burials are the themes. The remains of a more recent burial indicate that the cave was used of old for this purpose. The natives in many parts used to relate how the Barosi invading their land in their time had disturbed the graves and robbed them for their golden treasure, in order to destroy sinister spirits of earlier kings and at the same time enrich themselves.

There is further evidence of the sacral-manistic character of many of these paintings. In February 1929 we succeeded in entering and investigating several royal tombs of the old style. We found remarkable, cascade-like altars, sacrificial dishes and urns, great heaps of natural rock, carefully cleaned wall facings, especially in front of a deeply cut burial niche. Traces and remains of red colouring matter could be seen. A funerary priest we found later related how, as a small boy, he had brought to the cave the colours with which the great figure painting on the wall was touched up from time to time. Large and important funerary monuments of this kind were certainly not only portrayed on walls. It seems to me rather that other burial paintings have not survived because they were painted on ornaments. On the other hand we found several on deeply overhanging, chapel-like semicircular vaults, with a massive flat-topped block of rock lying under the wall painting. These chapel rooms with altar stones were described to me as Dende Maro (king's thrones). Two great works which we found in such places depicted the recumbent king, with a row of concentric circles below, filled with all kinds of spirit figures. Comparison with other paintings showed us that the "Dzivoa" or holy lakes, were represented thus in circles, protecting the sacrificial and otherworldly figures (cf. p. 198).

Landscape motifs play an important role (Pl. 16; Figs. 32–34). An amazing number of types of tree are shown (Figs. 28–31). This style of art is not afraid of complicated themes, and it is this above all which rightly differentiates it from the prehistoric art of earlier ages. One stands amazed before the renderings of trees, which although very stylized, manage to make the botanical categories quite clear. Then there are whole

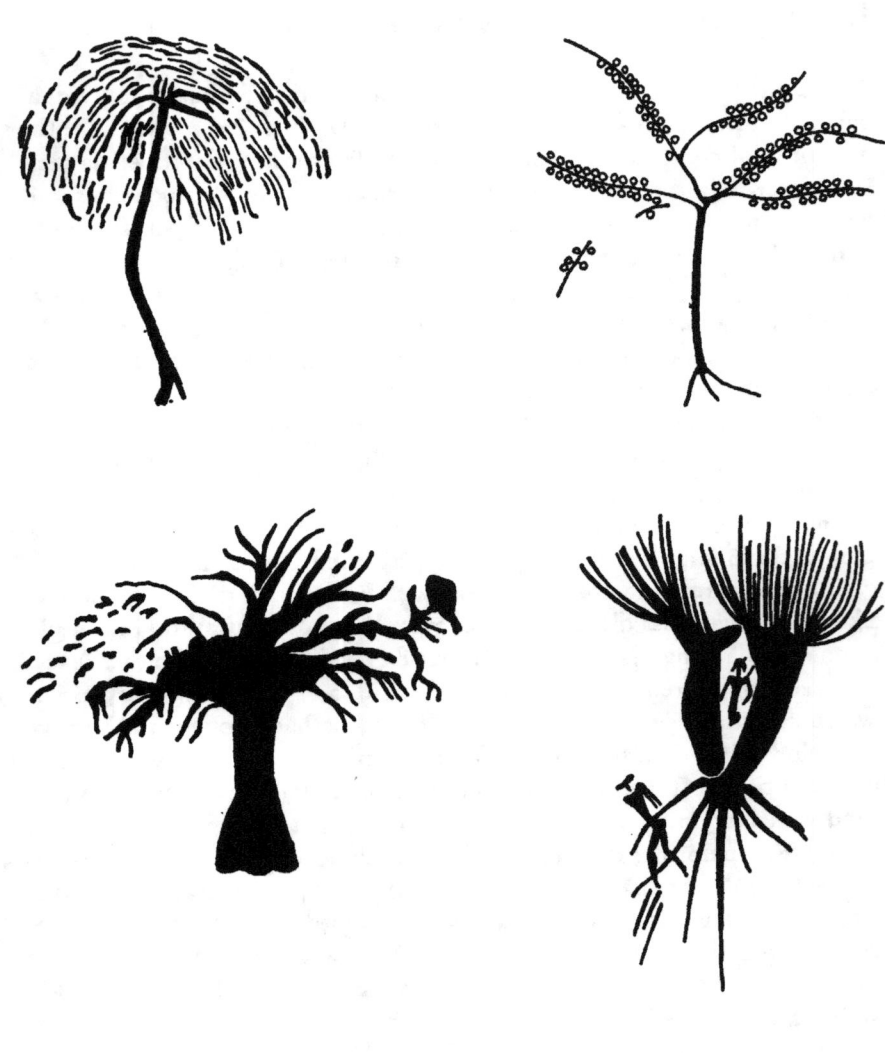

Fig. 28–31 Pictures of trees (rock paintings, Rhodesia)

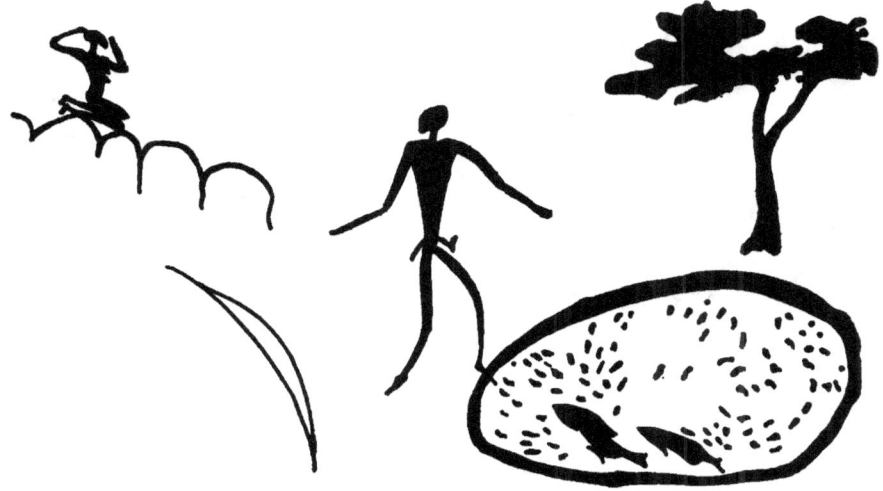

Fig. 32 Landscape with pond and people (rock painting, Rhodesia)

landscapes: a man springs over a great slab of rock to where another man, obviously dead, lies under a tree. And a more complicated scene: in the centre a man who has thrown down his bow behind him walks towards a circle, which clearly, from the two fishes and stippling in it, represents a pool (Fig. 32). On the bank to the right is a tree. On the left, behind the man who is hurrying down to the water, is a chain of rocks, on which a woman is kneeling, in a posture of lamentation. It seems possible that this painting represents a mythical theme.

The most distinctive element in the landscape pictures is the representation of rocks (Figs. 33, 34). One must turn to the striking natural patterns which arose from the decomposition of the hard layer of granite in Southern Rhodesia to find prototypes for this. The great, gently rounded blocks, 5–20 metres high and 2–5 metres broad, carved out by the alternating high day temperatures and night cold, by rain and drought, stand side by side like soldiers or lie across one another like sacks waiting to be carted. These gigantic natural features, when incorporated in monumental landscape paintings, led to the most striking representations. In one painting, five of these cucumber-shaped blocks are shown standing upright. The painting is in strokes, as described above, not yet linked with the flat surfaces. If one looks closely, one can see that the artist has worked from right to left. When the fourth block was finished, a small human figure was added and then the last block drawn in with fine strokes. One

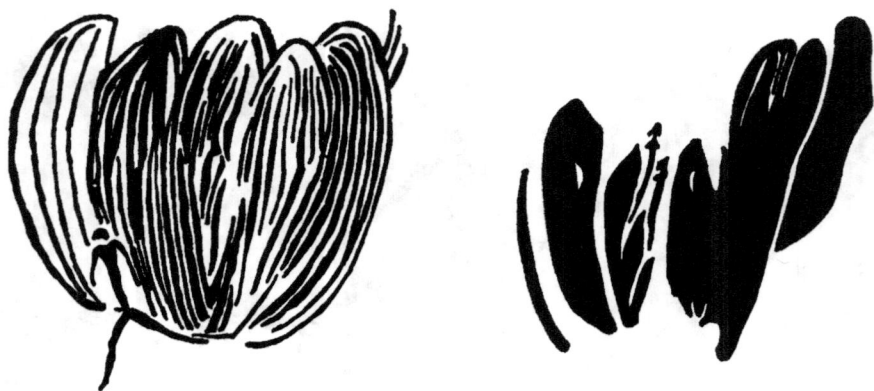

Fig. 33–34 Pictures of rocks (rock paintings, Rhodesia)

can see that these were only drawn in after the man by the way that the lines surround the man, and that therefore the artist deliberately planned a composition to include the figure; the painting seems to indicate that we should take it to represent a man who is striding out from a crevice between two rocks into the open.

Another picture takes us into the realm of fantasy: a strange crowd of women, children and leather bags surround the "rose" of the rocks. In yet another, from between the ghostly masses climb limbless spirits, familiar from other paintings. But we can only guess whether what is shown here represents rocks (and guesswork cannot always be trusted). To add to the uncertainty, there are many extremely strange objects in these scenes, which were possibly once derived from landscape elements, but have come so far from these that they could equally well be considered as giant cigar stumps, sausages, root tubers or cubes, or even slide rules. Here the original stylized natural forms have become geometric compositions, of which we are today unable to understand the various categories, and which we have therefore taken to calling simply "Formlinge".

If we now turn to the most important compositions with human figures, we might begin our study by considering a motif which occurs very frequently, and to which we have given the name "pietà" (Figs. 35, 36). Men and women are gathered with expressive gestures of grief or mourning round one or two recumbent figures. Clearly this is a representation of mourning for the dead. A great number of variations on this theme can be found among the paintings, so that we are justified in saying that this is one of the most common motifs in the classic cuneiform style. A comparison between works in this group should make it possible to

102

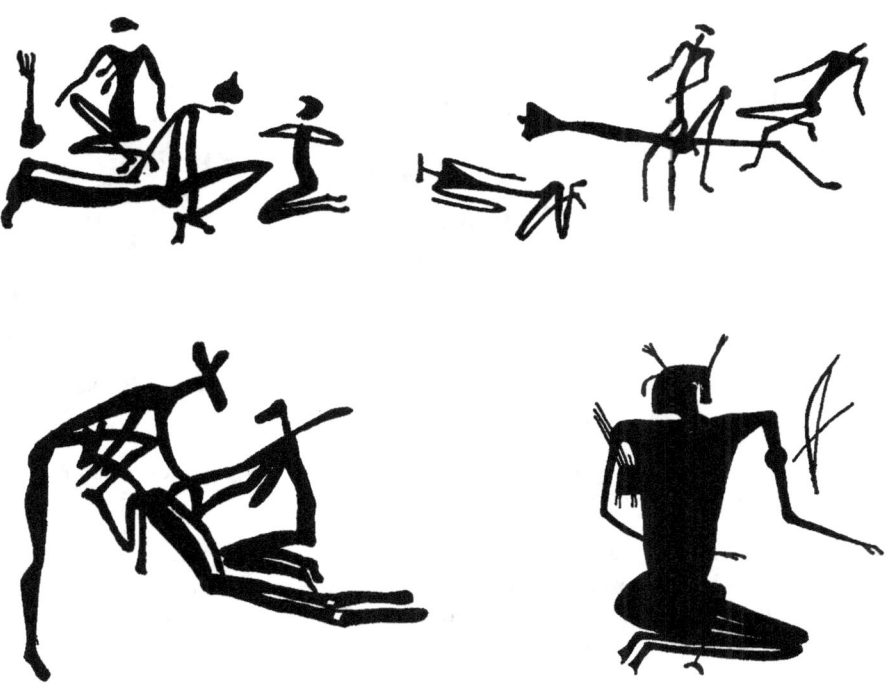

Fig. 35–36 Mourning for the dead (rock paintings, Rhodesia)
Fig. 37 Demonic beings grieving (rock painting, Rhodesia)
Fig. 38 Large seated man (rock painting, Rhodesia)

distinguish between their ages, and to chart the degeneration from the original clear and austere style to the softer style.

From here we come inevitably to the great monumental paintings in the original style, of which all the most significant are found near Marendellas and Rusapi, and therefore quite near the Makoni tombs. First the major monument A, a painting 2.62 metres in width and 1.72 metres high (Fig. 39). It is in four sections, and we will consider the top left section first. The meaning of the scene is easy to understand. Two men are hurrying towards a larger seated figure, to whom they hand their bows. We know from medieval accounts of the territory, that a king's enthronement was celebrated by the headmen bringing him their bows. Thus we may assume that the larger figure, distinguished by a different style of dress and the royal cloak over his shoulders, is a new king. It is a coronation ceremony. To the right of the group of three figures is another, smaller figure, facing to the right, in the posture of a mourner.

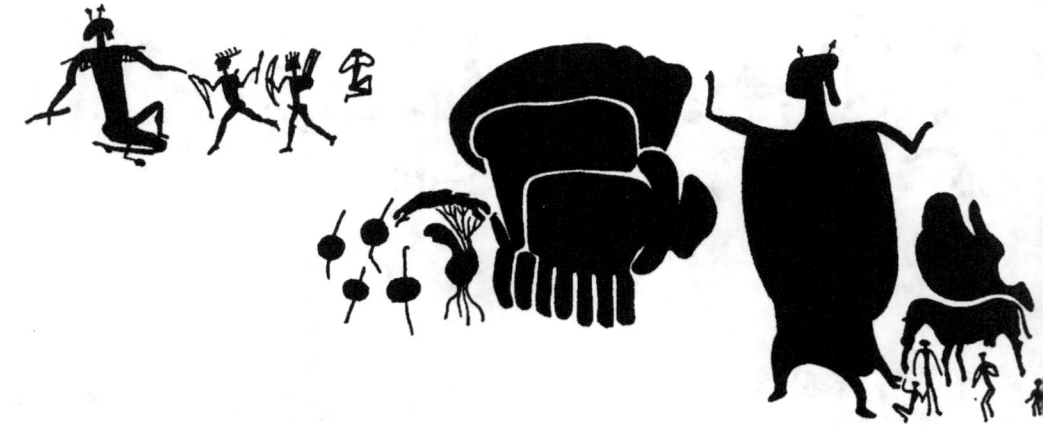

Fig. 39 Funeral obsequies of a dead king and homage to a new king. Rocks and plants interspersed (rock painting, Rhodesia)

The most striking of the three other sections is the largest, central one. A head, in apparel similar to that of the newly elected king, towers above a great five-fold decoration. By comparing this with similar representations in the caves near Mtoko, one can deduce that the flat surface represents an ox hide, and it was probably meant as the ox hide in which the king's corpse would be shrouded. If this is the case, the round bundle of the fourth section must be the tied up corpse, and the figures below, a zebra and several humans, are the sacrificial offerings. The zebra, at least, is represented as dying, or as a sacrifice, because a stream of blood pours from its nose and throat. There remains the interesting second section, which shows a massive structure above a short base, and beside this a tree, on which are balls on stems. The tree is so clearly depicted that it is easy to identify botanically. It is a Ngoja-tree, which has spherical pods with black seeds. These seeds were crushed for their oil, which was used solely for the embalming of corpses which were to be mummified. If we take the mass in this section to be a group of rocks (which is corroborated by a study of the meaning of this type of "Formling"), and surmise that the cave tombs of earlier kings were found in such rock masses, the meaning of the grieving posture of the small figure on the right of the first section becomes clear. This figure, which is in the background of the crowning ceremony of a young king, is mourning the king's predecessor, and the larger, right-hand side of the painting depicts the latter's burial.

Having solved the meaning of one of these monuments, it should not be difficult to unravel another. Let us take monument D, a broad, seated figure, who has laid aside his bow, with typical headdress, royal loincloth and bracelet. It is painted on a gently overhanging, beautifully smooth spread of rock. Beneath the wall is a cube-shaped block, like a sacrificial altar. I later learnt that such places (blocks under overhanging wall paintings) were called Dende Maro. This is the name for a stone throne. It was also explained to me by the descendant of the last Mukuabpassi priest, that this painting Monument C, corresponded exactly to the painting in the king's tomb of the Muonve.

Next, the important Monument B (Pl. 1). Here the king lies in the typical posture of the dead in the "pietà". Typical loincloth, body swathed in bandages, a horned mask on its head. The left hand stretches out towards an unidentifiable object. On its raised knee is a small bird. Round about, human figures walk or hover. On the right below is a larger figure surrounded by blocks of rock (?). Below the group, and separated from it by several parallel lines, is a confused mass of figures and sacrificial offerings. According to other prototypes these parallel lines may be taken to be Dsivoa, the banks of the mythical lakes of the other world.

We find something very similar on main Monument C. From the area of the Dzivoa lines, in which trees and ghostly figures are drawn, a procession of mythical beings climbs from the left-hand side to a central reclining figure on the right. Behind the latter on the right-hand side is a great "rose" of "Formlinge", and beneath that several trees.

Having attempted a very general interpretation of the most important examples of the classic cuneiform style, let us pass on to a consideration of a few more paintings which are not immediately comprehensible. One shows a broken line, which rises above a buried woman and runs up into a coiled snake (Fig. 40). Above to the left another female figure is bending forwards. In another painting there is again the corpse of a woman, lying under a tree, with a man beside her lifting his hands to heaven in prayer or making a vow (Fig. 41). A woman bends down from above, with many parallel lines ending in drops leading from her to the earth. One naturally assumes that here and in a series of similar pictures the lines and dots represent rain. So we might venture to suppose that we are concerned here with rainmaking sacrifices, possibly related to the accounts and myths of princesses sacrificed as the evening star goes down and rain beginning as the morning star appears (cf. p. 210).

However, even if many of these works remain incomprehensible to us today, they still belong unequivocally in style to the ones previously described and together make up a unified group, in the same organically evolved style. This style is only connected with the "bushman paintings"

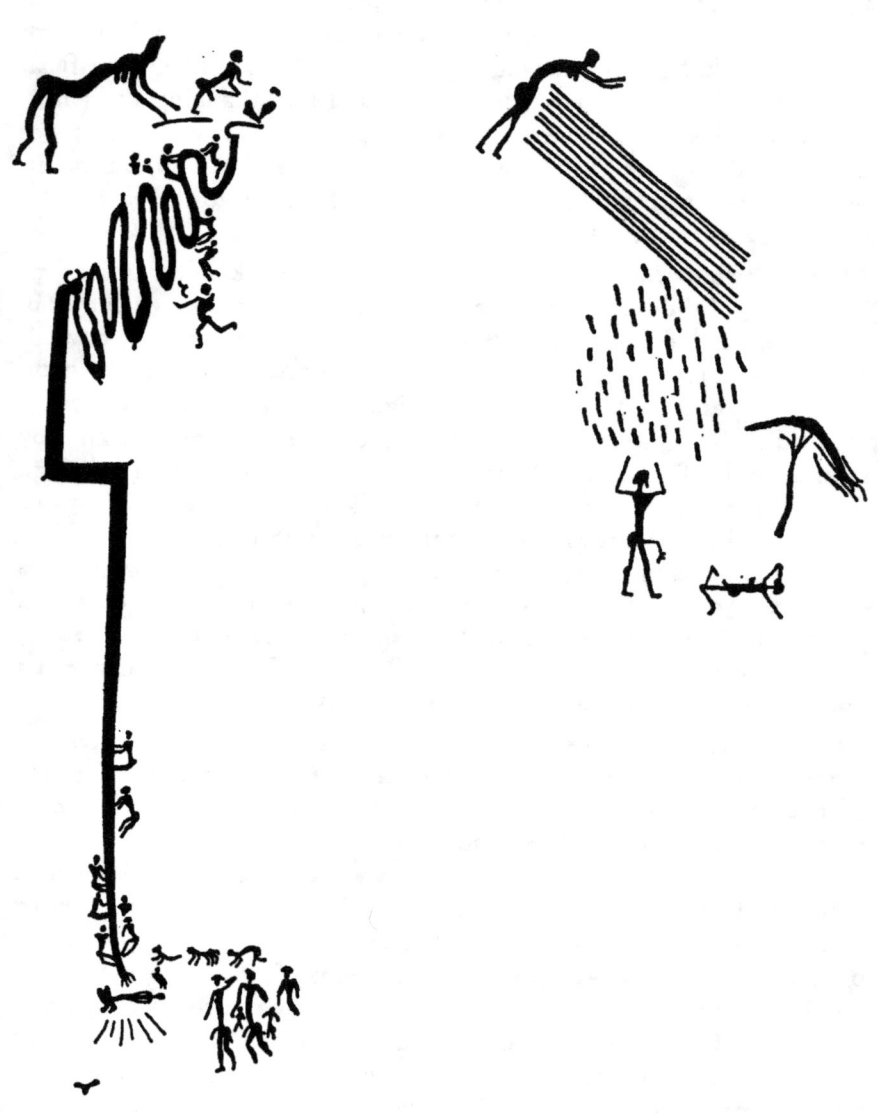

Fig. 40 Mythological scene (rock painting, Rhodesia)
Fig. 41 Mythological scene-rain ceremony (rock painting, Rhodesia)

of the south in that it may have influenced them at some point, both in the south and south-west.

This art of the northern style represents a world complete in itself, both in form and in context. The subjects of the art of the south are limited by man's place in his environment, and even the animal-men can be taken to represent the individual ideas of the artist rather than the generally accepted concept of a world order. In the northern, cuneiform-style works, however, there is a complete, well thought-out representation of a transcendental concept of existence. An existence in which the fact of death plays an important part; an existence in which the natural world, and the cosmos itself, is so meaningful that its various elements – lake or Dzivoa, trees and rocks – are represented. Thus we come to recognize that *this* art – even if we have to maintain the rather clumsy categories into which it has become customary to slot it – must no longer be regarded as "primitive". During that first period of culture, which we are accustomed to call "primitive", only human and animal forms are depicted, not the geographical, botanical and cosmic details of the world. The first "landscapes" appear with the beginning of a "higher culture". And so I do not hesitate to call these cuneiform works the works of a past advanced culture.

This higher culture began when men switched from a fleeting, undirected interest in everything animal and human to a concentrated effort in one direction, with fixed rules of thought and expression. This we can see in the works in the cuneiform style. The most important, described above, are the major works and royal scenes. They all appear to have served at the spiritual and funeral rites of the kings. The cleaned walls of the old tombs were covered with such paintings; the Muonve Cave was only one of many. An old Matebele in the Matopo hills told me how as a young man he had joined some robbers in the Marandellas or Charter district, and how one day the robber band had found a cave tomb, which was painted from top to bottom with great figures, and how they had hacked away at the magnificent wall and found a cave behind it with corpses and "much gold" (?). In this way, therefore, such art was used for cult purposes and had a highly mythical meaning.

There seems to be no doubt that this art in the south and east of Africa represented a high degree of culture. The oldest paintings are the most significant and the largest; and they are limited to a fairly small area, which today comprises the Mtoko, Rusapi, Marendellas and Charter districts, and earlier no doubt Gutu and Victoria. In both the latter, however, everything has been destroyed by vandals. Only the occasional discovery indicates that this distinct style was current here too. But even the fine paintings in the Matopo hills and near Salisbury, have already lost some of the great majesty of the "royal monuments".

One can trace how the classic style degenerated in many places, losing its clear-cut austerity. The cuneiform bodies became more and more cylindrical, the angular limbs became bent. The big figures declined in number, or rather, the powerful, fully shaped figures became pin-men, as can be seen from the three "pietà" figures. At the same time the motifs in the paintings changed. They became less and less intellectualized, until there were only paintings of elephant hunts and battles once more, with little feeling for the nuances of weapons, dress, and tools. And as this atrophy set in, the symbolical representations of rocks, water and other aspects of the natural world gave way to the "Formlinge", which for us are only significant as ornamental decorations of the flat surfaces. The new art was only a copy of the old.

In this way the art of a higher culture degenerated. Younger generations were not capable of achieving what their forebears had done. If we seek to relate the old works to other aspects of the culture, in order for instance to find out their relative age, we can find various means of corroboration.

We must look first at the intellectual relationship between these works of art and the "cosmic world view". This is not only apparent in the images in the royal monuments – the Dzivoa and rocks, the rain ceremonies – but also in the austere style, which expresses the cultural ideal of the god-king's state.

One should note also that the large paintings of this type were used to decorate the king's graves, and that they were not only painted on walls, but also on plastered wall niches. Here another point is worth mentioning. The art of using mud, making mud walls and mud plaster, was introduced into architecture with the "South Erythraean"* culture. The tall mud silos of south-east Africa originated in this way. All the early travellers have told us that the walls of the mud towers were painted with pictures, both in Southern Rhodesia and in Katanga on the Tanganyika (and still were in Bent's time). So the old fresco paintings spread here, and south as far as Basutoland, passing into a form of decorative craftwork. Painting in this style may surely have migrated here at the same time as the mud-wall and macadamizing techniques.

Finally, it is interesting to note the omission of one motif in the paintings

---

* Frobenius conceived the "South Erythraean Culture" as the southernmost outlier of a state-forming African culture with a developed ritual kingship.

of the classic style. We have seen what an important role the black bulls played in the mythology. But there is not the suggestion of a cow in any single painting. There are no domestic cattle. It must therefore have been an animal which was only used for religious purposes. We know from an account from the old Portuguese times that this was the position as regards cattle breeding. Only the king was allowed to raise cattle, and they were as valuable as gold. Yet at this very time the Hottentots in the south and the Wahuma in the north were driving their cattle across the African plains – although not the small, black breed, which from time immemorial had been a sacred animal in Southern "Eryträa"*. All this points to a very early date.

There are many other details in these first paintings which indicate an extremely early date. The Portuguese accounts, which are otherwise so accurate, say nothing about the sacred masks which the kings wore. Nor about the striking loincloth decorations and clothes of the prominent figures in the paintings. Clothing in the regions we are concerned with had already changed radically by the Middle Ages.

Taking all these points into consideration, it seems certain that the classical cuneiform style of art in South Africa must have begun at a time when the "South Erythraean" culture held sway in Africa in all its youthful stylistic vigour, affecting the whole way of life as well as the art.

* cf. p. 108.

9. African Hunters: The Mahalbi Culture*

In the Sudanese world of legend and myth, the hunters have a particular role. They represent not only a particular occupation, but also a particular culture. Even outside the world of legend, the different tribes speak of the hunters as a special tribal and cultural community.

An unusually light-skinned type of "Magussaua" are said to live in widely scattered groups in the great population basin between the Niger and Lake Chad, and particularly in the northern regions. The Hausa refer to them simply as Mahalbi, which means hunters. They wander around in small family-like groups, living in the bush and turning up now here, now there amongst the farmers. Although they are so widely scattered, however, they never lose contact with one another.

The Hausa say that these Mahalbi are not only very clever fellows, and a real blessing in the fight against beasts of prey, but that they are above all uncommonly gifted with magical powers. This is particularly apparent in the initiation of youths at the time of puberty and their introduction to their tribal functions.

Before their initiation, the youths may neither indulge in sexual intercourse nor hunt large animals. For the initiation ceremony they are taken into the bush, and there dancing and confusing noises are used to send the youths into a state of excitement. At the height of their ecstasy a leopard (or a leopard-like creature) suddenly appears. Its aspect is terrifying and the youths are frightened to death. This creature leaps on the youths and wounds them, particularly in their sexual parts, so that they carry the marks for the rest of their life. Some say that one of their testicles is torn off. Days of orgiastic celebrations then follow. This is the time at which certain buffalo horns are prepared, which serve the hunters as their most important magical device until the day of their death. Into these horns they pour the blood of the animals which they kill. The women are not allowed to come into contact with them, otherwise the most wild and dangerous animals will turn into beautiful women, and take bloody revenge on the hunter when he unsuspectingly yields to them. The youths have to leave the place of initiation in the bush on their heels, for if they left in the normal way, the wild bush creature would be able to follow them by the imprint of their toes. From now on the youths are in great demand as sleeping partners. The nearer they are to their time in the bush, the more fertile they are considered to be.

* From "Erlebte Erdteile", Vol. 7, 1929, pp. 31–59.

The youth has now become a hunter, and henceforth he must pour a few drops of blood from every animal he kills into his magical buffalo horn. As a hunter he should not pursue his game too greedily, but be content with a successful kill. Otherwise he will one day turn into a lion with the "evil eye".

In Adamaua it is related that the "hunters" in the region of Lake Chad and in Bornu are particularly light-skinned and quite different in appearance from the people of Adamaua. In these tribes, when a youth has killed his first antelope, he is put in a hole in the ground, where he is tortured, so that he loses a great deal of blood. One of the antelope's horns is removed and the blood poured into this. If it is a male antelope, then one of its testicles is removed and likewise placed in the horn. "Otherwise the beasts turn into women."

Numerous references can also be found in the western areas. Wandering Diulas tell of "light-skinned hunters" who travel in troops through the lands north of Senegal and far into the north, and who are neither Moors nor Berbers. There are many small groups which are all part of a large community. They readily eat wild berries and fruit, but never corn. Here again the first hunt and the age of puberty play an important role. After their first kill the youths are shut in a cave in the mountains, and here they must paint pictures on the walls, such as I saw near Bandiangara in the Homburi mountains. These pictures are painted with the blood of the shot antelope.

The Mande peoples also tell of tribes of hunters, both past and present. These play a large part in their legends, where we find mention of the "Kulluballi". The following story is now told about the first "Kulluballi". This hunter received his strength from an antelope. A lion and he were hunting it at the same time, and the little antelope said to the hunter: "Shoot me; break off one of my horns and pour my blood into it; then, when the lion attacks you, he will only scratch you but will not be able to kill you." The "Kulluballi" did as the antelope had advised him. He shot it and broke off one of its horns, then he poured the antelope's blood into the horn. Afterwards the lion attacked the Kulluballi, and tore open his sexual parts with its claws, so that a shred was ripped away. But the lion did nothing more to the Kulluballi, who set up his first house there and settled on the spot. He became a very great hunter ... The story has a noteworthy conclusion: "This custom is still said to be observed by the Bafulabe today."

The Tuareg and Hausa told us of tribes which hunt between Air and Mursuk. These people are said to live solely from their hunting and never to eat corn. Their men folk have no voice amongst them; the women are the dominant sex and own all the property. Men who are unsuccessful at hunting are considered worthless. They have to observe chastity as youths, and when they reach puberty, the older people take them southwards to regions where there are leopards. There they have to hunt and kill one or several antelopes. After that they are put in a hole in the ground, where they are beaten and scratched. Then they have to fight with a leopard or lion. The beast attacks them and when it tries to fix them with its gaze they hold out a horn full of antelope blood and it goes away. After this battle they are fully fledged hunters. They are now highly successful in their calling, since the little antelope has given them magical powers.

This tribe of hunters maintain that the father of all buffaloes, who is their patron, lives in Damergu. When the latter is well disposed towards one of the Mahalbi, he changes him into a buffalo cow and covers her. They are also very shy, and fear the evil eye. They say that lions and leopards were once men who had the evil eye. The Tuaregs also fear the evil eye, of course, but not to the same extent as these hunters. The latter also practise the custom of burning the hair or nail pairings of people they hate, which is common among the Tuareg women. The hunters' women, however, are even more formidable practitioners of this form of magic than the Tuaregs.

The hunters throw the bodies of their dead into stony chasms, so as to have nothing more to do with them, and on returning from such burials they walk on their heels. Salt is *never* used in their food. After a successful hunt, they drink the blood of their prey, having first poured a few drops into a horn which they always carry with them. The men are not allowed to dance, but when they go hunting, the women have to dance and wiggle their behinds violently. This puts the men into a state of excitement, and they then have to hurry off to the hunt. If a woman sleeps with another man while her husband is away hunting, the beasts tell the husband. These people maintain that blood is the essence of life . . . All this was reported as a true description of living customs, but gives much more the impression of a dim remembrance of a strange and mythical past.

More information was to be found in the eastern Sudan. Here the cattle raisers form a middle stage between the hunters and pure crop-growers, and this has a levelling effect. The completely self-sufficient hunter has more or less died out, but fables are told here too. Thus in 1926, the Bisharin told us that the southern Hadendoa had been particularly skilled hunters, and still are today. When a youth of their tribe reaches puberty, he has to go hunting and chase a gazelle to death. He must chase it until it collapses. He runs after it from morning to night, and has to keep right on its heels. He carries his sexual organ covered with leather so that the gazelle's glance does not fall on it when the animal collapses. If this happened the youth's life would be in danger. The reason why a lion carries its sexual parts pressed back between its legs when attacking an antelope is so that he can avoid the damage which would be caused by the glance of the dying animal. It is also said that the animals can turn into women, who can weaken and destroy the hunter, and for this reason he crushes one testicle or conceals it so as to appear impotent.

Many tales are told by the inhabitants of Kordofan. They tell of the leopard hunters on the borders of Abyssinia and say that when the latter discover a she-leopard's den and take out the young, they must 1) return from it on their heels, 2) not make water on the way, 3) not injure themselves or lose the slightest drop of blood and 4) not turn round, so that the leopard will not be able to follow them. The Kordofan hunters themselves, like those in Senaar, among the Bedjas or the Tuaregs, and in the Aures, treat their hair and fingernail trimmings with great care, since if these were destroyed with magical intent, they could destroy their owners also. On the other hand, they themselves gain unlimited power over their prey by pouring the blood from the animals they have shot into a magical horn. In this way the life of the animals is preserved. However, when a hunter has shed an animal's blood during the hunt, he must let the blood flow from his own arm as a deliberate penance. In this way the arm which wielded the weapon and shed the animal's blood is absolved. In addition the hunter of north Kordofan hides his sexual parts with the utmost care, so as not to be harmed by the evil eye of his prey. The immigrant Ababde hunters in Kordofan, on the other hand, are said to crush one of their testicles to protect them from the evil eye of the lioness.

Finally I will report what I heard in Kabylia and among the tribes of the Aures. One day they told me of the tribes "in the south". First an old man said that in earlier times their men used to wear a pouch over their sexual parts when hunting to protect them from the evil eye of the lion. Then he explained that the lion was a savage madman with the evil eye. Another declared that in former days each hunter had sacrificed a piece of his foreskin to the animals; this act of blood-letting and submission was intended to avert the revenge of the hunted beasts. For every panther hunter, both in former times and today, feared the revenge of his prey, which if it could not take its revenge when dead, could certainly do so while bleeding to death.

This is consistent with what the Kabyles have to tell about their ancient tribe of hunters, now apparently extinct. Today the Kabyles are an agricultural community, cultivating their flowers and fields, yet they have not entirely lost all the traits of a bygone hunting culture. Thus, after their death, the men who had been mighty and successful hunters during their lives, and had therefore practised a bloody trade like the butchers, were generally laid to rest somewhat apart from the others "in a quiet corner" of the cemetery. However, if an over-bold hunter accidentally fell to his death – which often happened in former times when panther, lion, buffalo and gazelles still lived high up in the mountains – or was even killed in a fight with an animal, such a man was not buried in the general cemetery under any circumstances. An exceptional hunter was honoured as long as he lived, and played an important part in the men's assemblies. For it was considered a bold undertaking to engage in the "trade of blood".

There was a complicated magical art involved in shedding blood without falling a prey to the revenge of the blood. The hunter poured a little blood from each animal he killed into a gazelle or buffalo horn. Before each hunting expedition he would take it to a place of sacrifice among the rocks, empty it with ritual gestures over the sacrificial dish and pray for the resurrection of the beasts he would kill, and for forgiveness for spilling their life-giving blood. This was a complicated and dangerous ceremony, and a great knowledge of exorcisms and magical words was needed ... As long as such a hunter lived he was treated with honour; his presence even gave a certain feeling of security. For his exorcisms and his blood magic were obviously a sign of strength. If however he perished in the practice of his trade, it was obvious that he had been defeated in his battle with the blood being. His death proved that he was being pursued by the revenge of the blood, and one could not tell how far this would go. The force of the revenge was evident and the protective strength of the hunter's magic was broken by his death.

The horticulturist Kabyles wanted nothing to do with the body of a hunter who had fallen a prey to the revenge of the blood. For this reason his corpse would be buried among the rocks, in the hunting region up in the mountains, and as near as possible to the place where death had overtaken him. The body was tied into a bundle with leather thongs – apparently in a crouching position. Then a crude stone pillar was erected, or failing that a tree trunk, to which the bundle was firmly tied. Nobody was to pronounce the name of the pillar, or if they did, only with some grains of corn in their mouth. This was advisable in any case as a means of protection against the dangers inherent in such a "burial". In addition, the horn in which the hunter had gathered the blood of the animals he had killed in his lifetime was laid near the body. Finally stones were heaped round the body, horn and pillar, until everything had disappeared and only a stone hillock was left. As he left, each participant threw one last stone over his shoulder onto the heap and then hurried home as fast as possible without once looking behind him. Whenever a hunter or any other man came past such a grave he would quickly throw another stone onto it.

Apart from their recollections of a special profession of hunting in the past, the Kabyles had many other related things to tell. When an old man was buried, who had been a great hunter in his earlier days, the young people went hunting, killed an antelope and brought it to the open space with the stone slabs, which was used for the men's assemblies and as a burial ground for the old. To one side of this place the kill was beheaded; one horn was removed from the skull and filled with the blood of the animal. This was laid by the body together with the horn of the dead man already mentioned above. A funeral banquet was then held, which was distinguished by a particular dish. The walls of the beast's intestines and stomach were filled with bits of blood, fat, liver and flesh and tied at the end. These "sausages" were then swung to and fro over glowing coals, just as Homer wrote of the shepherds' meals, and as is also customary among the Bedja. This particular dish could be eaten only by hunters or old men who had been hunters in their prime. The others consumed grilled pancakes of corn meal. Finally the Kabyles also tell of a large rock picture near Haithar, which represents the legendary original buffalo. Here, it is said, he spilled his seed into a dish, and it was from this that the gazelles were created. In any case the place was used by the hunters as a place of sacrifice, at which they made offerings to the buffalo as the lord of the animals.

It does not matter whether we regard all these statements as legends, memories, descriptions or even as inventions. They could no doubt be easily multiplied by writing down innumerable camp fire conversations, and they all add up to indicate a concept existing in the minds of the north, north-east and south African peoples. It is immaterial whether or not this concept expresses the reality of a quite specific type of humanity and culture – the fact is that it *exists;* and as an existing concept it is all the more noteworthy in that it exists chiefly in the minds of those people who do not identify themselves with the type of culture described, but rather describe it as something opposed to their own nature and way of being. But for this very reason it is all the more valuable to point out the inner conformity of all these statements, a fact which emerges most clearly from the following summary and conclusion.

There is first of all an astonishing conformity in the *type of people* described as the embodiment of these ideas. They are everywhere described as being particularly light-skinned, and in some cases even as blue-eyed and blond. But the nuances of colour are unimportant in relation to the overall agreement. Possibly the knowledge of a particularly light-skinned type of man, and the need for an explanation, have led to an exaggerated specialisation. I never heard it said that dark tribes were predisposed towards hunting, but I heard it said again and again, both in the northeast and the south (in the south Congo basin), that people with light skins showed a particular predisposition towards hunting. There was a particular man who visited our camp in the Kanioka district in 1905, of whom the Baluba and Bena Lulua both said: "That man is so white that he must be a good hunter." And the people of Angola said of the ruling family of the Bena-Ki: "Look how fair these people are! That means they are great hunters!" Moreover the social circumstances under which the hunters live are always described as the same. They wander around in individual groups, but still maintain contact with one another. They are hunters who live readily on the fruits of the savannah, but avoid corn. In particular, the complex of customs relating to the puberty of their youths shows an amazing consistency.

The description of the initiation ceremony begins with a significant detail. The youths are taken to a remote place, which is either a thicket in the bush, a hole in the ground or a cave. Here they are put into a state of ecstasy and then "maltreated". The reports show an unmistakable intention to shed blood, and the wounds inflicted on their bodies are above all directed at the sexual organs. The individual details are not altogether clear here. Some reports seem to indicate some kind of cutting, others mention that a shred of skin or flesh must be torn away, others indicate the removal or crushing of a testicle. The wounds are inflicted by the claws of a beast of prey, and the leopard seems to have been the animal most frequently involved. But the "game" also has its significance. Either at the beginning of the ceremony, or during or after it, an antelope or gazelle is killed, and one of its horns is broken off, to be filled in future with the blood of any animal killed by the hunter. As well as an antelope horn, a buffalo horn may also be used. Cave paintings are executed with the blood of the killed antelope. The whole ceremony divides the life of the youths into two directions. On the one hand they gain the right and the power to hunt big game, on the other their sexual life now begins. Before the ceremony they are not supposed to have had sexual intercourse, but after it they are considered particularly fertile. The end of the ceremony resembles a kind of flight. The youths must either walk away on their heels, so that they do not leave toeprints to indicate the direction they are taking, or else they must take care not to turn round or look back and thereby give an opportunity to anything that may be following.

The main features of this complex of customs show a strongly magical sense of life. This is particularly evident in a series of attitudes and behaviour which can be summed up in the phrase *"pars pro toto"*. The parts of a living creature include not only its hair and nails, claws, horns, and blood, but also its glance and its name. Taking possession of a part gives power over the whole. Possession can result not only from taking hold of the creature with one's hands, but also from a call or summons, and above all from a glance. The call invokes the magic of names, while the glance is the most sinister. The eye which grows dim in death is something to be feared. But the blood is the most important. Blood is identified directly with life. When the hunter pours the blood of his game into his magical blood horn, he has also taken possession of his fate. For beasts of prey, however, there is also a protective formula: *do ut des*. The hunter gives a drop of blood from the arm which has wielded the weapon, and by giving in this way he also gains the right to take. Absolution begins and the guilt is wiped out. The way in which blood and the animal's glance are related to sexual life is strikingly clear. The beast of prey takes possession of the hunter's sexual parts by ripping them open. In this way all further claim on him is removed and the possibility of a wild animal weakening the hunter in the form of a woman is avoided. *Post coitum omne animal triste!* This weakness is feared, and sexual intercourse before the hunt is forbidden. The glance of the hunted animal must not fall on the hunter's sexual parts. The fear that the game could turn itself into a woman and seduce the hunter reappears here. This would seem to explain the first appearance of the pouch covering the penis . . . Just as blood and the glance become symbols of power and life, that which is bloodless, cold and sightless turns into the opposite. The human corpse is done away with, and all possibility of any influence emanating from it removed by its being tethered far up in the mountains, thrown into a chasm or covered with stones.

The relationship of the hunter to the animals is fateful and decisive. First of all there is the lion or leopard which figures in the puberty ritual. The beast of prey decisively invades human life. With a blow of its claws it emphasises the youth's entry into sexual life and brings him in a certain sense to the moment in which he gives himself up to weakness in the sexual act. Above all there is a somewhat obscure relationship between the piercing glance of the beast of prey and the sexual life of man. "The youths", we were once told, "must go through the initation ceremony when the buffaloes are on heat." It is during this ceremony that the hunter wins his blood horn. The hunters obtain their magical resources from antelopes and gazelles. Again and again it is said that the wild animals can turn into beautiful women and lure the hunters to destruction. This appears in the legends of many tribes – the Djur, Basari, Nupe, Ankoi, Yoruba, Mande, Hausa, Bashama, Bosso-Sorokoi, Muntshi, Kredj and Kordofan. We also hear of a very close bond existing between the hunter and his game: when the women go with other men at home while their husbands are out hunting, the animals inform the husbands of their misdeeds.

To sum up, it can be said first of all that we have here a series of descriptions of customs and attitudes, which are so uniform in type that we may talk of a particular "style". This is the style of the Mahalbi culture. Secondly, however, both in the details of the various accounts and in the spirit which emanates from them, we find a form and movement which bear unmistakable similarities to what I have described as the "Hamitic" culture*.

If the Mahalbi culture is seen as a variant of the great Hamitic culture, the question arises of where to place it in the overall course of its development. No culture lives in such isolation that it can remain forever independent. The Hamitic culture (such as I discovered it in a surprisingly austere form among the Bedjas) is uncommonly well defined in its pronounced tendency towards rationalism, a magical sense of life and the rejection of everything mystic and irrational. Yet the example of the Kabyles alone shows that it must at least have gone through periods of enrichment, which it perhaps rejected again subsequently, but which must once have been of considerable significance. For the Bedjas too still have (admittedly tenuous) links with their country's rich heritage of rock pictures. The origin of such enrichments remains an important area of research in cultural prehistory. In the Mahalbi culture, the Hamitic culture appears with different features, which perhaps enable us to get a glimpse of bygone cultural relationships and opposing influences.

---

* Frobenius uses the term "Hamitic to describe the basic culture of the northern Africans, who partly speak Hamitic languages. He makes a basic distinction between this and the "Ethiopian" culture, i. e. that of the African negroes. (Ed.)

10. African Hunters: Bushmen and Hunting Spirits*

How easily the problems of describing the "origins of art", or the "origins of poetry", seem to have been solved in earlier days! And how very different the picture that emerges today, when thorough-going research has started to discount the prejudices of a subjective attitude in assessing the results produced by observation. Seen from the subjective point of view of those who think rationally and realistically, the spiritual life of so-called "primitive peoples" seemed utterly simple and intelligible. But as soon as this premise, which rested on purely subjective thinking controlled by the ego and emanating from the ego, was removed, this marvellous simplicity vanished – leaving behind a fair number of very strange elements. It became evident that in constantly staring at the facts, man – and in this case European man on the "pinnacle of civilization" – in his search for sublime scientific knowledge had been enticed into a world of magic as weird as that once experienced by man in his earliest forms of culture, which are most alien to us.

What a wonderfully simple picture the explorer – scientifically trained to observe the facts strictly – used to paint of the hunting methods of a Bushman in South Africa! In the foreground stands the statement that the Bushman knows every detail of his prey's life; that, as a good huntsman, he stalks it; that he then carefully aims his arrow at the right spot in the springbok's neck. Then comes a description of how the Bushman camouflages himself to look like an ostrich, in order to get as close to his prey as possible; how he skilfully disembowels the dead springbok, and so on. But what kind of truth do we find when we examine such a springbok hunt more closely?

For several decades W. H. J. Bleek took down accounts given by Bushmen in their original language and in 1911 some of them were published by L. C. L. Lloyd under the title *Specimens of Bushman Folklore*. They are a veritable treasure-trove for anthropologists and students of literature alike. Let us reprint some passages from this book and interpret them, so far as it is possible to grasp the meaning of a translation that the writer of this article finds very difficult to decipher. For instance, we hear from one Bushman: "As we want our prey to die, we must pay attention to the animals we hunt. For game does not die if we pay it no attention. We

* From "Kulturgeschichte Afrikas", 1933, pp. 280–286.

proceed as follows: when we have wounded an animal we are hunting, we do not eat anything that can run fast, for we do not want the wounded animal to run quickly away. But if we eat meat that can run fast and is fleet of foot, the wounded animal gets up and behaves like the meat we have eaten [i.e. it rushes away]. This means that our prey will behave in the same way as the food we have taken. So the elders preserve only the meat of animals that are not fleet-footed. They [certainly] do not give us just any food. They will give us only food which they know will strengthen the poison [meaning the action of the poison] so that the poison may kill the prey. When we are hunting a chamois-buck, they give us no springbok meat, because the springbok runs by day and by night. So the prey would also run day and night, if we were to eat springbok meat. For the springbok does not sleep at night, but roams about. The elders do not allow us to hold springbok meat in our hands if we are also holding a bow and arrow. The same characteristics would be transmitted to the bow. The huntsman must step aside while the springbok is being disembowelled."

It is also interesting to hear that children are on no account allowed to play on a springbok's pelt, and that great care is taken in throwing away gnawed bones. Another explanation runs: "My grandfather placed the bones from the forelegs and the shoulderblades and horns of the springbok between the posts of our hut. Otherwise the index finger of our right hand could easily receive a wound. If our hands grasped the horns of the springbok, our index finger would be wounded, and we would not be able to bend our bow when hunting. So we sew our index finger into a finger-stall made of the pelt, which the women have softened and then sewn. When the finger is wrapped up like that we bend our bow."

If the reader extracts the essential core from this account – and I must admit that I do not fully understand it myself – he will find that he is dealing with a stage of intellectual outlook in which there is no division of consciousness between the individual and his environment. So the characteristics of the food that man eats are transmitted to the animal he hunts. If he eats springbok meat, the animal he hunts will take on the characteristic features of a springbok. If he takes some nourishment that would enhance the action of poison on his arrowheads, the action of the poison in the wounded animal would also be increased. In other words, the essence, or nature, of things has a greater effect than their actual reality. But the strong links between all phenomena are not in this case something that man simply accepts and surrenders to, venerating it in all humility as in "Ethiopian" culture (see p. 30). Here the universal interrelationship of all phenomena leads man to avoid danger, and in so doing and in exploiting the factors inherent in this inner interrelationship, to create an instrument for his own use.

What course the development of such a mentality was bound to take will be explained in the next section. Here, however, is one of the characteristic tales told by the Bushman:

"The mantis* assumes the likeness of a doe antelope. The mantis is a creature that deceives children by transforming itself into a doe antelope. It pretends to be dead and stretches itself out immediately in front of the children, who are just starting to pick gambroo [a type of maize], because it hopes the children will cut it up with a stone knife.

The children noticed her as she lay there, with her horns thrown back. The children said to each other: 'There lies an antelope. It is dead.' The children jumped for joy and said: 'Oh, our antelope! We shall have a gorgeous meal!' They broke off some stone knives and then they skinned the mantis. The antelope's hide jumped quickly out of the children's hands. They said to each other: 'Hang on to the hide!' Another child said: 'The antelope's hide has pulled at me.'

Her elder sister said: 'It looks as though the antelope has no wound, so it probably died a natural death. Although it is fat, it has no wound.'

Her elder sister cut off one of the antelope's shoulders and laid it on a bush. The shoulder got up all by itself, and sat down nicely [on the other side of the bush], where it was comfortable to sit. She [then] cut off a leg and put it down [on a bush]; it was lying nicely on the bush. She cut off another shoulder and put it on another bush. It got up and then sat down on a smooth branch [part of the bush], as soon as it felt that the bush [where the child had placed it] was prickly.

Another elder sister cut off the antelope's other leg. They talked to each other as follows: 'The antelope's flesh is moving; that is why it is disappearing.'

They divided their burden. One elder sister said to the other: 'Cut off the antelope's neck, so that your younger sister can carry the head, because your elder sister over there can carry the back, as she is a big girl. We must go home now, because we have cut up the antelope. Its flesh jumps out of our hands and sits down nicely somewhere else.'

They now loaded themselves with the antelope flesh. They said to the

---

* *Mantis religiosa* – the "praying" mantis – an insect of the Mantidae family, lives on smaller insects – flies, grasshoppers, caterpillars.

smallest child: 'Carry the antelope's head, so that father can roast it for you!' The child hung the antelope's head round her neck, and called to her sisters: 'Wait a bit and help me.' The child was lying with her back on the antelope's head. The head is heavy. Her sisters did help her. The children really believed that the antelope's flesh was moving. It did not seem to be antelope's flesh, for the flesh of the antelope was like human flesh; it was moving.

They set off, they went home. The antelope's head slipped down, because the praying mantis likes to have its head on the ground. The child picked it up again. The antelope's head pushed the strap away from the antelope's eye. The head whispered. It whispered to the child: 'Oh, child, the strap is just in front of my eye. Take away the strap. The strap is closing my eye.' The child looked back. The mantis winked. The child whimpered. Her elder sister turned round to her. 'Come quickly, we're going home.'

The child called: 'The antelope's head can talk.' Her elder sister scolded her. 'You're lying, come on. We're going. You're trying to tell us a pack of lies about the antelope's head.'

The child said to her big sister: 'The antelope winked at me. The antelope wanted me to take the strap away from its eye. The antelope's head looked at me like this from behind my back.'

The child looked back at the antelope's head; the antelope opened and shut its eyes. The child said to her elder sister: 'The antelope's head must be alive, because it can open and shut its eyes.'

As she walked on, the child loosened the strap. The head fell to the ground. The mantis scolded the child, complaining about its head. It scolded her: 'Oh, oh, my head [It complained only about its head]. Oh, you wicked little person, hurting my head!'

The sisters dropped the flesh of the mantis. The antelope flesh sprang back together, quickly uniting to form the lower part of the back. The head of the mantis placed itself on top of the mantis's neck. The neck perched itself quickly on the upper part of the spine. The upper part of the spine perched itself on the back of the mantis. The mantis's leg leapt forward; it attached itself to the mantis's back. The mantis's breast ran forward; it attached itself at the front of the upper part of the mantis's spine. The mantis's shoulderblade ran forward and attached itself to the mantis's ribs. The other shoulderblade ran forward, because it felt that the ribs of the mantis had joined together when they were racing each other.

The children ran on. It – the mantis – got up from the ground and ran and chased the children – it was whole – its head was round – and then it felt that it was a human being. So it moved on in shoes, wiggling its shoulderblades.

It saw that the children had reached their house. It turned round quickly, and, pushing forward with its shoulderblades, it went down to the river. At is walked along the river bed, its steps made a soft noise in the white sand. It quickly climbed out of the river over there and came back from the other side of the house [its own house]. It returned, passing the front [of the house].

The children said: 'We saw a dead antelope. We cut up this antelope with stone knives; its flesh was trembling. The antelope's flesh jumped quickly out of our hands. It sat down nicely on some bushes that it found comfortable. Then the antelope found that its head was moving forwards, whispering as it did so. When the child sitting over there carried it, it stood talking behind her back.'

The child said to her father: 'O, Papa! Do you think that the antelope's head didn't really talk to me? While I was walking, the antelope thought it could look into the hole across the nape of my neck, and then the antelope's head said to me, would I remove the strap from its eye. Because the strap was lying across its eye.'

The father said to the child: 'Did you by any chance cut up the old gentleman, the mantis, when it was pretending to be dead?'

The children answered: 'We thought of the antelope's horns, of its lovely pelt. The antelope had not been wounded by an arrow, so the antelope thought it could speak. That is why it came and pursued us, when we had taken off its flesh. Its flesh sprang together, and in so doing it fitted itself into place, so that it could hold the antelope's back together, as if it had been mended. The back then attached itself to the rest.

That's why the antelope ran forward; its body was dead, because it had no pelt (the pelt in which it had lain before us), and it swung its arms like a human being. Then, when it saw that we had arrived home, it swept about. It ran, so that you could see the white soles of its shoes, faster than the wind, and the sun was shining on its soles. Then it ran into a little river, to get behind those hills over there.'

Their parents said: 'You have cut up the old man, Tinderbox-Owner. It [the antelope] came out quite quietly back there.'

The children said to their parents: 'It jumped about, it ran very quickly. It always looks as if it were coming over that small hillock over there, when it sees that we are about to arrive home.

It told the little one everything; the antelope's head spoke to her as she carried it. Then she told us about it. We put our pelts over our shoulders, so that we could run away fast.

While its flesh ran to join its [the antelope's] back, it pieced itself together. It got up and ran, and, moving its arms rapidly, it pursued us. We then began to feel tired of being chased, and it really was moving its arms about.

Then it ran down to the little river and thought it would run the length of the little river, all the time swinging its arms. Then it gathered up some wood and came out. All this time we were sitting and feeling exhausted, because it had fooled us. It knew that everybody had seen it when we had carried its legs and when it had lain stretched out dead before us. It wanted us to be annoyed; particularly the little one here, who carried its head; that's why it looked up with really pleading eyes. First it was dead; afterwards it opened and shut its eyes and kept on talking from afar [when the children were running away]. It talked while it was mending its body. Its head talked, while it was piecing its body together. Its talking head reached its back; then it placed itself at the top end [of the neck].

Then it ran on; it will go on deceiving us [at home], when we have cut it up with stone knives. It pretended to be dead, so that we would cut it up. We ran away.

Were are angry and exhausted and our hearts are burning from this. Therefore we will no longer worry about food. We will stay together at home.'"

11. The Civilization of the Kabyls*

Berbers and Arabs

As a result of the numerous migrations of populations which have engulfed northern Africa over the centuries, two distinct ethnic groups have come into being: the Arabs and the Berbers. Though living cheek by jowl and settled throughout the area at random, they may be said to embody diametrically opposed ways of life. The two groups – each the end result of a prolonged mixing of races – predominate in the area to such an extent that, leaving aside recent arrivals in the wake of colonial ventures belonging to our own age, they utterly overshadow the remnants of outside ethnic groups – such as Jews and Turks – which have survived in northern Africa. Arabs and Berbers are divided by more than language. Both must be seen as the end result of a prolonged process of development and blending of peoples; neither may in any way be regarded as a distinct race. What distinguishes Arab from Berber is a spirit, an outlook, most clearly reflected in the role of the mosque in their respective lives. Nowadays, Berbers and Arab alike are Muslims. However, to the Berber his *jemaa,* or mosque, remains to this day the meeting place of the local menfolk – the community centre. This is not only where religious services are held, but also where the men formally discuss the affairs of the community; moreover, it serves as a guest house for visitors. The *jemaa* thus embodies the spirit of solidarity which holds the local community together, and the religious observances and rites which take place there reflect this feeling of unity. To the Arab, on the other hand, the mosque is the symbol of a universal, worldwide, unifying religion. To the Arab *any* mosque is a centre of Islamic observance, which does not vary from place to place. To the Berber, however, the mosque is the symbol of his native soil. For the Arab, there is only one universe – *the* universe; for the Berber, his homeland is a microcosm within a macrocosm. Universally valid ideals and beliefs are part of the Arab way of thought, while the Berber outlook is made up of a series of individual beliefs and myths about the origins of the universe. The creative force of the Arabs found its expression in the philosophy of Islam. The Berbers' view of the supernatural has in fact given Christendom many of its early holy fathers.

"The Arab gobbles up the Berber" goes the proverb – and how true it is! The Berber language is disappearing from one oasis after another, from

* From "Volksmärchen der Kabylen", Vol. I, 1921, pp. 3–51.

one district after another. Arabic has made a virtually clean sweep. To this day, we can observe this process in the area between the Ammon Oasis [Kufra] and the Atlantic coasts of Morocco. The Berbers are fast losing their separate identity. The flatter the landscape, the more suitable for breeding camels, the more rapid this process is.

Conversely, the more mountainous and rugged the terrain, and the less suitable for keeping beasts, the slower it is. It follows that the Berber nation has managed more or less to hold its own along the northern fringes of Africa only in eastern Morocco and in the area of the Djurdjura mountains, in so-called Kabylia. The mighty Djurdjura range, crowned by a 3,200 metre (10,000 ft. approx.) peak, covered in eternal ice and snow, runs east from the city of Algiers. The range is divided into several chains by deep ravines. The streams and rivers, flowing through gorges ranging in depth from 200 to 2,000 m. unite to form the Sebaou river, which has its estuary at Dellys. This is mountain country in the true sense of the word.

The mountains of Kabylia are huge, and not in height alone; the land-scape is as un-African as one could possibly imagine. Oak, ash and euca-lyptus abound. The gardens are planted with vines, fig trees and oleanders, with wheat and barley as undercrops. Often, as I wandered through Kabylia, it struck me that the flora of Great Kabylia might well be the last surviving trace of a pattern of life which once upon a time was characteristic of the whole of the Maghrib, a pattern which has found its last refuge in these mountains, just as the spirit of the Berbers – who at one time predominated throughout North Africa – survived in a pure form here and here alone.

The Kabyls who dwell in these mountains were not always so called. The word "Kabyl" is derived from the Arabic and is used to designate people whose sibs are organized on a village-by-village basis. One legend tells us that the Kabyl used to be known as *Imazigh* (plural: *Imazighen*). They have themselves all but forgotten the name. I myself only came across it by chance in a fragment of an old legend about the creation of the universe. However, the name *Imazigh* is common to all the Berber peoples and has survived in the expression *"tamashirt"* – which is the name we use for the Berber script.

Linguistically, and probably also racially, the Kabyls are Berbers like all the settled peoples in the lands north of the Sahara. They are, how-ever, distinguished by one singular trait: the Kabyls are Berbers who have proved capable of absorbing and assimilating other ethnic groups.

We know of several Arab tribes which have made their homes in Kabylia. Africans, Byzantines, Romans – even Frenchmen – have settled there and became Kabyls. Let me emphasize that this is not a mere hypothesis or a description of fortuitous, isolated occurrences in the past. No, this is a phenomenon of capital importance! Just consider: while all the other Berbers are being absorbed by a population wave which engulfed the area in the recent past, with the result that they are losing their identity before our very eyes, the Kabyls, alone among the Berbers, have succeeded, not only in maintaining their distinct character but in actually absorbing the newcomers.

To understand this phenomenón, you must bear in mind what I said at the outset: the distinguishing mark of the Berber is his form of culture, his way of thinking. The Berber psychology closely reflects the viability of plant life. It dies wherever cultivated lands – as has happened in most parts of northern Africa – are engulfed by the desert. It stays alive, inviolate and inviolable – wherever nature has set bounds to the – normally victorious – advance of the desert. The mountain country round about the proud Djurdjura can thus be likened to an island where the last remnants of the ancient Berber ways have survived in their entirety. We may therefore say that the characteristics of the Kabyls were once upon a time shared by all Berbers, who probably predominated throughout northern Africa before its landscape was parched and taken over by the desert.

An immense number of new traits – many of them foreign – have been added to the ancient civilization of the Kabyls. However, when you take a closer look, you invariably realize that the civilization of the Kabyls is the dominant force, capable of imposing its style on the newer influences, which it has succeeded, since time immemorial, in absorbing and transforming to comply with its own ways.

The architecture of the Kabyls

While it is true that the Kabyls have preserved in a concentrated form all the many and diverse features of Berber culture, it would be quite wrong to think that this is obvious to the casual observer at first sight. We must emphasize that before you can uncover the valuable original Berber features, a great many products of modern, alien – above all present-day – civilization have to be stripped away.

By way of an example – which will at the same time afford the reader an insight into the structure of Kabyl society – I propose to describe the settlements and dwellings of the people. All Kabyl villages are built on hills, and mostly on passes. The outlines of houses, gables and roofs always fit snugly into the surrounding landscape. I saw but few of the storage towers standing out above all other buildings – a feature common to the villages of other Berber peoples. Occasionally the top floor of a building or a *saqf* spanning the width of a street provides a prominent feature of this kind. The true Kabyls have no towns; their settlements consist of hamlets, as well as small and large villages. The villages are in turn made up of individual homesteads; occasionally one sees isolated farms situated some distance from the nearest village. Normally, however, the homesteads are grouped closely together into tight settlements.

The typical modern Kabyl dwelling is devoid of any noteworthy features. It has mud walls; the pitched roof is covered with tiles imported from France. Wooden shuttering is generally used to build the walls, rather in the manner of our own concrete buildings. The European-style roof frame of beams and rafters, as well as the ceilings, rests directly on the "cast" walls. The house itself is divided into rooms by means of partition walls and doors; the outside walls have glazed windows. Inside, there are a few Byzantine-Arabian chests, European iron bedsteads and European kitchen utensils, plus some pieces of furniture, including perhaps a cradle of ancient design, suspended from the ceiling by four ropes like the pans of a pair of scales.

The visitor will have to travel a few hours into the interior of the country, away from the garrison towns set up by the French, to see architecture of a different type. At Bani Yanni, for example, he will see houses all of which, as elsewhere, are covered with roofs of European design, including the tiles and the timber structure underneath. However, the ceilings and rafters do not rest on the walls but on posts which at the same time help to support the walls themselves. As for the interior, it is divided, following an ancient design, into living accommodation for the owner's family and a stable.

To see houses built according to genuine, traditional Kabyl design, the tourist must continue his journey for a few hours more, penetrating further inland, e.g. as far as Tirual, where he will find quite unspoilt old buildings. The entire village follows the contours of a concave mountain pass. Here, tiled pitched roofs give way to barrel-like, vaulted ones. Each house, each homestead, is carefully adapted to suit the economic life and clan structure of the village. Individual homesteads consist of anything from one to five houses, depending on the number of families. All are designed along the same lines, although their appearance may vary considerably according to the wealth of the inhabitants and the standard of maintenance.

The basic design of the house is determined by the timber frame. This consists of four square wooden posts rammed into the ground. The corner posts are grooved at the top so as to support two heavy beams which protrude beyond the pair of posts on the opposite side far enough to carry the roof of an adjoining stable. These main beams are linked by means of curved beams. The walls – which are not weight-bearing – reach up to the eaves. In the past, they were of wattle and daub between wooden posts. Not till recently has it been the practice to build them of a mixture of mud and stones. This makes them stronger and thus better able to support the roof structure. In the past, the roof covering consisted entirely of mud spread over wattle matting which in turn was fastened to the roof beams. Since the latter were curved, the roof itself was slightly vaulted, and this ensured that any rain water would drain off easily.

The interior of the house is divided roughly into three rooms. The door, fitted into one of the two longer walls of the rectangular structure, leads straight into the living room. This has a hole in the centre for a hearth. On the left, there is a parapet made of clay carrying an array of jars, and on the right a shelf with huge storage urns which contain part of the grain harvest. Let me say right away that to this day the Kabyls do not store the whole of their grain reserves in these urns. For they also have silos in the fields, as well as various hiding places. These silos are conical pits with the walls sloping inwards towards the top.

Below the shelf carrying the storage urns are three holes. To one side there is a large door leading downstairs and above it a small window-like door opening into the loft. The latter, extremely narrow door leads to the *tarrisht* – the four-poster bed, while the larger door leads to the stable, which is on a lower level than the living room. The cattle and donkeys can push their heads through the holes beneath the shelf carrying the storage urns.

A large part of these houses, which outwardly appear so simply constructed, may, however, be occupied by a secret room, the *baerka*. Where there is such a room, there is an opening in the parapet carrying the jars, which is usually hidden by means of these same splendid painted jars so that its presence is concealed from the stranger. This is, in fact, exactly what is intended, for the opening gives access to the *baerka* pit. Like the silos, this is of conical design. It serves as a hiding place, not only for the most precious jewels of the family, but also for any fugitive in need of asylum.

The *baerka* pit may, however, also be a full-sized cellar, its outline corresponding exactly to the living room above, its ceiling and the upper room supported by a system of posts. Access to the cellar is afforded either by a ramp-like sloping passage from the stable or – as with the normal *baerka* pit – by way of a hole in the jar shelf, and a post with notches cut into it to provide a foothold. These *baerka* cellars enable whole groups of people – or a herd of cattle – to be concealed for a while. The *baerka* pit is an ancient Kabyl institution. In the past, the pits were also used to house the Kabyl's primitive oil presses.

There are also subterranean dwellings to be found in Kabylia, as well as natural and artifically enlarged caves. Dug into the slopes of low hillocks, these dwellings have two entrances: a door which affords level access to the dwelling and an entry hole which leads into it from the upper part of the hillock by way of a sloping shaft fitted with a wickerwork ladder.

The subterranean dwelling I visited in Kabylia was anything but a "dark hole in the ground". The walls were expertly surfaced and painted. The side rooms were pleasantly decorated and all the passages carefully finished. The Kabyls certainly gained my respect as cave-dwellers.

This subterranean architecture, which the Kabyls go to so much trouble to keep secret, used to be commonplace among the Berbers. The cave dwellings in the Garyan mountains at Tripoli are well known. I saw ruins of similar structures in the Majirda valley in Tunisia, as well as near Silla. They are also to be found in Morocco and have fathered a host of architectural idioms in the oases. However, nowhere has this type of architecture been preserved in so pure a form, and with such splendid detail finish, as among the Kabyls. Moreover, nowhere else has this style of underground construction been blended so remarkably well with surface structures as for instance, in the house of Ayt Bou Mahd.

It has long been my impression that nearly all peoples have two types of huts: one for permanent use and the other intended to give temporary shelter while travelling, occasionally for a single night only – and which can therefore be put up quickly. The two types are more often than not built on different lines. The huts of the Berbers, I found, likewise conform to two distinct patterns: those intended for permanent settlement consisted of a cube-shaped timber frame and walls made of stone or hollow brick. They also have huts for use during journeys, though nowadays more and more Berbers have taken to using the Arab woollen fabric tent. It is only rarely that they erect their "old *jirbi*", as the French used to call the Berbers' temporary straw huts.

The Berbers' "old *jirbis*" were quite unique: the inner structure consisted of two wooden posts, set $1^1/_2$ to 3 m. apart at the base and meeting at an angle. The protruding top ends were linked by a horizontal cross-tie. Curved twigs were fastened at right angles to either end of the cross-

130

tie and stuck into the ground. In this way an oval-shaped hut was constructed. This oval shape – occasionally supplemented by a ½ to 1 m. high dry-stone wall containing a spiral entrance passage, must be regarded as the basic feature of the Berber hut. I am convinced that in prehistoric times the same construction was used not only for temporary shelters around a timber frame but also for permanent dwellings supported by stone pillars. I have found several ruins indicating that such buildings did exist. The framework – consisting of two forked posts and a cross-tie – which, translating literally from the Arabic, I propose to call "gallows", had a certain mythical significance among past generations of Berbers. In the Aures country I came across the proverb: "If a man enters under the same gallows with his feud enemy, he must harm him no more." The injunction applies even where the "gallows" merely serves as the door-frame of a stone house. Moreover, amulets are tied to the "gallows" which, according to circumstance, may bring either good or ill luck to those who pass beneath them. It used to be considered particularly important to suspend a few bundles of seed grain stalks from the gallows; this was thought to bring luck to the occupants.

All this "gallows" lore has virtually disappeared. This was only to be expected, since the types of timber suitable for the construction of "gallows trees" are vanishing from the lands of the Berber peoples, together with the rest of the plant cover. Hence roofs tend increasingly to be supported by walls rather than forked posts. The "gallows" usually consisted of two posts, but occasionally three or five would be used. Where this was done, the tallest post was always placed in the centre. The cross-tie, which formed the ridge of the structure, was regarded by the Kabyls as the main part of the house. According to the brief note I made of Kabyl mythology on the subject, the "gallows" – and especially the ridge beam – were considered the father of the house and were known as *"tatheleth"* (strangely enough, a noun of the feminine gender!). This combined in a "sexual union" with the *"ishgua"* – the forked support struts.

Architectural features which among the rest of the Berbers either decayed, vanished altogether or have become flat and insipid, continue to develop among the Kabyls, retaining their original style pure and undiluted. This strikingly reflects the contrasts between the extinction of the Berber national spirit in the great plain on the one hand and the powerful concentration of that spirit within the narrow confines of Kabylia on the other. It is as if a mighty, vigorous plant with a great spread of branches had withered and died after first condensing all its power in a single grain seed which has preserved the species from extinction.

The memory of how the nation's architecture developed lives on quite unmistakably in the Berber legend of creation. The nation's ancestors lived *underground*, in a cave dwelling; it took later generations to begin building above ground. This shows how deep the roots of historic development and knowledge go.

The patriarchal sibs and age groups

The Berber spirit has continued to flourish so vigorously among the Kabyls that they have been able to preserve its essential features faithfully. This applies not only to the aspects of their civilization described in earlier chapters, but also to their social institutions, despite the fact that one would have expected Islam to make its strongest impact in precisely this area. Islam and its laws, which mould society, hold undisputed sway, subject to no exception. That much is clear from such works on the subject as Hanoteau's and Letournent's "La Kabylie et les coutumes Kabyles". Yet these laws are only the tools of society; they are the form, not the content.

The Kabyls' entire social life is based on a patriarchal sib structure. All male descendants in the male line of succession – i.e. grandfather, father and his brothers, the sons and their male cousins descended from their father's brothers – belong to the same sib. The sib also includes women who have married into it – though they are bereft of all rights and privileges. It does not include their brothers, fathers, etc. Since all women are *a priori* denied all rights, the sib as a body consists to all intents and purposes exclusively of men.

The sib members frequently live in close proximity, often in large farmsteads or separate sections of villages. These *imaulan* are subdivided into age groups. As regards the outside world, they are linked by a common duty – the blood feud.

In the past, the *imaulan* were strictly divided into age groups consisting of (1) old men; (2) *patres familias* (the "true men"); (3) young men; and (4) the immature boys. Young children, whether boys or girls, were classed with women, not men. The various age groups each had distinct tasks.

The fourth group, the immature boys, had to perform ceremonial games on feast days. This may at first seem strange, precisely because they were regarded as immature. It was, however, explained on the grounds that they had as yet spilt no blood, that they were therefore not yet pursued by the spirits of vengeance and that, being innocent of both bloodshed and sex they were, in a sense, wholly pure and free of sin. These boys, being *still pure*, were, therefore, regarded as suitable executants of religious rites, while the old men, being *again pure*, were regarded as suitable instructors of the young.

The manner in which the boys used to grow into youths and later into young men eligible to attend the men's meetings can be expressed very simply: by shedding blood and by a period of abstemiousness. Ancient folk tales shed further light on these customs: they speak of solicitous fathers who sought to shield their children from their first encounter with bloodshed for as long as possible by bringing them up in isolation, and of evil old hags who did their utmost to encourage them to fight. One thing is certain: a young Kabyl was permitted to marry only after he had been involved in bloodshed, whether in battle or while hunting wild beasts. It was considered that until then a young man might be pure; but his seed would be infertile. Not until he had performed a blood deed did a man's seed become fertile. In other words every victory in battle, every enemy vanquished, adds to a man's magic powers. It is clear from the Kabyls' folklore that such was their belief.

It is also certain that in their view the magic powers required to beget children resided solely in the man and in no way in the woman. To this day, women are merely regarded as temporary vessels. I once heard an old Kabyl make the wholly characteristic statement: "Just as *Itherter** allowed his seed to drop into a stone dish, so does man drop his seed into woman. Woman is like the stone dish from which sprang live gazelles. The stone dish was *Itherter's* wife." In other words, man is the positive, creative factor and acquires his creative power only through a deed and the purification following that deed.

Let us now consider the men's assembly. Every old Kabyl village – indeed every group of farmsteads and even every isolated farm – has at least one *tajmai't* – an outdoor meeting place with a circle of stone seats. This is where the men hold their sib, village, tribal or tribal alliance meetings. Women are strictly barred from attending. In addition to these outdoor meeting places in the village outskirts, each village has a "men's house", now called *jemaa*, which also serves as a mosque and guest house for visiting friends. The *jemaa* in no way shares the exclusive nature of the *tajmai't*.

The *tajmai't* meetings are attended by all men belonging to age groups (1) to (3). The old men recount their experiences, the men state their views.

---

* Mythical ancestor of the buffalo.

The youths listen in silence. All questions of law and property, all issues touching upon the common good, are discussed and decided at the *tajmai't*. This is also where the old and the young foregather of an evening for lessons, imparted in the form of legends and folk tales. It is within the *tajmai't* that the ancient culture of the Berbers lives on.

There used to be two other institutions in addition to the *tajmai't*: the *thimamorth* and the *tashluit*. The *tajmai't* was reserved for the discussion by menfolk of purely practical issues, and the institution has survived throughout the area to this day. The location of the *thimamorth* and *tashluit* was probably always a closely guarded secret, for this is where ancient pagan rites were practised. Once Islam, with its strict dogma, had emerged victorious, these institutions had to be concealed, and indeed in many places they scarcely survive even as a memory.

The *thimamorth* was where trials for criminal offences were held. It was also the place where the men of the (1) and (2) age groups met and where the members of age group (2) were initiated – after appropriate sacrificial rites – into the secrets of the myth of creation.

As for the *tashluit,* it was a mysterious meeting place reserved for the exclusive use of members of the senior age groups. Other men were admitted only to attend the burial of an old man. The *tashluit* had a flagstone floor and was surrounded by a single row of stone seats. Old men who had gained special recognition for their wisdom, kindness and purity were buried beneath the slabs. The bodies were dressed in robes which are no longer to be seen nowadays, made of a fabric woven from reed fibre. A long slit was cut into the centre, through which passed the head, the upper body and arms; the legs down to the knees were covered front and back by the robe, which was held together around the loins by a belt. If the dead man was known in his younger years for his prowess as a hunter, the young folk would go out and kill an antelope and take it to the *tashluit.* The carcass was beheaded close by. One horn was detached from the skull, filled with the blood of the dead beast and buried beside the old man's body. From the antelope's blood, liver, a few pieces of meat and a little water, a special dish was prepared. From the skin of the beast – and if it was a male also from its stomach – a pouch was made which was filled with various victuals. A fierce fire was then lit between two upright stones, so that the latter became very hot. When the fire had all but burnt itself out, the cooking process could begin, the embers being kept alive by logs added from time to time. If at any time the flames flared up too high, they were beaten down with a wooden club.

The food was cooked as follows: a spit was stuck through the pouch and, supported at either end on the two upright stones, was turned round and round. Thus was the sacred funeral meal prepared for the dead huntsman. Later it would be eaten by the old men foregathered in the *tashluit* – provided they had themselves hunted during their younger years. Those of the old men present who had never taken part in hunting would participate in the meal only by eating a few pieces of flat bread baked on a stone slab. In general, old men who had not been hunters in their younger years tended to stick more and more to a vegetarian diet as they grew older, especially at *tashluit* meetings.

The effective leaders of the sib and the managers of its property – which would considerably exceed the sum of its members' private wealth – were the men of age group (2). The old men, for their part, were responsible for keeping an eye on the sib's spiritual life, saw to it that traditions were kept up and supervised all sacrifices and sacrificial games.

This is how power was divided between the various gatherings of men. In the past, these divisions were strictly observed throughout, both in the spirit and the letter. Nowadays, the mosque has in many ways superseded the meeting-place of man – at all events, their variety has been reduced – and they have been in part suppressed. The upshot has been that the existence of diverse power groupings is no longer so strongly expressed in terms of formal display, nor is it possible for the demarcations between the groups to be enforced by means of a rigid ceremonial. Nonetheless, the various groups continue to exist as such. They have matured and gained unquestioning acceptance so that – unlike more recent social institutions – they no longer require the support of formal customs. Nowadays, they exert their influence automatically – and all the more effectively. The same is true here as in other areas of social life. In our society too, the meaning of many phenomena becomes clear only when we have studied the formal customs with which they were associated in their initial stages.

The Kabyls no longer require any outward display of the importance of the male age groups: they have become an essential part of their national heritage. Many a decision taken by them, ostensibly in accordance with "Islamic law", makes sense only when we call to mind their older and more vigorous traditions, which live on under the cloak of Islam.

From caste to party

The sib – and, within it, the age groups – are the foundation of the whole of the old social structure of the Kabyls. A group of sibs formed a village; several related villages together made up a tribe and an association of several tribes constituted a federation. States in our sense of the word did not exist. A European-style Kabyl prince would have been unacceptable to the Berbers in the long run. We find that, consequently, all attempts in the remote past to establish ruling dynasties invariably collapsed, the dynasties themselves never having a more than problematical, shadowy existence, consisting wholly of formal ceremonial and dependent on the influence of foreign powers.

However, each village had its leader, nowadays known by the Arabic word *amin* but formerly called *agelith*. This is an elective office. The *amin* is supported by the *tam'en*, the leader of the sib group. In addition, the federations have their leaders, who are also elected, and then there also are the various party leaders who owe their office entirely to personal influence. All in all, we thus find that there is no such thing as an hereditary office; all appointments depend on the confidence inspired by the office-holder and his personality. As a result, he enjoys an utter and complete independence.

With the sibs combining into villages, villages into tribes and tribes into federations, there is an incentive for the leaders to pay heed to higher interests. Let us therefore call this progression – which results from a social structure based on sibs and men's age groups – the vertical line. The federal principle governs the association of the various age groups within a sib group, as it governs the federation of tribes.

This vertical line of progression is, however, crossed by another line, symbolizing a different concept of society and of social structure. And since it bisects the first line at right angles, I propose to call it the horizontal line of development. To say that society is divided into four castes is probably as fair a way to describe the situation as can be devised.

The first caste used to be that of the *igelithen* (singular: *agelith*). This was the property-owning aristocracy as it were, consisting of the leaders of the sib groups and villages. Its members owned the land, commanded troops in war and were the heroes of the nation's "legendary age". In the eyes of the people the word "*agelith*" stands for excellence, truth and wisdom. Today, there are no more *igelithen*. Nowadays the Kabyls use the word "*l'harr*" to describe a nobleman, while the *agelith* has been replaced as leader by the *amin*.

It is particularly interesting that these *igelithen* were not only feudal lords and warlords, but also "lords of the fire", and hence – so the legend has it – the *ishadethen* i.e. the blacksmiths, were included among them. In this respect, Berber society differs radically from its Arab counterpart. Not only does the nobleman tower in Arab society above the nomad, the wanderer through the desert and the peasant; to an Arab no one could possibly occupy a more lowly place in society than a blacksmith. Among African Arabs, the blacksmith is at the bottom of the social pile in terms of professional prestige. Among the Kabyls, on the other hand, he continues to this day to enjoy a position of great respect, and his profession is highly esteemed. That this should be so is easy to understand once we call to mind that the blacksmiths used to be regarded as members of the nobility.

The *l'hasos* made up the second caste, consisting of sibs considered impure, which had lost their property. They were looked upon as impoverished successors to the *agelith* caste – as people who had come down in the world. In the eyes of the Kabyls, such people are unable to preserve their purity, and that is why they set up a caste of their own, the second caste. The word *"l'hasos"* continues to be fairly widely used in popular parlance – it describes a person regarded as a defector, one who is unreliable, and also perhaps one who is foolish.

The third caste were the *ishamassen*, the serfs. While the *l'hasos* still ran their farmsteads – albeit in pawn to the members of the *agelith* caste – and enjoyed complete freedom in their personal and family life, were able to change their abode and place of work, the *ishamassen* had forfeited that freedom. They belonged, body and soul, to an *agelith*, whose land they worked. For their labour they were paid with a share of the crop – figs, olives, grain, etc. Where the master owned a large farmstead, they would occupy a little outhouse or room. Where the master's farmstead was small, they would live in smaller enclosures.

Over the years, the *ishamassen* have become free labourers, for as the property of the *agelith* diminished, that of the poorer people grew. Barter has been replaced by a money economy, and consequently it is open even to an ordinary labourer to attain a measure of prosperity. Since there was no slavery for light-skinned people, this development could proceed comparatively unhampered.

The fourth caste consisted of the *isharasen* and the *ishenaijen* – the guilds of leather workers and bards, respectively. It would seem that among the Kabyls leather work used at one time to be regarded as the exclusive province of women. I have been told that the leather shroud of the dead used to be made by their daughters or daughters-in-law; also that it was the duty of the women to make the leather tents. They were responsible not only for making the skin sheets but also for erecting the tents.

Those who worked in leather were consequently regarded as belonging to a "female" trade. There is another interesting tradition connected with this craft. True to the patriarchal spirit of the society to which he belongs, the Kabyl is named after his father. The *isharasen*, however, are said to have been formerly compelled to call themselves after their mothers. The leather workers of our own day deny this, of course, and are likely to be quite put out when asked about it. There is another reason why the *isharasen* are of some interest. Among the Tuareg and peoples along the Niger, the leather workers – the *garase* and *garata* – are also considered to constitute a separate caste.

There is little I can say about the *ishenaijen*, the singers or bards. Their guitars have been silent for a long time now. Their disappearance coincided with that of the *agelith*, of the "great battle" and the hunt for big game. It is said that they used to follow the *igelithen* and to sing about their deeds. I have been unable to discover anything in the nature of a major epic. There are no more *ishenaijen* in the old sense of the word; they have been displaced by Arab itinerant singers of various sorts.

Lastly, there were slaves – negroes and people of part-negro blood. They could be bought and sold and were held in utter contempt. They did not form part of the caste structure.

Within the sib groups, the various castes tended to overlap. Each group of sibs was presided over by the "chief nobleman", "the" *agelith*. Every sib was headed by an agelith and contained *l'hasos, ishamassen, isharasen* and *ishenaijen*, as well as negroes and part-negroes in most cases. The expression *ashrum* (plural: *eshrumen*) was applied in the first place to the caste. Since, however, each sib group as a whole was known by the name of its *agelith* chief, and since the concepts of "pure" and "impure" in a racial sense were gradually disappearing, the importance of the *ashrum* tended to recede, while that of the "village quarter" and of the secret federation of several sib groups came more and more to the fore,

In bygone days, each federation – a body not unlike our political parties – was presided over by an *agelith* – a nobleman. The names of the last *igelithen* to head such parties are still well known among the people. They were two brothers who died one hundred years ago. Since then, the position of chief of a federation has ceased to be hereditary. The secret federations gradually lost their caste nature, which they had inherited from the sib groups, and turned into political parties. Two such bodies confront one another everywhere in stiff and unrelenting opposition.

Nowadays, the Kabyls give their various parties the same unbending loyalty all Berbers used to give to their sib and caste – a quality which is highlighted in Ibn Khaldun's history of the Berber peoples, and is shared by the Tuareg inhabiting the regions further south. In the old days, when the caste system still held sway, a person of impure descent, of "mixed race" in a caste sense, was known as *l'hasos*. Nowadays this label is attached to people who have deserted their party to join another. The secret federations no longer exist. They function quite openly, and every man, through his sib, belongs to one party or another and promotes its cause not only in private but also in public.

The Kabyl is ready to do anything for his party. He is at all times ready to give up both time and money for its sake; he is ready to fight and, if need be to die, for it. A Kabyl who is away from home for any length of time invariably calls on fellow members of his party, one after another, and partakes of their hospitality. As soon as he is back home, he makes a point of inviting his erstwhile hosts for a return visit without delay. These reunions of fellow federation members are not held in the *tajmai't*. Unlike the age groups, they do not have "club premises" of their own. They meet either in the home of the leader of the federation or in a wood – as a rule one belonging to the leader. This is a survival of the caste system, which once upon a time used to thrive and flourish in the settlements.

The political parties are thus in no way tied to the age groups. These two institutions frequently cut across one another, and this is indeed why I have referred to a "vertical" and a "horizontal" stratification of society.

12. Tales from the Sudan*

Gassire's lute (Mali)

Four times Wagadu was built and stood there, in splendour. Four times it was destroyed so that there was no trace of it to be seen. Once it was lost through vanity, once through faith being broken, once through greed and once through strife. Four times Wagadu changed its name. First it was called Dierra, then Agada, then Ganna and finally Silla. Four times Wagadu turned its face in a different direction: once it looked North, once West, once East, and then South. For every time Wagadu was erected on earth, visible to men, it had four gates: one to the North, one to the West, one to the East, and one to the South. These were the cardinal points whence Wagadu derived its lasting strength, no matter whether it was built of stone, wood and earth, or whether it lived only like a shadow in the mind and the memory of its children. For Wagadu was not actually built of stone nor of wood nor earth. Wagadu was the strength that dwelt in the hearts of men. At times it could be recognized because there were eyes to see and ears to hear the blows of swords and the clang of shields. Sometimes it could not be seen because it had fallen asleep, exhausted and bewildered by the lack of human restraint. Four times Wagadu fell asleep; once by vanity, the second time by the breaking of faith, the third time by greed and the fourth time by strife. But if Wagadu were to be re-discovered for the fourth time, it would live on in man's mind with such vigour that vanity, lack of faith, greed or strife would never again be able to harm it.

Hoooh! Dierra, Agada, Ganna, Silla! – Hoooh! Fasa!

Every time when, by the fault of man, Wagadu perished, it rose with a new kind of beauty, a beauty that served to enhance its splendour. Vanity brought with it the songs of the minstrels, imitated and praised even today. Loss of faith brought the nations vast quantities of gold and precious stones. Greed brought in its train the art of writing, an art practised by women in Wagadu. But it is strife that will bestow on the fifth Wagadu the ability to endure as do the rains of the South and the rocks of the Sahara. For every man will then have Wagadu in his heart, and every woman will carry Wagadu under her heart.

Hoooh! Dierra, Agada, Ganna, Silla! – Hoooh! Fasa!

The first time Wagadu was destroyed by Vanity. At that time Wagadu

* From Atlantis, vol. 6, "Spielmannsgeschichten der Sahel", 1921, p. 53–60, 106–111; vol. 4. "Märchen aus Kordofan", 1923, p. 9–17.

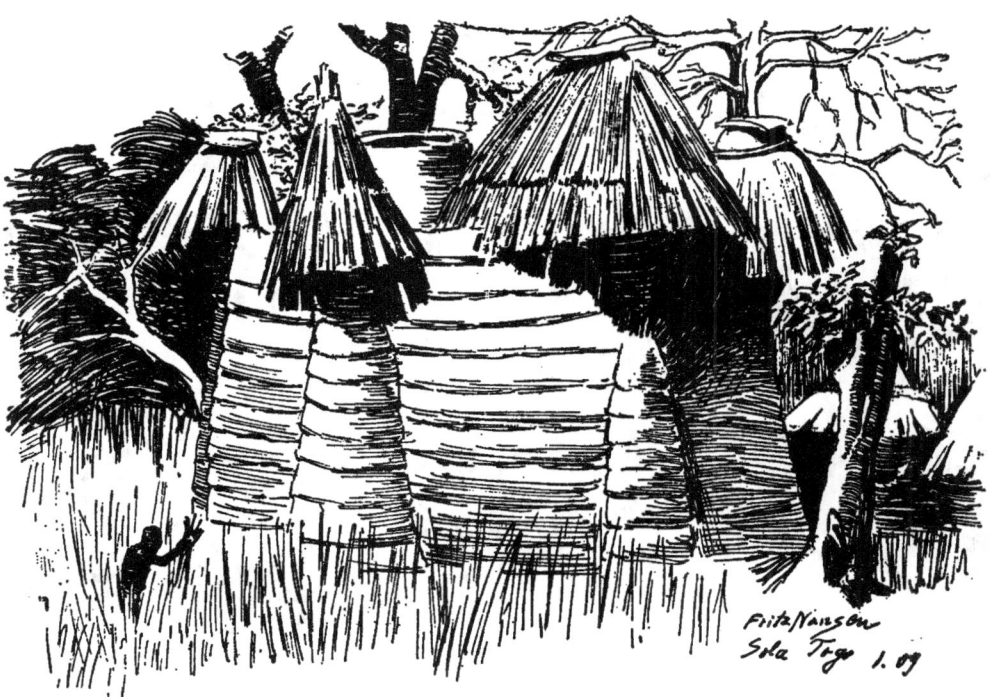

Fig. 42 Rural clay "castle", Sola, Togo

faced North, and its name was Dierra. Its last king was called Nganamba
Fasa. The Fasas were strong. They lived to an old age. Every day they
fought against the Burdamas and the Boromas. They fought every day of
every month. The fighting never ended. It was from this struggle that the
Fasas derived their strength. All of Nganamba's men were heroes (Gana),
and all the women were beautiful and immensely proud of the strength
and the heroic deeds of the men from Wagadu!

All the Fasas lived to an old age, unless they were killed in single
combat against the Burdamas. Nganamba was very old. He had a son
called Gassire, and he too was quite old already for he had eight grown-
up sons. They in their turn also had children. All of them lived at the same
time, and Nganamba ruled over his family and the Fasas as well as over
the base Boromas. Nganamba reached such an old age that under his rule
Wagadu fell into ruin and the Boromas once more turned to thieving. They
became the slaves of the Burdamas while the latter claimed the right of the
sword. Had Nganamba died sooner, would Wagadu have been lost for the
first time?

141

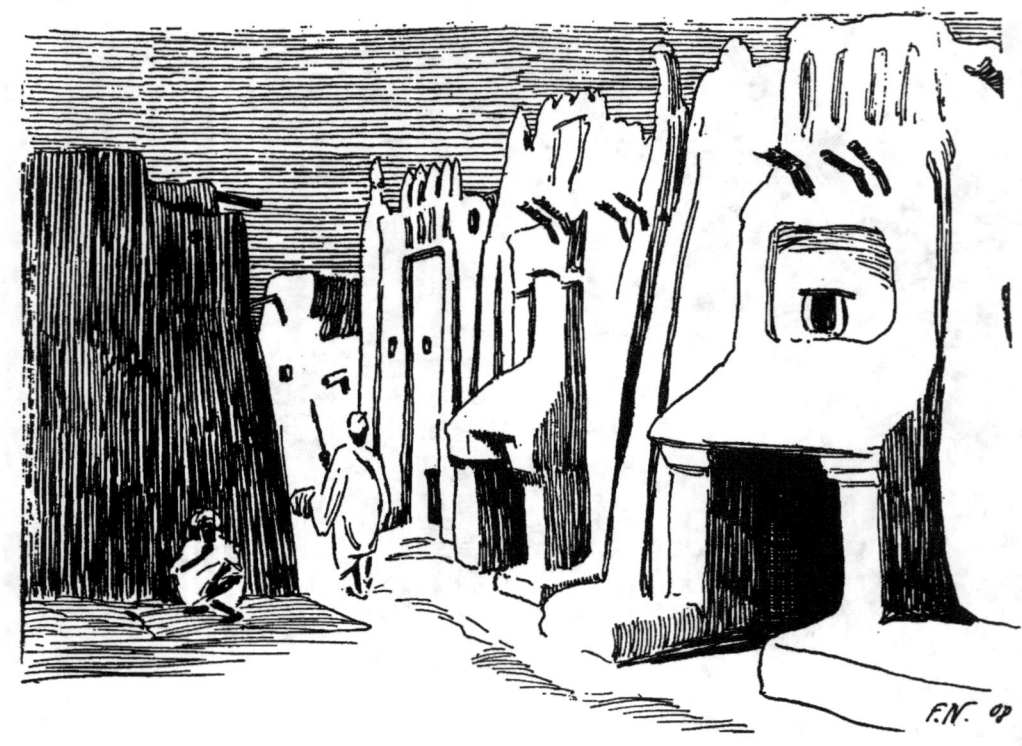

Fig. 43 Street in Djenné, Mali

Hoooh! Dierra, Agada, Ganna, Silla! – Hoooh! Fasa!

Nganamba did not die. A jackal was gnawing at Gassire's heart. Every day he secretly wondered: "When will Nganamba die? When will Gassire become king?" Gassire waited as impatiently for his father to die as a lover awaits the rising of the evening star. Whilst fighting like a hero against the Burdamas during the day and chasing the faithless Boromas, Gassire thought only of the fight and of the sword, the shield and the horse. But in the town in the evenings, sitting in the circle of his men and his sons, Gassire lent his ear to the heroes who praised his deeds. Yet his heart was not in it; it listened impatiently for Nganamba's last breath. His heart was filled with despair and yearning.

Gassire's heart yearned for his father's shield that he could carry only after Nganamba's death and for the sword that would adorn him only after he had become king. With every day that passed, Gassire's wrath and impatience increased. When Gassire lay down at night a jackal was

142

gnawing at his heart. Grief was choking him. One night Gassire jumped up, left the house and went to Kiekorro, a wise old man who had more knowledge than anyone else. He entered his house, saying: "Kiekorro! When is Nganamba, my father, going to die? When will he bequeath to me his sword and his shield?" The old man replied: "Ah! Gassire! Nganamba will die, but he will not bequeath his sword and his shield to you! You will play the lute. Others will inherit the shield and the sword. But because of your lute-playing, Wagadu will be ruined . . . Ah! Gassire!" Gassire said, "You are lying, Kiekorro. I see that you are not wise. How could Wagadu be ruined whilst its heroes win all their battles? Kiekorro, you are a fool!" The wise old man said: "Ah! Gassire, you do not believe me. But your way will lead you to the partridges in the fields. You will understand their language, and then you will know your way and the way of Wagadu!"

Hoooh! Dierra, Agada, Ganna, Silla! – Hoooh! Fasa!

The following morning Gassire again went with the heroes to fight against the Burdamas. Gassire was angry. He called out to the heroes: "Stay behind here! Today I want to fight the Burdamas by myself." So the heroes stayed behind. Gassire rode out alone against the Burdamas. He threw his spears. Gassire charged among the Burdamas. Gassire brandished his sword. He hit one Burdama to his right and one Burdama to his left. Gassire's sword cut like a scythe in a cornfield. The Burdamas took fright. Terrified, they screamed: "This is not a Fasa, it is not a Ganna! It is a Damo *!" The Burdamas turned their horses. They threw away their spears and took flight.

Gassire called the Gannas and said to them: "Bring me the spears!" The Gannas came forward and collected the spears. They sang: "The Fasas are heroes. Gassire always was the greatest hero of the Fasas. He always achieved great things. But this day Gassire has surpassed himself." Gassire entered the town on horseback. The men rode behind him, singing: "Never before has Wagadu conquered so many spears as this day."

Gassire allowed the women to bath him. The men gathered but Gassire did not sit down with them. He went out into the field where he listened to the partridges. He stepped close to them. One partridge was sitting in a shrub. The young ones were sitting in the grass. The partridge was singing: "Listen to the Dausi**! Listen to my exploits!" The partridge was singing about its fight with the snake! It sang: "All creatures must die,

---

* A terrifying creature unknown to the singer.
** Heroic song.

be buried and decay. Kings and heroes die, are buried and decay. I too shall die, be buried and decay. But the Dausi, the tale of my fights, will not die. It will continue to be sung and will outlive kings and heroes. Hoooh! How fortunate am I that I was able to perform such heroic deeds! That I am able to sing the Dausi! Wagadu will perish. But the Dausi will endure and live on!"

Hoooh! Dierra, Agada, Ganna, Silla! – Hoooh! Fasa!

Gassire went to the wise old man. "Kiekorro!" he said. "I was in the field. I understand the language of the partridges. The partridge boasted that the song of its heroic deeds would survive Wagadu. Tell me whether people, too, know the Dausi and tell me whether the Dausi will last longer than life and death!" The wise old man replied: "Ah! Gassire! You are walking fast towards death. Nobody is able to prevent it. As you cannot become king you will become a Diare*. Ah! Gassire! At the time when the kings of the Fasas still lived by the sea, they too were great heroes and they fought with people who had lutes and sang the Dausi. Often the Fasas were frightened because of the enemy's Dausi. They themselves were great heroes. They themselves never sang the Dausi because they were the first. They were Horro** and the Dausi is sung by the Diare. No longer did they fight as heroes for the day, but as drinkers for the evening's fame. But you, Gassire, unable to be the second of the first, want to be the first of the second. That is why Wagadu will perish." Gassire cried: "Then let Wagadu perish!"

Hoooh! Dierra, Agada, Ganna, Silla! – Hooh! Fasa!

Gassire went to a smith and said to him: "Make me a lute!" The smith said: "I will, but the lute will not sing." Gassire told him: "Smith, you do your work and leave the rest to me." The smith made the lute and took it to Gassire. Gassire seized the lute and played it. But the lute did not sing. Gassire asked the smith: "What is the matter? This lute does not sing!" The smith replied: "I told you so!" Gassire demanded: "See to it that the lute sings." The smith said: "I can do no more. It is up to you now." Gassire asked: "What am I to do?" The smith replied: "This is nothing but a piece of wood. It cannot sing if there is no feeling in it. It is you who must give it a heart. The piece of wood must go into battle with you. It must resound at the stroke of the sword. The wood must suck in the blood that trickles down, blood of your blood, breath of your breath. Your pain must become its pain, your glory its own. The wood

* Minstrel.
** Noblemen.

must no longer be like the wood of the tree from which it was hewn. It must be as your own flesh and blood. That is why it must live not only with you, but also with your sons. It is then that the sound coming from your very heart will echo in your son's ears and will continue to live in the people's hearts. And the blood that gushes from his heart will drip down on your body and will go on living in this wood. This is why Wagadu will perish!" Gassire said: "Then let Wagadu perish!"

Hoooh! Dierra, Agada, Ganna, Silla! – Hoooh! Fasa!

Gassire called together his eight sons. "My sons," he said to them, "today we are going into battle. But the blows of our swords are no longer to die away in the Sahel. They are to be known for ever. The Dausi is to sing of me and of you, my sons, and praise us before all other heroes. You, my eldest son, and I – we shall be the first to fight this day!"

Leading the heroes into battle, Gassire rode at their head with his eldest son. He had slung his lute over his shoulder. The Burdamas approached. Gassire and his eldest son rode up to them. Gassire and his eldest son were the first to join battle. They were far ahead of the other heroes. Gassire did not fight like a man. He fought like a Damo. His eldest son did not fight like a man. He too fought like a Damo. Gassire was drawn into a fight against eight Burdamas. The eight Burdamas harassed him greatly. His eldest son joined in the fight and killed four Burdamas. One of the Burdamas pierced his heart with a spear. The eldest son fell off his horse, dead. Gassire was angry. Gassire screamed loudly. The Burdamas took flight. Gassire dismounted. He lifted his son's body and laid it across his shoulders. That was how he rode back to the other heroes. The blood from the heart of his eldest son dripped on to the lute that Gassire was carrying on his back. That was how Gassire, riding at the head of his men, entered Dierra on horseback.

Hoooh! Dierra, Agada, Ganna, Silla! – Hoooh! Fasa!

The eldest son of Gassire was laid in his grave. All Dierra mourned him. The casket in which the body lay was red with blood. In the evening Gassire took his lute and played it. The lute did not sing. Gassire's anger was roused. He called together his sons: "My sons," he said to them, "tomorrow we are riding against the Burdamas!"

For seven days Gassire rode into battle with his men. On the morning of each of these seven days one of his sons rode with him as he led his men into battle. On each of the seven days Gassire carried back to the town the body of one of his sons, carrying it across his shoulders and on the lute. So it came about that every evening the blood of one of the sons dripped onto the lute. At the end of the seven days of fighting there was deep mourning in Dierra. All the men and women wore white and red clothes. Everywhere the blood of the Boromas was flowing. All the women mourned. All the men were angry. Before the eighth day of battle dawned, all the men of Dierra assembled. "Gassire," they said to him, "there must be an end to this fighting. We are prepared to fight if needs be. But there is no sense or limit to your fury for battle. Go and leave Dierra! Some of the men will join you and will leave with you. Take your Boromas with you and your cattle as well. As to the rest of us, we prefer life to glory. For sure, we do not ask for a life without glory, but we do not want to die for the sake of glory."

The wise old man spoke: "Ah, Gassire! This is how Wagadu perishes for the first time!"

Hoooh! Dierra, Agada, Ganna, Silla! – Hoooh! Fasa!

Gassire and his last – his youngest – son, his wives, his friends, his Boromas went out into the desert. They rode across the Sahel. Many men accompanied him as far as the city gates. Many of them returned. Some of them accompanied Gassire to the Sahara.

They rode far – day and night. They came to a lonely place, and that was where they halted. All the Gannas as well as the women and all the Boromas were asleep. Gassire's youngest son was asleep. But Gassire was awake. For a long time he sat by the fire, and then he too fell asleep. Suddenly Gassire was roused from sleep. He listened intently. Close to him Gassire heard a voice. It sounded as if it were coming from inside himself. Gassire listened. He began to tremble. He heard his lute singing. The lute was singing the Dausi.

When the lute had finished the Dausi for the first time, Gassire's anger vanished. Gassire wept. When the lute sang the Dausi for the first time, Wagadu perished for the first time.

Hoooh! Dierra, Agada, Ganna, Silla! – Hoooh! Fasa!

Four times Wagadu was built and stood there, in splendour. Four times it was destroyed so that there was no trace of it to be seen. Once it was lost through vanity, once through faith being broken, once through greed and once through strife. Four times Wagadu changed its name. First it was called Dierra, then Agada, then Ganna and finally Silla. Four times Wagadu turned its face in a different direction: once it looked North, once West, once East, and then South. For every time Wagadu was erected on earth, visible to men, it had four gates; one to the North, one to the West, one to the East, and one to the South. These were the cardinal points whence Wagadu derived its lasting strength, no matter whether it was built of stone, wood and earth, or whether it lived only like a shadow in the mind and the memory of its children. For Wagadu was not actually built of stone, nor of wood nor earth. Wagadu was the strength that dwelt in the hearts of men. At times it could be recognized because there were eyes to see and ears to hear the blows of swords and the clang of shields. Sometimes it could not be seen because it had fallen asleep, exhausted and bewildered by the lack of human restraint. Four times Wagadu fell asleep: once by vanity, the second time by the breaking of faith, the third time by greed and the fourth time by strife. But if Wagadu were to be re-discovered for the fourth time, it would live on in man's mind with such vigour that vanity, lack of faith, greed or strife would never again be able to harm it.

Hoooh! Dierra, Agada, Ganna, Silla! – Hoooh! Fasa!

Every time when, by the fault of man, Wagadu perished, it rose with a new kind of beauty, a beauty that served to enhance its splendour. Vanity brought with it the songs of the minstrels, imitated and praised even today. The loss of faith brought the nations vast quantities of gold and precious stones. Greed brought in its train the art of writing, an art practised by women in Wagadu. But it is strife that will bestow on the fifth Wagadu the ability to endure as do the rains of the South and the rocks of the Sahara. For every man will then have Wagadu in his heart, and every woman will carry Wagadu under her heart.

Hoooh! Dierra, Agada, Ganna, Silla! – Hoooh! Fasa!

Sirrani Korro Samba and Samba Ta Samba – the lady and the minstrel (Mali)

Sirrani Korro Samba was married to a woman from Tomma Korro. One day he was travelling with her to Tomma Korro to visit his parents-in-law. She was riding a pack-ox, he was riding his horse. He had given his wife a slave who was carrying her belongings. They arrived at Tomma Korro where they stayed for three days. They feasted well and as much mead had been made, every day Sirrani Korro Samba became drunk.

On the fourth day he said: "Today we'll return, and you, my wife, shall ride ahead on the pack-ox. I'll stay on here for another couple of hours for I want to finish off that good mead. I'll join you about midday. Mount your pack-ox now and ride ahead." So his wife set out with her slave.

There were sixty men from Segu on the road at that time. They had been hatching some small enterprise but their luck was out, so they were riding about, ill-humoured and without any boody. Among those sixty men were to be found some who had already made a name for themselves as heroes. There were Massassi Diadierri, Fulbe Malia, Djaora Gundaunda, as well as Sira Obassi and Bosso Mamadu Amadu. And, most important, there was Signana Samba, the Dialli*. He was said to have been given his name in the following way: whenever he asked for a gift – as is the custom with the Dialli – and was promised something for the next morning, he would squat at the door of the house and wait until he had received the gift. He had plenty of perseverance and patience.

So those sixty men from Segu came riding along the highway, greedy for any loot they could plunder, for they did not want to return to Segu empty-handed. One of the men looked into the distance. "Hoo!" he exclaimed. "Isn't that a man riding along on an animal loaded with goods?" The others too looked into the distance, "No," they replied, "it's not a man. It's a woman. She's riding on a pack-ox. She's sure to be beautiful and wealthy, for she has a slave walking beside her." Others thought: "Let's show the woman the way to Segu then. That will teach her something about the ways of the world." Others again thought: "Our unsuccessful enterprise might end tolerabley well, after all."

The sixty horsemen came galloping up to the wife of Sirrani Korro Samba and formed a circle around her. "Now then, what sort of robbers are you," she asked, "not leaving a decent woman in peace? Aren't you ashamed to be standing around here in the sun with robbery in your minds? For I can guess what you're thinking." Astonished, one of the sixty men said: "Woman, what gives you the courage to talk like this to sixty of the noblest heroes from Segu?" The wife of Sirrani Korro Samba replied: "Oh, what kind of noble heroes are you then, to dare to talk so boldly to a woman? Just you wait a while – my husband will soon come and teach you to fart with fear. That will quickly put an end to the courage you need to face a woman!" Signana Samba the minstrel strummed on his guitar, saying: "Even if this woman's husband doesn't belong to the Pui, one ought at least to sing the praises of her gift of the gab. Woman, who is your husband?"

"You ask who my husband is?" said the wife of Sirrani Korro Samba. "Do you really want to meet him? If so you'd better quickly look for the mouseholes in the field and for the birds' nests in the trees so that you can hide there together with your little horses. From such hide-outs you can best make my husband's acquaintance and stand a chance of not getting under his horse's hoofs." Massassi Diadierri said: "Woman, you

* Minstrel.

148

simply must accompany us to Segu so that the king can be informed of this extraordinary affair. Is there anybody who has ever heard such a bird singing? Forward to Segu!"

"Make haste," said the woman, "so that you can make your escape. For over there I can see my husband coming. He's very drunk and it's dangerous to cross him when he's in that state. See to it that you're gone, for it would be a great pity if sixty heroes should come to harm – heroes who are so brave that they dare to molest a woman on her own in broad daylight. Just move on. I see now that my husband is exceedingly drunk." One of the men from Segu said: "He must be a strange kind of hero. Tell us whether he's a god or a hyena!" They all repeated mockingly: "He must be a god or a hyena!" The woman replied: "If you creep into a mousehole he will seem like a god to you," she replied. "If you slip into a bird's nest you might think he is a hyena."

Sirrani Korro Samba came trotting along. He heard the quarrel and looked up to see what it was about. The sixty men from Segu withdrew and watched him from a distance. With an effort Sirrani Korro Samba straightened himself in the saddle, for he was very drunk. Then he took his shot gun, fired it into the air, first to his right, then to his left, and finally in front of him. Then he took his tobacco pipe out of his pocket and began to puff, calling to the men from Segu: "Hoo! What a nuisance you are!" and again: "Hoo! What a nuisance you are!"

One of the heroes from Segu came riding along at full speed. He fired at Sirrano Korro Samba. But he did not hit him. Calmly Sirrani Korro Samba fired his gun into the air. The other man shot and missed again, and then a third time. Sirrani Korro Samba now took aim. He shot the other man off his horse. He reloaded, took aim and shot down a second man. He reloaded, took aim again and shot down a third and fourth man. The men from Segu now began to take flight. Then Sirrani Korro Samba urged his horse forward and gave chase and took three of them prisoner.

So a great many people were wheeling around in that wide open space, and many shots were fired. Signana Samba, the Dialli of Segu, strummed on his guitar. "You heroes from Segu!" he sang. "Do not forget what you owe to your name! Heroes from Segu! Do not forget that there are sixty of you who have been poisoned by a woman's tongue, and now you are to be slaughtered like sick men! Just remember that you are heroes, you sixty men from Segu!" The hero from Kalla pursued the fugitives. Then the Dialli rode up to the woman and said: "If ever this story is to be told in the Pui – as it deserves – then a minstrel must be found who will tell the tale. To be sure, those fugitives who are taking to their heels will not make it known themselves. If the minstrel tells his tale in the Pui, he will sing of the brave woman he met. But by then he will be so far away from her that she won't be able to give him a present!" So the wife of Sirrani Korro Samba removed one of her heavy golden ear rings and gave it to the Dialli.

Sirrani Korro Samba returned with his three prisoners and handed them over to his wife. To the men he said: "Watch out that my wife doesn't fall from her pack-ox with fright when she sees you heroic fellows beside her."

Then they moved on again on their way.

Signana Samba caught up with his fleeing comrades, who had gathered under a tree. He sat down with them and plucked his guitar, saying: "One against sixty!" The heroes looked at him. "Surely you won't say anything about this business to the king?" one of them said. Signana Samba took out the golden ring he had received from the wife of Sirrani Korro Samba and hung it on the neck of his guitar. Plucking his instrument again he said: "One against sixty!"

The heroes withdrew behind a tree. Massassi Diadierri said: "He means that the man from Kalla was by himself, whilst there were sixty of us. He's certainly going to let the king know about it." But Fulbe Malia said: "He means that he has received a golden ring from the wife of the man from Kalla so that he would sing about her in the Pui. But he also means that there are sixty of us, and that he'll keep quiet about the incident if we give him sixty golden rings." Thereupon they came to an agreement and went back to Signana Samba. Massassi Diadierri told him: "If you don't let the king and the other people know what happened then each of us will give you a golden ring when we return to Segu." Signana Samba asked: "Are you really going to give me the rings as soon as we are back home?" The others promised: "Yes, we will."

They returned to Segu. "Are you bringing me good news?" asked the king. "Yes, we are," the Dialli replied. "We have cleansed the house and with a good broom swept away all those who did not belong there." The king said: "I don't understand," The minstrel asked: "Do you know the song of the Pui – One against Sixty?" "No", replied the king. The minstrel continued: "It is the very song your heroes are preparing for you."

Some of the men at once gave the Dialli the promised gold rings. Some did not. When Signana Samba happened to meet one of those who were slow in keeping their promise, he would strum on his guitar and sing: "One against sixty!" And if the man behaved as if he did not understand, then the other would ask him: "Do you know the woman who sings such

150

strange songs? Do you know the man before whom some hide in holes in the wall, others in bird's nests? Do you know the man who seems a god to some, a hyena to others?" One after another all the men paid their due, and some of them even paid for those who had been killed in battle or had been taken prisoner. So it came about that, after some time, Signana Samba the Dialli had received his sixty golden rings from them.

Now and then the king would hear a word or so about this matter. He said to Signana Samba: "Hadn't you better tell me what's going on?" The minstrel replied: "I must first discuss the matter with the others. All of them must be consulted, for it concerns every one of them." In the evening the men gathered together. The Dialli had brought with him his sixty-one golden rings, letting them dangle from the neck of his guitar. "What has been happening then?" the king asked. Signana Samba replied: "One against sixty." All the men looked at him. The Dialli asked Massassi Diadierri: "How does one keep one's word – half or fully?" Massassi Diadierri replied: "One keeps it fully." The other said: "One against sixty. Was I not promised that sixty golden rings would be given to me immediately on our return? Was there no delay, and were things not made awkward for me? Was there no plotting under a tree?" Signana Samba the Dialli strummed his guitar and began to sing: "I am singing before a great king. Will the great king give sixty golden rings to the poor minstrel?"

Thereupon the king sent for sixty golden rings and gave them to the minstrel, who thus received a hundred and twenty-one golden rings in all, and in the Pui told the tale of Sirrani Korro Samba and the sixty heroes from Segu.

Later they also sang about Samba Ta Samba. This is what happened: With Samba Ta Samba, his youngest brother, Sirrani Korro Samba once engaged in a fight against robbers who shot his horse dead. As the elder brother lay on the ground, Samba Ta Samba said to him: "Quickly mount my horse and ride behind me." Sirrani Korro Samba replied: "No, I would rather die than ride behind you like a woman." Three times Samba Ta Samba pleaded with his brother to ride behind him.

Three times the brother refused. But as the enemy approached he accepted the offer. He jumped onto the saddle behind Samba Ta Samba, and so was saved.

Thus it happened that Samba Ta Samba too came into the Pui.

The destruction of Kash (Kordofan)

Four kings ruled the vast realm of Kash. One of them ruled in Nubia, the second in Habesh, the third in Kordofan and the fourth in For. The richest of all was the Nap of Napht(a) in Kordofan. It was he who owned all the gold and copper. His gold and copper were brought to Nubia and from there were carried away by the great kings of the western world. From the East, envoys came across the sea in ships. In the South, the king ruled over many nations. These forged weapons of iron for him and sent slaves by the thousand who lived at the court of the Nap.

Although the Nap of Naphta was the richest man on earth, his life was the saddest and shortest any man could have. For he was allowed to rule his country for a few years only. Throughout his short rule the priests observed the stars every night, made sacrifices and lit fires. Not for a single night must they discontinue their prayers and their sacrifices. These were never to be stopped, not even for one night, or they would have lost sight of the stars' movements and would not have known when, according to their rules, the king had to be killed. For a long time things went on in this manner. Every day, year after year, the priests studied the stars and foretold the day when the king had to be put to death.

Once again the day had arrived when the king had to die. All the fires in the land had been extinguished. The women were confined to the houses. The priests lit the new fire. They proclaimed the new king, who was the nephew of the king who had just been put to death. The new king was called Akaf and it was during his rule that the old customs of the country were changed. Yet people say that it was these changes that caused the subsequent destruction of Napht.

The first task a Nap had to undertake was to decide who should accompany him on the way to his death. The Nap chose them from among his favourite courtiers. To begin with, he had to choose the man who would lead the others. Now it so happened that some time ago a king from the Far East had sent across the sea to the court of Naphta a man who was famous for his skill in telling stories. This man, called Far-li-mas, had just arrived as a slave at the court of the Nap. King Akaf liked Far-li-mas and he said: "He is to be my first companion. With his tales he will entertain me until my time is up. He will make me happy even after my death."

When Far-li-mas learned what the king had decided he did not take fright. He simply said to himself: "It is God's will."

In those days it was the custom in Naphta to maintain a fire constantly. Even to this day the custom still exists in remote villages in For. To feed the fire the priests always chose a young man and a young girl. Their task was to guard the fire and to lead a chaste life. These two young people were also put to death, but not at the same time as the king. They were killed when the new fire was lit. As the new fire for King Akaf was lit the priests chose the youngest sister of the new king to guard the fire. Her name was Sali. On hearing that she had been chosen Sali was frightened, for she was much afraid of death.

For a time the king lived happily, enjoying the wealth and the splendour of his country. He spent the evenings with friends and with visitors who had come to Naphta as envoys. But before long God implanted in him the thought that with each happy day he came one day nearer to his certain death. The king was afraid. He tried to banish these thoughts from his mind. But he did not succeed. King Akaf became very sad. Then God gave him the second idea: to make Far-li-mas come and tell him a story.

Far-li-mas was sent for. "Far-li-mas," said the king when he arrived, "the day has come when you are to cheer my spirits. Tell me a tale." Far-li-mas replied: "Your order shall be obeyed even before you have uttered it," and he began to weave his story. King Akaf listened. His guests listened. They forgot to drink. They forgot to breathe. The slaves forgot to serve at table. They forgot to breathe. Far-li-mas's tale was like hashish. When he had finished, everybody was overwhelmed in a blissful swoon. King Akaf no longer thought about death. None of those present had noticed that Far-li-mas had narrated throughout the night. As the guests left the sun was rising.

The following day King Akaf and his guests could hardly wait for the evening, when Far-li-mas would tell another story. Each evening Far-li-mas had to tell a story. The news of his fairy-tales spread at court, in the capital and throughout the country. With every night Far-li-mas improved his art of story-telling. Every day the king made him a present of fine clothes, and the guests gave him gold and precious stones. Far-li-mas became rich. When he passed through the streets he was followed by a retinue of slaves. People loved him. They began to bare their breasts before him.

The news of Far-li-mas's wonderful tales spread everywhere. Sali too heard of them. She sent word to her brother, the king. "Let me listen to Far-li-mas's tales too for once," she asked ."Your wish shall be fulfilled even before you utter it," the king replied. Sali arrived, eager to hear the story. Far-li-mas saw Sali and lost his senses. He saw nothing but Sali. Sali in turn saw nothing but Far-li-mas. "Why don't you speak?" asked King Akaf. "Don't you know any more tales?" Far-li-mas forced himself to take his eyes off Sali and began to narrate. At first Far-li-mas's tale was

153

like hashish when it produces a gentle kind of trance. But then his tale became like hashish when it puts people to sleep after passing through a state of unconsciousness. After some time the guests fell into slumber, and so did the king. They heard the tale only as if in a dream until in the end they were completely carried away. Only Sali remained awake. Her eyes were fastened on Far-li-mas. Her eyes absorbed Far-li-mas. She was completely enraptured by Far-li-mas.

When Far-li-mas ended he rose. Sali rose. They walked towards each other. Sali embraced Far-li-mas, saying: "We do not want to die, do we?" Laughing, Far-li-mas looked into Sali's eyes and said: "The will is yours. Show me the way." Sali replied: "Leave me now. I will search for the way. When I have found it I will tell you." Sali and Far-li-mas took leave of each other. The king and his guests were still asleep.

The following day Sali went to the head priest and asked: "Who determines the time when the old fire is to be extinguished and the new one is to be lit?" The priest replied: "It is God who decides." Sali asked: "How does God make his will known to you?" The priest answered: "Every night we observe the stars. We never lose sight of them. Every night we see the moon and from day to day we know the movements of the stars in relation to the moon. In this way we foresee the hour of the king's death." Sali said: "Have you to do that every night? What would happen if you did not watch the sky for one night?" The priest replied: "We would have to make a sacrifice if nothing was seen for one night. If we could see nothing for several nights we would not know where we stood." Sali said: "Does that mean that in that case you would no longer know when it was time for the fire to be put out?" The head priest replied: "In that case we could no longer fulfil our task."

"God's works are great," said Sali. "But the greatest of his works is not his writing in the sky. The greatest of them is life on this earth. I learned that last night." The priest asked: "What do you mean?" Sali replied: "God gave Far-li-mas the gift of telling stories better than anybody else before him. That is greater than the writing in the sky." The head priest said: "You are wrong." Sali argued: " You know the moon and the stars. But have you heard the tales of Far-li-mas?" The priest said: "No, I have not heard them." Sali spoke again: " How then can you judge? I tell you that in listening to them you will forget to gaze at the stars." The head priest said: "Sister of the king, that is your opinion." Sali urged: "Prove to me that I am wrong. Prove that the writing in the sky is greater and more important than life on earth." The priest said: "I shall prove it."

The head priest sent word to King Akaf: "Allow the priests to come into the castle tonight to listen to Far-li-mas's tales from the setting of the sun till the rising of the moon." King Akaf agreed. Sali sent word to Far-li-mas: "Tonight you must narrate as you did last night. This is our way."

As evening fell the king called together his guests and the envoys. Sali came and sat by his side. All the priests came. They bared the upper part of their bodies and prostrated themselves. The head priest spoke: "The tales of Far-li-mas are said to be the most wonderful work of God." King Akaf said: "Judge for yourselves." The head priest said: "Forgive, O King, if at the rising of the moon we leave your house so that we can fulfil our duty." King Akaf said: "Do whatever is God's will." The priests, the guests and the envoys all sat down. The hall was crowded with people, and Far-li-mas made his way between them. "Begin, my companion in death," said King Akaf.

Far-li-mas looked at Sali. Sali looked at Far-li-mas. Again King Akaf said: "Why don't you speak? Don't you know any more tales?" Far-li-mas wrenched his eyes from Sali. As the sun was setting he began his tale. His tale was like hashish which clouds men's minds. His tale became like hashish which makes men swoon. Finally his tale became like hashish which smothers the senses altogether. As the moon was rising King Akaf and his guests and the envoys lay slumbering, and all the priests were fast asleep. Only Sali was awake. She willed Far-li-mas into speaking words that became ever sweeter.

Far-li-mas's tale came to an end. He rose. Far-li-mas went up to Sali. Sali went up to Far-li-mas. "Let me kiss these lips whence come such sweet words," said Sali. They drew happiness from each other's lips. "Let me embrace thy body the sight of which gives me strength," said Far-li-mas. Wide awake and with their limbs entwined, they lay among all those slumbering people, so happy that they thought their hearts would overflow. Sali was jubilant. "Do you see the way now?" she asked. "I do," replied Far-li-mas. So they went away. Only sleepers remained in the castle.

The following day Sali came to the head priest. "Tell me now if you were right to condemn my words?" she asked. "I won't give you an answer today," he replied. "We will listen to Far-li-mas once more. For yesterday we were not duly prepared." Sali said: "Let it be so." The priests made the sacrifices and they said their prayers. The fetters of many of the oxen were loosened. All day long the prayers in the temple continued. In the evening all the priests came into the palace of King Akaf again. In the evening Sali again sat by her brother. In the evening Far-li-mas began his tale. And before dawn the king, his guests, the envoys and the priests, all of them listening in ecstasy, had fallen asleep. Yet in their midst lay Sali and Far-li-mas who, their limbs entwined, were drawing happiness from each other's lips.

Every night the same thing happened.

At first news of Far-li-mas's tales had spread among the people. Then it was rumoured that the priests were neglecting their sacrifices and their prayers during the night. Everybody was seized by deep anxiety. One day a highly respected man from the town met the head priest. The highly respected man said to the priest: "When will the next festival be celebrated this year? I would like to undertake a journey but I want to be back in time for the festival. Tell me therefore when it will be." The priest was embarrassed. It was many days since he had seen the moon and the stars. He knew nothing about their movements, so he said: "Wait another day, then I shall be able to let you know." The highly respected man thanked him. "I will come to see you again to-morrow," he said.

The head priest called together his priests. "Which of you," he asked, "has observed the movements of the stars recently?" None of the priests replied. All of them had been listening to Far-li-mas's tales. Once more the head priest repeated his question. "Is there not a single one amongst you who observed the movements of the stars and the position of the moon?" All the priests kept silent until at last a very old one rose and spoke up: "All of us were carried away by Far-li-mas. None of us will be able to tell you on what days the festivals are to be celebrated. Nor can we tell you when the fire is to be extinguished or when it is to be lit afresh." Horrified, the head priest said: "How could this happen? What am I to tell the people?" The old priest replied: "It is God's will. But if Far-li-mas has not been sent by God, then let him be killed. For as long as he lives and tells his tales everybody will listen to him." The head priest repeated: "But what am I to tell the people?" Then they all fell silent and dispersed.

The head priest went to Sali. "What was it you said on the first day?" he asked. Sali replied: "I said: 'God's works are great, but the greatest of his works is not his writing in the sky. The greatest of them is life on this earth.' You scolded me because of what I said. You told me I was wrong. Now then, tell me today whether I was lying." The priest said: "Far-li-mas is against God. Far-li-mas must die." Sali said: "Far-li-mas is the king's companion in death." The priest said: "I will speak to King Akaf." Sali said: "God dwells in my brother, King Akaf. Ask him what he thinks."

The head priest came to King Akaf. His sister Sali was sitting by his side. The priest bared himself before the king, and threw himself to the ground before him, saying: "Forgive me, King Akaf." The king said: "Tell me what is worrying you." The priest replied: "Talk to me about Far-li-mas, your companion in death." The king said: "At first God made me think of the approaching hour of my death and I was frightened. Then God reminded me of Far-li-mas who had been sent to me as a gift from the country in the East beyond the seas. By the first thought God implanted in me he had disturbed me greatly. By the second he cheered my soul and made me and all the others happy! That is why I have given many fine garments to Far-li-mas. My friends have given him gold and precious stones. He has distributed among others many of the gifts he has been given. He is rich, as is his due, and everybody loves him as much as I do." The head priest said: "Far-li-mas must die. He disrupts the order of things." King Akaf said: "I shall die before Far-li-mas." The head priest said: "God shall decide this matter." King Akaf agreed: "So be it. The people must see for themselves." The head priest left. Sali spoke to the king. "King Akaf, my brother, the end is near. Your companion in death will be the one who can awake you to life. But I ask you to spare him. For I must have him if I am to find happiness in this life." King Akaf said: "So take him then, Sali, my sister."

Messengers passed through the town, proclaiming everywhere that the same evening Far-li-mas would speak to all the people in the large public square, between the king's palace and the priests' houses. A throne screened in veils had been erected there for the king. In the evening crowds thronged together from all directions and settled down in a circle. Many thousands of people had gathered. The priests came and settled down. So did the guests and the envoys. Sali sat down next to the veiled king. Far-li-mas was sent for.

Far-li-mas came. His servants walked behind him, clothed in shining garments. They settled down, facing the priests. Far-li-mas threw himself to the ground before King Akaf. Then he too sat down.

The head priest rose, saying: "Far-li-mas has disrupted the order of things in Naphta. Tonight it will be made clear whether this was God's will or not." The priest sat down. Far-li-mas rose. He looked into Sali's eyes. Then he took his eyes off Sali and gazed beyond the crowd. He looked at the priests, saying: "I am a servant of God. I believe that he loathes everything that is evil in the hearts of men. Tonight God will judge."

Far-li-mas began his tale. The words he spoke were sweet as honey.

His voice was to the people as the first rain in summer is to the thirsty earth. From Far-li-mas's mouth came a perfume finer than musk and incense. Far-li-mas's head blazed like a light, the only light in the dark night. At first his tale was like hashish that delights the waking. Then it became like hashish that shrouds the dreamer in darkness. But towards morning Far-li-mas raised his voice. Like the rising Nile, his words surged into the hearts of men. For some his words had a soothing effect, as soothing as if they were entering paradise. But for others his words were frightening, as frightening as the apparition of Azrael, the angel of death. Some were filled with happiness, others with horror. As morning dawned, the voice increased in power, and echoed even more loudly. People's hearts reared up against each other, as in a fight. They rushed against each other as clouds do in the sky in a thunderous night. Lightning shafts of anger and blows of fury met each other.

As the sun rose Far-li-mas's tale came to an end. An unspeakable surprise filled the bewildered minds of the people. For, as the living looked around, their glance fell upon the priests. The priests lay on the ground, dead.

Sali rose. She threw herself down before the king. "King Akaf, my brother," she said, "God has judged. This is the end of the path. Oh King Akaf, my brother, remove thy veil, show thyself to thy people and complete the sacrifice thyself. For those who lie here have been destroyed by Azrael, acting upon God's orders." The servants removed the veils from the throne. King Akaf rose. He was the first king whom the people of Naphta had ever seen. Their king was as beautiful as the rising sun.

The people were jubilant. A white horse was brought which the king mounted. To his left walked his sister Sali-fu-Hamr, and to his right walked Far-li-mas. The king rode to the temple. Arriving at the temple, he seized an axe and with it he made three holes in the holy ground. Into the holes Far-li-mas threw three seeds of corn. Then the king made two holes in the holy ground. Into these Sali threw two corn-seeds. At once the five seeds shot up and they grew before the very eyes of the people. By midday the ears of corn on all five plants were ripe. In all the farms of the town the fathers loosened the fetters of the oxen. The king put out the fire. All the fathers in the town put out the fires in the hearths. Sali lit a new fire and all the maidens came and took from it for the new fire.

From that day no more human beings were killed in Naphta. Akaf was the first king of Napht who lived until it pleased God to call him to himself at a ripe age. After his death Far-li-mas succeeded him on the throne. Under him Naphta reached not only the summit of its fortunes but also its end.

King Akaf's reputation as a wise and well-advised ruler soon became known in all countries. All the sovereigns sent him gifts and wise men asked for the king's advice. All the great merchants settled in the capital of Naphta. On the sea to the East King Akaf had many great ships that carried the products of Naphta all over the world. The mines of Naphta could not always deliver enough gold and copper to fill the holds of the ships. At the time when Far-li-mas succeeded King Akaf the fortunes of the country reached their highest peak. Its fame resounded through all the countries lying between the oceans of the East and the ocean of the West. But together with fame, greed now also grew in the hearts of men. After the death of Far-li-mas the neighbouring countries broke their alliances and made war on Naphta. Naphta was defeated. Naphta was destroyed, and with it perished the strongest castle in the great kingdom. The great kingdom fell apart. It was over-run by wild races. People forgot the copper and gold mines. The cities disappeared.

Nothing remained of Naphta except the tales of Far-li-mas which the latter had brought with him from the land beyond the sea in the East.

This is the story of the fall of the land of Kash whose last inhabitants lived in the land of For.

13. The Religion of the Yoruba *

Obatalla the god of the sky (and Olufan)

We begin with the couple from whom the world descended, which originally consisted of Obatalla, the god of the sky, and Odudua, the goddess of the earth. In some localities, particularly on the coast, these two deities are still very well-known in this form, but in the north they have undergone radical changes and are actually fading from memory in many places. In Ibadan Odudua is not venerated at all, and in Ife she has been transformed into a male. Obatalla, however, survives in distorted form under the name of Osha-la Osha = Orisha, la = Obatalla), and the only priest from whom I was able to gather any information on the matter was not even sure whether Oshalla was male or female.

There are said to be some places where Oshalla is definitely regarded as female, in which case we should be presented with the phenomenon of the god of the sky and the goddess of the earth having changed places. But in the central area of the Yoruba country a new name crops up that seems to be entirely absent in the south, that is, Olufan. The priest told me that 'Osha (= Orisha) Olufan is the real name of the god Oshalla, and Olufan means chief, or special.' Olufan or Oshalla is the sky, and has neither father nor mother. On the other hand he is also described as being lord and master, though the offspring of Oshalla.

The wild confusion of views about this deity seems to reflect the absence in this area of any clan claiming direct descent from him. But, just as in the south, there is a great deal that recalls the simple and straightforward legend of the sky god as the father of all and the earth goddess as the mother; an illustration of this is the fact that Oshalla is represented by two gourds on top of one another, covered and painted white. Where the legend still clearly survives in the minds of the Yoruba, this is a symbol representing the integration of the universe; the lower gourd represents the earth and the upper the sky above it. Even though the full content of the legend has been lost, there are all sorts of indications that originally it was everywhere the same.

Oshalla's descendants are forbidden the consumption of palm wine and dog and goat flesh. The principal sacrifices to the gods are sheep, snails, hens and kola. Oshalla is outstanding among the gods as a god of fertility. When a married woman wants a child she goes to Ille-Shole (or

* From "Die atlantische Götterlehre", Atlantis vol. X, 1926, pp. 189–192.

Sharre), where neither palm wine may be drunk nor dogs' flesh eaten. This is the site of the small round temple of Oshalla, which I continually saw reproduced in various forms in the farms. In it the women make sacrifices and pray for their wishes to be granted.

The great five-day festival of Oshalla is celebrated by the whole population every fourteen months (i. e. once a year). Each morning while the festival lasts a woman is chosen by the deity, and this is regarded as a great distinction. She is forbidden to speak. Silently she picks up the water pitchers, and silently she takes them down to the stream, and on the way she may greet or speak to no-one. Silently she draws the water and silently she carries it back, ignoring everyone she meets. Inside the temple the water is poured into the god's big jar, after which she is released from the obligation of ceremonial silence and may talk to anyone she pleases.

An attribute of Osha-la's is a sacred drum, called an *egvi*. I saw a whole series of specimens of these drums at Bangba, a locality near Ife. They were carved in various shapes, and every specifically male specimen was accompanied by another that was specifically female. They were obviously the object of extreme veneration. These and similar drums are vigorously beaten during the festival week to set the time for the dances, in which everyone joins. Someone or other is always said to be inspired at these festivals, and such people are then called *elegun oshalla*. The *orisha* enters the head of the *elegun* and speaks through him, and what the *elegun* then says is law. Through him the god proclaims his will, that must be acted on immediately, and he gives the people precise instructions what to do or not to do to gain his favour. His pronouncements refer above all to women who have hitherto vainly wanted a child, which they are now promised. The fortunate ones are given new names and must immediately make a thank offering of a sheep. But goats must never be sacrificed to him.

When those inspired by the god oracularly pronounce glad tidings on important matters, the officiating priests, who in some places are called *adye* and elsewhere are known as *obo-orisha,* present them with valuable clothing, tin armbands, etc., etc.

In Ibadan these festivals are less celebrated than they are in neighbouring towns, and, as mentioned above, Odudua is completely unknown there.

The frequent fusion between Obatalla and Olufan is strange, and complete vagueness in the matter prevails. It took me a considerable time to track down the origin of the shadowy figure of Olufan. I was given a first clue at Ife, where the priest three times repeated the word 'Allah' outside the entrance to the temple. A priest from Ilesha then told me that Olufan's worshippers were forbidden to eat goats, dogs and horses. These are forbidden foods to Mohammedans. This made it clear to me that the word 'Olufan' was nothing but 'Al(u)fan' or 'Alfa'. 'Alfa' is the term applied by the Yoruba and by Muslims to forbidden foods, which leads to the conclusion that Orisha Obatalla, the supreme deity of the Yoruba, has become identified with the God of Islam. Thus a phenomenon has taken place that is by no means unusual in mythology. The Muslims have made a transference of the kind that is often made by modern Christian missionaries. When missionaries go to a new country they generally quickly discover that the indigenous population recognise the existence of a supreme deity, and to smooth the path for an understanding of the Christian God they say; 'Our God is the same as your Olorun. You must worship him every seventh day.' The institution of Sunday insinuated itself among many Christianised Yoruba in this way, and it became the custom to worship Olorun, who used not to be worshipped there at all. In the same way the Muslims said: 'Our Allah is the same as your Obatalla or Oshalla. If you wish to worship him, you must avoid eating the flesh of goats, dogs and horses.' Thus Alfa imperceptibly established itself and gave rise to the god Olufan.

Shango the thunder-god and the legend of his death

Of all the gods in Africa none has such a well-developed mythology and cult as Shango, the thunder-god of the Yoruba. The first king of the country was his offspring, and his descendants still have the privilege of providing the country with kings.

Shango, according to the coastal saga, was the most important male born in Ife of the universal mother Yemaya. He is a powerful, mighty, warlike god, of a type well calculated to satisfy the imagination of an ambitious tribe in this part of the world. He is the god of the thunderstorm. When he flings his thunderbolt the lightning flashes, and he burns down farms and towns, splits trees, and strikes down men. He is cruel and terrible in his magnificence, but he also brings blessings through his mighty deeds. For the torrents of rain he brings down from the black clouds give fertility to the parched earth and the fields. Men therefore fear him, but they also love him. They fear his anger, but pray for his approach. They picture him as riding a horse (which they call a ram, because it is so swift and lively), carrying a hammer, the hammer of thunder, and surrounded by his wives, who are the rivers and lagoons. For he is the god who brings water down from the skies, and rivers swell

162

when he dismounts. He lives in a palace of shining brass from which the lightning flashes, and he possesses a powerful medicine. As a result of his taking this medicine, flames flash from his mouth whenever he opens it. His wife Oya, the River Niger, stole some of this medicine, according to legend, with the result that fire flashed from her mouth too. The angry god chased her, striking down the gods who stood in his way, until finally, at sunset, he was unable to overcome the last resisters and sank down into the earth. All the peoples of the Yoruba country have stories about the great god Shango. Many of them are contradictory, but the basic picture remains, broadly speaking, the same. One point on which there is no agreement is the country of his origin, but we shall find it possible to clear up this important point. Here are some legends about him.

In Ibadan I was told that Shango's father was Oronyan(g) and his mother Yemodia; Oranyan(g)'s father was Laro and Temodia's father Aussi. Oronyan(g) was a great warrior in the Yoruba country. He once made himself master of Ilife, but was driven out again. He went to the Oku territory, where Yemodia, who was of Takpa (i.e. Nupe) stock, lived, and he married her there. She remained his only wife; he did not follow the usual custom of taking a second wife. Shango was born in the Nupe country. Oronyan(g) became king in Oduma-ushe, but Shango was king in ancient Oyo.

When Shango was king in Oyo, he had two *ironse* (high officials or courtiers). One was Mokva (or Mogba), and the other Timi Agbali-Olofa-no. As Shango loved warfare above all things, he often sent out Mokva and Timi to make war and destroy towns. He was so bellicose that in the end the people of Oyo gathered together, saying: "Our king is destroying the country all around. But we want a king who gives us, not slaves, but food." They sent a deputation to Shango, saying: "You are king no longer. You have been too severe, too cruel, you are evil. You must cease to be king." Shango listened to the deputation. "I see all that," he said. "Mokva will explain it to you later. I am a great *oni-sheggo* (magician). No-one can force me to do anything. But I am tired of this miserable life." Shango went away. He took a rope with him and went into the bush. He tied the rope to a certain tree. Then he hanged himself. He hanged himself by the rope.

The people came to the tree. They saw and heard what had happened. "Is that Shango? Is that Shango? Is that Shango?" they said. "Was that the King of Oyo? Was that the King of Oyo? Was that the King of Oyo?" "Has Shango hanged himself? Has Shango hanged himself? Has Shango hanged himself?" Mokva heard this, and said to the people: "If

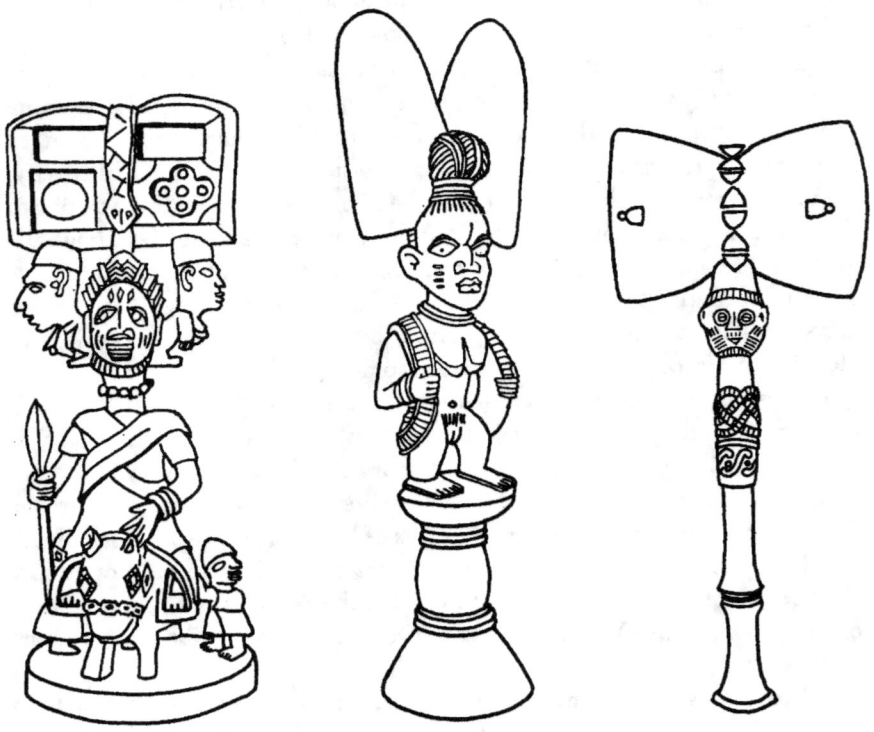

Fig. 44 Statue of the god Shango
Fig. 45 Shango stick
Fig. 46 Thunderbolt symbol

Shango hears how you talk about his death, he will burn down your houses; for he is not dead. I will explain to you how all this came about."

Mokva also said:

"Every day Shango sent out Mokva and Timi to make war and destroy peoples and towns. In the morning he said: "Go and do this and that". We went and did what he said. In the evening we came back and said: "We have done what you ordered," Shango answered: "No, that is not enough. Tomorrow you must go out again and do more." We went out every day. Shango spat fire out of his mouth and told us to go. We went and did what he said. One day Mokva and Timi, the two of us, came and said: "The day before yesterday we went out and destroyed a town as you ordered. Today we went out to destroy a town. We had to do it all, we had to do it all. But you breathe fire out of your mouth. That is all."

Then Shango said: "I see you are discontented with my will, but I am so strong that you must do what I require of you. I shall prove that to you. You came to complain about it together and to tell me that I do nothing. So I shall force you to fight each other." So we fought each other; we could not do otherwise. We were both strong, and our swords were good. In the end Mokva killed Timi. I killed Timi. Timi, Mokva's friend, died. Mokva then said to Shango: "You forced me to kill this man. But this man was not my enemy. So now I shall kill you." Shango said: "What? You want to kill me? You think you can kill me? Call together the people of the town. Speak to the people. Listen to the people. And see what happens then." I, Mokva, called together all the people.

Mokva said to the people: "Every day King Shango sent out Mokva and Timi to destroy towns and kill people. Mokva and Timi grew weary. Mokva and Timi came to complain. Shango forced Mokva and Timi to fight each other. Mokva and Timi fought. Mokva killed Timi. Mokva said to King Shango: "You forced me to kill Timi. Timi was not my enemy. Now I shall kill you." Shango said: "Call the people together."

I Mokva have called the people together and now you are here and must decide."

The people said: "Shango must leave the country in five days' time." That was what the people said to Shango. Shango took a rope and went into the forest. That is what happened. It is true, nobody could have killed Shango. Shango went of his own free will.

Thus Mokva spoke to the people. He said: "In future if anyone says: "Shango hanged himself", ogu medicine must be put in his house to burn it down." Mokva chose fifty other mokvas (that is the title by which the priests of Shango are known) and put ogu in every house in which a man said: "Shango hanged himself". After Shango's death two chains grew out of his grave; that was because of his powerful medicine. Shango climbed up to heaven by those chains. His magical power did not come from himself; he learnt and inherited it from Adya Ganti. Adya Ganti was Oronyan(g)'s grandfather (?), i.e., Shango's great-grandfather. That was how he learnt to produce the fire that flashed from his mouth. Shango's only wife was (according to the belief in Ibadan) Oya, the lagoon. Oya was a great and mighty huntress and pursued her craft with tremendous skill. She hunted all the wild animals in the bush, leopards, antelopes and elephants. She had a younger brother who accompanied her everywhere on her hunting expeditions. After Shango married her and later hanged himself, she changed herself into the River Niger.

A man from Ilesha gave me this additional information: Oya was

Shango's wife; as his wife she still precedes him and sweeps the way clear before him. She had been married before. She had been married to Ogun. But Ogun was bad, so she ended by running away to Shango, and she was married to him and stayed with him. Oya was the mother of Shango's children, i. e., the mother of the Alafine, the royal clan in Oyo. In her present form she lives with Shango in heaven. When the time of the festivities in her honour approaches, i. e., in December or January, many people go to the river and sacrifice to it. The priests and priestesses of Oyo always kill sheep for the goddess, but never goats. Killing goats or consuming their flesh is forbidden.

Many legends describe the god's descent to earth. There are some stories about him that must be mentioned. Once, when Mokva was at war, Shango ordered the people of Oyo to make a pile of timber no less than twenty-four feet high in the middle of the road. Palm kernels were thrown on it and palm oil poured over it. When everything was ready, Shango kindled the pyre, and when it was blazing he threw Mokva on top of it. Mokva was burnt to ashes, but promptly changed back into a living man again. Shango was very surprised at this, and said: 'What Mokva can do, I can do too. But I do not want to be a man, but an *orisha*.' He took his loin-cloth and sixteen cowrie shells and went into the bush and hanged himself from an *anyo* tree. That was how he turned into an *orisha*, for he went up to heaven; and cowrie shells were sacred to him, because people threw them for him; and Mokva became his first priest.

Even more interesting is another legend about the two warriors, because, apart from anything else, it begins by referring to some principles of Shango's which contrast strongly with the usual lack of moral precepts among these tribes. It comes from the Ibadan area and is as follows:

King Shango was born in the Takpa country. Firstly, he insisted on his people's speaking the truth and detested lies. Secondly, he did not want them to poison one another. Thirdly, he did not want them to rob one another, going into each other's houses in the towns and taking away things that did not belong to them. Shango, who is now an *orisha*, kills anyone who disobeys these three commandments. He comes in an *ara*, a thunderstorm, and kills the guilty with the stone *ara-dung*, which is our thunderbolt.

In his lifetime Shango was an *oni-sheggo* and climbed up to heaven by a chain. He killed himself, and this came about as follows. When he went to war he had two *enondye* (representatives or messengers), one of whom was very bad while the other was very good. The bad one was Edshu and the good one Ossenye. One day Ossenye said to King Shango, who was living in Oyo, that Edshu had said that Shango must not come back. Edshu was then in Kushi in the Yoruba territory. So Shango set out to meet Edshu at Kushi. But on the way he hanged himself from an *anyo* tree, for which reason the people, when they call on him, still call him *obaka-su*. Shango then climbed a chain to heaven.

There is no difficulty in recognising in these two royal officials Edshu, the chief supervisor of the gods, who is often described as a mischief-maker, and Ossenye, who stands for the blessed power of the shamans, the magic, divinatory power which is the only means by which even the gods are able to communicate with men. I observed that the moral precepts, mentioned above, strike one at first as un-African, and shall therefore repeat a story I heard among the prople of Oyo. According to one of them, who was a member of the royal family, the Alafini are undoubtedly descended from Shango the thunder god. There were, however, two Shangos. The elder was Shango Takpa or Shango Taba, and the younger Mesi Shango. The former's name alone shows that he must have come from the Nupe country, while the latter came from Borgu. He came into the Yoruba country at the head of the Alledyenni and became the first *mesi*. Now, in all old legends and stories *mesi* means king. It is a title no longer used today, and the story is that Mesi Shango's dynasty was overthrown by the Takpa Shangos, who ruled in their stead, thus deposing all *mesis*. Mesi Shango is always represented as riding a horse, and he was the first ruler to be represented in this way. Shango Takpa, however, was thought of as wearing a ram's-head mask. There are two such masks in Oyo which serve as the lid of a box in which the god's fire medicine was kept.

The legend here clearly distinguishes between two dynasties, the older of which was temporarily displaced by the younger. The former is associated with visualising the god in the form of a ram possessing magic medicine; the latter visualises him as a horseman, and above all associates him with moral precepts, the idea that men should lead good lives.

The cult of the ram-headed thunder-god

No god in the Yoruba country can compete with Shango in the number of sacrifices and ceremonies dedicated to him. The great festival in his honour takes place every fourteen months, as the Yoruba count them, that is, in November. Celebrations take place in every farmstead belonging to a descendant of Shango, with a *mokva* officiating. The poor sacrifice a ram and then celebrate for three days; the rich sacrifice many rams and the celebrations go on for weeks. At Ibadan we had a neighbour who was an *omo-shango*, a descendant of the god; he was rich and fond of display and went on sacrificing rams for three weeks; the beating of drums assaulted our ears until we left for Ife. Everyone offered up a ram or rams, but the actual sacrifice had to be carried out by a *mokqua* or *mokva*. In return he was given his share of the food prepared for the feast, which he took home. Unfortunately no-one would give me permission to attend the celebrations.

If the private family sacrifices are so impressive in their way, the communal celebrations must be spectacular. All the senior and most respected members of the Shango community gather at the venerable *mokva*'s farm, and all sorts of sacrificial animals are brought along, above all, of course, a number of elderly and dignified rams. Goats are also included, because only the priests of Oya are forbidden to eat goats' flesh; the ban does not apply to the children of Shango. Chickens are also brought, as well as jugs of palm wine and maize beer, packets of kola nuts, etc., etc. The sacrifice begins, blood flows over the god's thunder axe, and is splashed on the altar, the pitchers and the images of the god. The sacrifices seem to take place according to a certain system, because I found bloodstains only at a few points in the temple and on the altar, especially, as I mentioned, on the 'lightning stone' and the altar cover.

When the sacrifices have been completed the feast begins. Only the officiating high priest has to fast, pray, and devote all his thoughts to the god; he distributes his share of food to the members of his household. His primary task is to seek an intimation from the god as to who is to consult the oracle. For the high priest does not himself consult the oracle of Shango. The individual who does so is chosen by the deity, who enables the *mokva* to divine his wishes. There are two ways of consulting the oracle. The first is by throwing sixteen cowrie shells, which is said to be the more usual method in the south; the second is by breaking and throwing a number of kola nuts. The latter method, which is called *aqua-obi* or *agba-obi*, is much the more common in Ibadan. In either case everything depends on whether more pieces fall on the flat or on the convex surfaces. This answers the vital question whether or not the god is well-disposed, and whether the community or some special personalities can look forward to an especially eventful or happy or unhappy year. If the god is evidently ill-disposed, more sacrifices are made, and feasting and drinking go on until the next phase, which is the dance.

This is initiated by the beating of the drum. Shango dances are not mere pleasurable social events, but a ritual practice, impregnated with deep meaning. The whole community waits tensely to see whether a 'great' and 'meaningful' phenomenon will or will not take place on that particular occasion. This consists of an individual's direct inspiration by the god, which takes place suddenly, unexpectedly, out of the blue. I spoke to a man who was the object of universal respect because a few years previously Shango had entered into him and spoken through his mouth. He was an unpretentious individual, who made no impression of deceitfulness or calculation of any kind. On the contrary, he spoke with such warmth and naturalness about the great event in his life that I was unable to detect the slightest sign of fraud or simulation on his part. I asked him to tell me what had happened, and he told me quite simply that he had been dancing like everyone else. He had been dancing very energetically. Some people near him had been wondering whether an *elegun shango* (inspired individual) would appear that day. Someone had remarked that you never could tell, even from the *agba-obi*, and the person himself never knew in advance, because it might happen to anyone. Then a very strange feeling had came over him, he felt he had to dash into the *banga* and pick up an *ose shango*, and he had no knowledge whatever of what happened after that. It had been most agreeable. In the evening he had drunk a great deal, and he had gone to sleep drunk. Next day he had been an object of universal respect, and only then had he been told what had happened to him the day before. I think this story is worth repeating; it is not necessarily all lies and deception.

The accounts given by those who have experienced the atmosphere of exaltation at such celebrations all concur. Shango unexpectedly enters the head of one of the dancers, who may be a man or a woman. The person thus inspired enters the *banga* and picks up an *ose shango*, one of those handsome, carved cudgel-like objects, or a *sere shango*, a rattle used in the god's service. He or she begins dancing in front of everyone, and his inspiration is immediately evident to all. An individual inspired by Shango, or, indeed, by any *orisha*, dances entirely differently from anyone else. He is followed by the man beating the sacred *batta*, and then by everyone else. He leaves the temple yard and dances towards his house and everyone follows him. Everyone knows and says that he is a friend (favourite) of Shango. At his home he pays for the rams and cowrie shells, the kola and the drinks, thus making his gratitude apparent to all. If another individual is also visited by the god, the procession follows him to his house too. A number of persons can be thus inspired, but only one at a time and never simultaneously, and the words that they speak are accepted as oracular wisdom.

169

In Ibadan the procession also always makes its way to the house of whoever is *bale* at the time, and more dancing takes place in the yard. The *bale* honours the individual visited by the god. He takes off his *akitayo*, the headgear that is the symbol of his office, and places it on the ground before him. That is the highest honour that such an important personage can pay anyone, as his brow, unless an executioner's sword suddenly severs his head from his body, must never touch the ground.

The *mokva* and the *bambeke* do not accompany the procession but stay in the temple, praying. The *bale* sends them his tribute through the inspired person, who is referred to only as 'Shango himself' or *elegun shango;* this tribute takes the form of a red robe, cowrie shells and kola nuts. These gifts are distributed among the priests, who in turn, make gifts to members of the community.

Inspiration by the deity is often commemorated by a change of name. In some places it is the custom for all those present to assume new names.

When this takes place the old name is never used again. But during the time of his inspiration the inspired individual is always called 'Shango' or 'Shango himself', or something to that effect, and referring to him by his old name is not permitted.

All sorts of strange and ancient rituals take place during these days of festival. One of the most interesting is the fire dance. This was described to me as follows. The fire-dancer has an *adyere* (fire-pot) or only an *agba* (basket) on his head, containing *yena shango*, Shango's fire. After some apparently random circuits, he is filled with magical powers which may easily enable him to perform miracles. He may, for instance, pick up some earth which turns to salt or cowrie shells at his touch. Or he may cut off one of his own ears; the sacred fire burning on his head puts it back. Or he may cut out his tongue, which the sacred fire causes to grow again. Or he may tear out one of his eyes, burn it in the fire and eat it. But it reappears in its place again, and he is able to see as well as ever. The fire-dance takes place during the great seven-day festival to the accompaniment of the *batta*.

In all these things there is a highly important point that we should note. The ability to perform such miracles in Shango's honour does not derive from the god himself, but is granted by the *ossenye* or *ose(e)nye* bestowed by *ada-ushe*, the shaman. Ossenye has been described as an *orisha*, but he is no more a god in our sense of the word than is Sigidi or related phenomena. The Yoruba themselves misuse the word *orisha*, and Ibedyi as well as Oro and Egun have been described as *orisha* in spite of the fact that neither their form nor level of development provide the slightest justification for it. So far as *ossenye* is concerned, it is not a god but a force that is the 'activating' and 'miracle-working' magical power of the shamans and, as we mentioned above, links every priestly action with the deity involved.

At the end of the day on which so many marvellous things have been done in honour of the thunder god, the fire-pot is returned to the Shango priest, who extinguishes the flames. Before the fire is lit again a year later, the shaman first has to prepare the dancer's head and the upper part of his body to make him immune to the flames. Without *ossenye* there can be no miracle. The god himself received his magic powers through a shaman, and it was this that caused him to breathe fire from his mouth when he was king. When the Shango fire-dance takes place at the time of the winter solstice, all fires are extinguished and all the men take a brand of Shango's fire home with them. That is how Shango worshippers celebrate the New Year.

As with all ancient and widespread systems of worship, there are a large number of superstitious accretions. Thus since Shango's death the plant *ogbo*, also called *ogungun*, *odidin* or *tete*, has the reputation of being an excellent remedy for all sorts of illnesses and of curing those struck by lightning or taken ill in thunderstorms. Shango himself is said to have introduced the remedy and shown his people how to mix it with palm or nut oil and apply it. The same must apply to the *batta*, the drum that is beaten in his honour, and to 'Nini's death', with which a magic spell is associated. I was told that Shango had a son named Nini. Nini often went to war, and eventually he was killed. The people beat the *batta* and announced everywhere: "Shango's son Nini is dead." But since then it has been forbidden to mention Nini's death when one of Shango's descendants dies.

Like every totemic group belonging to this widespread, socially integrated cult, the Shango community, the descendants of the thunderer, have their own *evuo*, or dietary laws. The Omo-Shango are forbidden to eat the flesh of *eku* or *ego*, the mouse, or of *esuro*, the squirrel. Their exogamic marriage laws are peculiar. After what we have stated above, it is intelligible enough that no son of Shango should be allowed to marry a priestess of Oya, the god's former wife, who as a goddess still flies in the wind ahead of him (the thunderstorm), sweeping the way clear for him, and in general that intermarriage should be forbidden to the children of Shango. In regard to the laws governing the marriage of *mokva*, priests, the situation is different. In some places a *mokva's* wives may be daughters of Shango; in others they must be. This recalls the fact that in a number of noble clans and families in the Sudan princes marry their own daughters.

More should be said about the ritual objects associated with the god. His emblems appear on practically every royal doorway: first of all the stone axe (thunderbolt), then *ose shango*, of which there is an extraordinary variety, and finally *sere shango*, longhandled dancing rattles that obviously derive from the shape of bottlegourds, and finally dancers using these objects. These emblems all assert the divinity of the ruling family. *Ibauri shango*, or priest's hats, adorned with cowrie shells, are displayed on the altars, and *laba shango*, big, handsomely designed leather bags, of which I was unable to discover any explanation, are hung on the temple walls. Here and there the plaited belts that are thrown over those inspired by the god are to be seen. Holy water is contained in *oko-shango*, sacred pots decorated with all sorts of figures, sometimes with very definitely phallic ornaments. A rich variety of emblems are displayed in the temple and also on the way to the fields, always expressing a prayer for fertility-bringing storms and rain without loss of human life through lightning.

Whenever a peasant finds an old stone axe in his fields he carefully picks it up and deposits it with his seed-corn or on the altar as the god's symbol and instrument, praying that his fields will always be borne in mind and that he will be granted rain and good harvests.

Our reference to the stone axe as a 'thunderbolt' will have recalled our own ancient mythology, but the parallelism is doubly striking when we discover that the god's favoured food is chicken and mutton. Shango loves and favours the ram. On the last day of my stay at Ibadan, while I was inspecting the horse that had been made ready for me in the yard, it pawed the ground in high-spirited fashion. A Yoruba old man looked at it with approval and said something obviously very complimentary about the animal. I asked what it was, and to my surprise I was told that he had compared its friskiness with that of 'Shango's ram'. In reply to further questions, the man said: 'Shango stands on rams when he travels across the sky in the thunderstorm, and ram is his favourite food.' I mentioned above that in Oyo Shango is represented by a ram's mask beneath which his sacred, luminous medicine is concealed.

Edshu and the structure of the universe

Among all the many wood carvings we brought back from the Yoruba country nothing aroused more interest than the oracle boards used in the

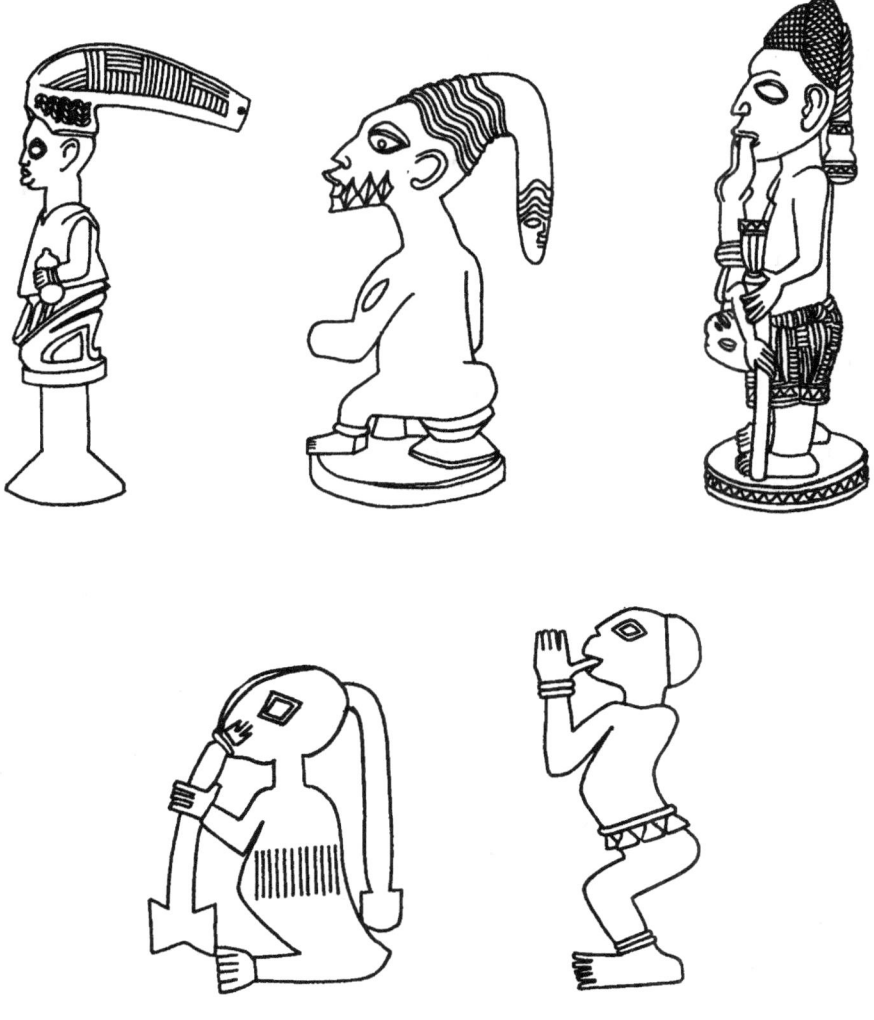

Fig. 47–51 Pictures of the god Edshu

173

worship of *Ifa*. These are generally circular but sometimes square wooden boards, the broad edge of which is generally richly carved, so that they bear some resemblance to our own bread boards.

These boards are the ritual object most sacred to the Yoruba. For every day at sunrise 'dice' are thrown on them, and the way they fall yields information about the day in prospect.

The carvings on the edge of the board are very varied, both figuratively and ornamentally. But their outstanding features are soon evident even to an untrained eye. They are nearly always, as it were, divided into four, and the four quarters are often represented by four animals, a tortoise, a crab, a fish and a spider. But on one side a head is always prominently displayed, sometimes with hands to the right and left of it, so that it looks as if a man were climbing up over the edge.

This is the head of the god Edshu, who presides over the *Ifa* oracle, and it always faces east. All *Ifa* worship is really Edshu worship. We must therefore find out something about Edshu in order to grasp the significance of the *Ifa* cult.

The black and white missionaries who advanced into the interior from the coast to teach the Yoruba the doctrine of salvation taught them that Edshu is the devil. Wherever a missionary has been in Yoruba the people nowadays talk of Edshu the devil. But if one goes to their farms and gains their confidence, one hears things such as: 'Yes, Edshu did much mischief; he often made people make war on one another; he shifted the moon and carried off the sun, and made all the gods make war on one another. But Edshu is not evil. He gave us the best things that there are; he gave us the *Ifa* oracle, and the sun. Without Edshu the fields would produce nothing.' So we must pay some attention to this Edshu, and to begin with we must banish from our minds any idea of equating him with the devil, with whom he has nothing whatever to do, or of attributing to him wickedness in the mediaeval sense of the word. All such ideas are totally misconceived. Edshu is a cheerful character who gets up to mischief, but above all he is a benefactor of mankind, for he gave it the *Ifa* oracle; and I shall relate the legends about him in the form in which I had them from a man who lived on the border of the Kukuruku country.

The coming of the Ifa oracle – Once upon a time long, long ago, the gods were very hungry. Their sons wandering about the face of the earth did not give them enough to eat. The gods were also discontented and quarrelled with each other. Some gods went out hunting. Others, particularly Olokun, the god of the sea, went out fishing. But, though they brought back an antelope and a fish, this was not sufficient to sate their

174

appetite for long. The gods had been forgotten by their offspring, and wondered how they could get men to feed them again. Men no longer made burnt offerings, and so they suffered from hunger. Edshu set out. He first consulted Yemaya. He asked her for something which would enable him to win back men's favour. Yemaya said: 'You will have no success. Shankpanna* has scourged men with illness, but they do not come and make sacrifices to him. He will kill all men, but they will not bring him any food. Shango sent men lightning. He killed men. But men do not trouble about him, they die and make no sacrifices to him. So you had better try something else. Men are not afraid of death. Give them something that is so good that they will long for it enough to want to stay alive.' Edshu went on his way. 'What I did not get from Yemaya I will get from Orugan,' he said to himself. He went to Orugan. Orugan said: 'I know why you have come. The sixteen gods are hungry. The sixteen gods must be given something that delights them. I know something of the kind. There is a great thing that consists of sixteen palm kernels. If you acquire the sixteen palm kernels and learn to understand what they say, you will be able to win men back again.' Edshu went to a place where there were palm trees. The monkeys gave him sixteen palm kernels. Edshu looked at the sixteen palm kernels, but did not know what to do with them. The monkeys said to him: 'Edshu, you do not know what to do with the palm kernels? Let us give you a piece of advice. You acquired the sixteen palm kernels by stealth, now go about the world and enquire everywhere about their meaning. You must go to sixteen places to find out what the sixteen palm kernels mean. At each of the sixteen places you will learn sixteen maxims. After a year you must be able to understand sixteen times sixteen maxims. Then return to the sixteen gods. Teach them your knowledge, and then men will learn to fear you again.' Edshu did as he was bidden. He went to the sixteen places, and then returned to heaven.

He taught the gods what he had learned. The gods said it was good. Then the gods taught this knowledge to their offspring, who were then able daily to divine the future and the will of the gods. When they saw all the bad things that lay in the future and the sufferings they could avoid by making sacrifices, they again started slaughtering animals and burning them as a sacrifice to the gods. That was how Edshu brought the *Ifa* (palm-kernel) to mankind. After his return he stayed with Okun, Shango and Ibatalla, and the four watched over what men did with *Ifa* kernels.

* The god of smallpox.

The worship of Edshu. – Edshu is worshipped especially by the northern Yoruba tribes. In the south, particularly in the coastal region, he loses his identity in that of Elegba, a phallic god. The northern Yoruba believe he came from the Niger, i.e., from the east. Sometimes I was told that he came with the sun, sometimes that it was he who brought it. In some way or other he is certainly connected with the sun. He is the bringer, not only of the sun, but also of the Ifa kernels. According to the Ifa legend, he also first brought mankind Olokun glass beads. He is thus a 'provider'.

He is everywhere held to be a kind of leader or supervisor of the gods, in particular the sixteen whose mother, according to the coastal legend, was Odudua. But his supervisory role is restricted to keeping order, as it were, in the Yoruba Olympus. His worshippers claim that without him the other *orisha* would be helpless and ineffective. As the descendants of the other gods made no comment on this claim but modestly looked aside, they so to speak tacitly acknowledged the superiority of this peculiar deity. But it would be quite wrong to regard him as reigning over the other gods. Instead he should be regarded as responsible for the maintenance of good order among them, rather like the strict master of ceremonies of King Arthur's Round Table in the Parsifal legend. His home is at every crossroads, where clay spheres are set up in his honour, as they are in the farms of the high priests of the Ifa worship; at definite seasons of the year dances and processions take place round them. Portraits of Edshu are frequent, and these, whether they appear on doors or boards or anywhere else, follow a definite pattern when his full form and not just his head is shown. In the first place, he is always shown in profile, which is peculiar to him alone. He is invariably shown with disproportionately big feet. Also he is always shown naked, but sexless. He always has a long pigtail, and he also has something in his mouth or his hand, and often he has a stick on his shoulder. Very often he has a tobacco or signalling pipe in his hand. If he has nothing else to put in his mouth, he puts his thumb in it. Very characteristic are the portraits that show him with snakes growing out of either side of his head. He is the god with the strongest personality in the Yoruba pantheon.

The northern Yoruba also insist that he is the god of troublemaking. He causes trouble everywhere. When many people are gathered together, he inevitably intervenes and causes strife between them. His real element is fire, or flames. If a house is burnt down, he has certainly had a hand in it. His real home is in a subterranean *ina* (i.e., fire). I was actually told that he lived in mountains inside which was an *ihu* (i.e., cave) that was

176

filled with fire. From time to time a mountain breaks open and the aged Edshu – he is always thought of as an old man – comes out in the flames. Thus a dark memory of volcanic eruptions seems to survive in these stories. He is also connected with fire in as much as no sacrifice can be made to him without it. Thus a place where an object sacred to Edshu is to be placed is always first purified with fire and ashes. The same practice was observed in the worship of Orun, the sun, which, however, has practically died out. Edshu is above all restless and perpetually travelling about. In the Okme country the bird sacred to him is *equo*, the owl. The *evuo* of the Edshu families is *adi*, the black oil obtained from burnt palm kernels.

Edshu's misdeeds. – In the beginning Olokun (the sea god), Orun (the sun god) and Oshu (the moon god) each had a home of his own. Olokun lived in the river, i.e., in water. Oshu used to leave his house every evening and go out into the world, now this way and now that. But Orun mounted high into the sky over his house every morning and came back again in the evening.

One day Edshu went to see Olokun and said to him: 'Your house is not good. Come with me, I will show you something better.' Olokun said: 'Well, then, show it to me.' Edshu next went to see Oshu and said: 'Your house is not good. Come with me, I will show you a better one.' Oshu said: 'Well, then, show it to me.' Next Edshu went to Orun and said: 'Your house is not good. Come, I will show you something better.' Orun said: 'Well, then, show it to me.' Edshu took Olokun to Oshu's home, Orun to Olokun's, and Oshu to Orun's.

Oshalla was the chief of all the gods. He lived at a crossroads, where he had his house, and every day he saw Orun passing by and every night he saw Oshu. But next day he saw Oshu passing in broad daylight. 'What is this?' he said. 'You come by day?' Oshu said: 'An old man came and it was his fault.' Oshalla said: 'Oshu, go straight back to where I put you, and send the old man to me.' Oshu went. After nightfall Orun appeared. Oshalla saw him, and said: 'What is this? You come by night?' Orun said: 'An old man told me he would take away my life if I did not go this new way.' Oshalla was still talking to Orun when Olokun arrived. Oshalla said to him: 'What are you doing here? Why are you not in the water?' Olokun said: 'An old man told me to come this way.' Oshalla said: 'Well, go straight back to your house and by the way I told you. Orun, go straight back to your house and do the work that I told you to do.' Orun went home and Olokun went home. Edshu went to see Oshu and said to him: 'Oshu, if you do not do my bidding today, I shall kill you. So go to

Orun's house, and to avoid quarrelling with Oshalla, make a big détour round his house.' Oshu said: 'If that is your wish, I must do so.' Oshu set out. He made a big détour round Oshalla's house and came to where Orun lived. Orun saw him coming and said to him: 'What are you doing here? Do you live here?' Oshu said: 'Why do you not leave your house and give it to me?' Oshu and Orun started quarrelling, and Edshu appeared on the scene. Edshu said to Oshu: 'Why do you put up with this?' And to Orun he said: 'Why do you put up with this?' Orun and Oshu started fighting, and Oshalla heard them and went towards the spot. When Edshu saw him coming he went to meet him and said: 'I have settled the dispute already, so you can go back home.' Oshalla went home.

Then Edshu went into the water to Olokun and said: 'Come out, or I shall take your life.' Olokun said: 'You did not give me life.' Edshu said: 'Come out, or I shall take your life.' Olokun came out. Edshu showed him the way into the bush. Oshalla heard that Olokun had come out of the water and gone into the bush. Oshalla gave Shankpanna a blade of grass and said: 'Go to Olokun. Olokun has gone into the bush against my will. Tell Olokun that he must never again go back into the water; for he was not with me when he left the water which I gave him as a home.' Shankpanna took the blade of grass. He took it to Olokun and said: 'Oshalla sends you this blade of grass. You left the water against his will. Turn into an *oke* (hill).' Olokun turned into a hill. Then all Olokun's children came out of the water to search for Olokun on the hill. Edshu met them on their way. Edshu said to them: 'Go through the bush to your father. Do not pass Oshalla's home.' Oshalla heard them. He saw that Olokun's children avoided passing his home and turned them all into monkeys. Since then Olokun's children jump about in the form of monkeys.

Then Oshalla summoned Shankpanna and said to him: 'Go and fetch Edshu.' Shankpanna set out. He came to a crossroads, and asked: 'Where is Edshu?' 'Edshu is at the market,' he was told. He took his *auvo* (bullrush broom, used for ceremonial purposes) and went to the market where he was told Edshu was to be found. He met him and said: 'Oshalla sent me to you to punish you.' He took his bullrush broom and started striking at Edshu with it. But Edshu took his *ogo* (shoulder stick) with which he warded off the blows, and he struck at Shankpanna. Orun heard the blows and the combatants' words. Orun said: 'Shankpanna is fighting with Edshu. I must go to Shankpanna's aid.' Orun came to where they were fighting, and said to Shankpanna: 'If I open my eyes, Edshu will not be able to see. So I shall do that first.' Shankpanna said: 'That is good. Do so.' Orun opened his eyes as he walked towards Edshu. Edshu was blinded, and

Shankpanna struck him with his broom. Edshu could not defend himself. Oshalla saw this. Oshalla said: 'All small children should go to Shankpanna and Orun and rejoice, because Shankpanna has beaten Edshu.' All small children went and said: 'Skankpanna is strong in battle.' Meanwhile Shankpanna went on striking Edshu. All Shankpanna's blows left wounds (weals) on Edshu's body. Edshu ran to the river to bathe. He bathed, and when he was in the water he said: 'Shankpanna's blows will be transmitted through the water to all men who bathe in this water and they will burn like fire. He who bathes in the water in which Edshu washed the weals left by Shankpanna will get smallpox and smallpox scars.' So Edshu's revenge was transmitted to men and has remained alive among them.

This legend is full of cosmological ideas, and strife takes place among the gods, but there are a whole series of stories in which the sheer pleasure of story-telling has gained the upper hand to produce the most varied accounts of the god Edshu's mischief-making activities. The following story comes from Oyo and contains what we shall later see is a very important feature.

In olden times Olorun first created *enya*, man, and then the god Edshu. Once there were two men who were great friends. When they went out they dressed exactly alike. Everyone said: 'Those two are the best of friends.' Edshu saw this. 'Those two are the best of friends,' he said. 'I shall cause strife between them, and that will be a good beginning for a big *idya* (dispute, palaver).' The two friends' fields were next to each other and were separated by a path. Edshu used to walk along this path in the morning, wearing a black *filla* (cap).

When Edshu was ready to start the quarrel, he made himself a cap of green, black, red and white material, so that it showed a different colour from each direction, and one morning he put it on when he set out to walk down the path between the fields. He also took his tobacco pipe but, instead of putting it in his mouth as usual, he put it at the back of his neck, as if he were smoking through the back of his head. Also he took a stick, as usual, but carried it the other way about, not in front of his chest, but behind his back. The two friends were working in their fields. They looked up for a moment. Edshu called out a greeting to them. They responded, and went on with their work.

Later they walked back home together. One said to the other: 'The old man (Edshu) went the opposite way along the path between the fields this morning. I noticed it because of his pipe and his stick.' 'You're wrong,' the other one replied. 'He went in the same direction as usual, I saw which way he was going.' The first one said: 'But that's not true; I saw his pipe and his stick too plainly to be mistaken. Also he was not wearing a black cap today, but a white one.' 'You must be blind, or you must have been asleep,' the other one said. 'He was wearing a red cap.' The first one said: 'You must have been drinking palm wine this morning not to have seen the colour of his cap or the direction in which he was going.' 'I haven't touched a drop of palm wine today,' the other one said. 'But you seem to me to have gone crazy.' The first one said: 'You're insulting me, telling me nothing but a pack of lies.' 'It's you who are the liar,' the other one replied. 'This isn't the first time I've noticed it.' He drew his knife and struck out with it and wounded the other man, who also drew his knife and stabbed at his head. Both ran away, and both were bleeding when they came into the town. The people saw this and said: 'The two friends have been attacked, this means that war is in the offing.' 'No,' one of the men said, 'that liar is not my friend.' The other one said: 'Don't believe a word that liar says. The lies come flying out as soon as he opens his mouth.'

Meanwhile Edshu had gone to the king of the town, and he said to him: 'Ask the two friends what is the matter with them. They have been cutting each other's heads open with their knives and making them bleed.' The king said: 'What? Those two friends, who always wear the same clothes, have been fighting? Bring them here.' The two friends were sent for, and the king said to them: 'You are both in a bad state. What set you quarrelling?' They said: 'We quarrelled about what happened on the path between our fields.' The king said: 'How many people walked along your path, then?' 'One man, who goes the same way every day. But today he went in the opposite direction, and he was wearing a white cap instead of a black one,' one of the friends said. 'He's lying,' the other one exclaimed. 'The old man was wearing a red cap and was walking in the same direction as usual.' 'Who knows the old man?' the king asked. 'It was I,' Edshu said. 'The two quarrelled only because I wanted them to.' He pulled out his cap and said: 'I wore this hat. It is red on one side and white on the other. It is green in front and black at the back. It looks different from every direction. I put my pipe at the back of my neck. So I walked in one direction, but it looked as if I were walking in the other. The two friends were bound to quarrel. It was my fault. Starting quarrels is my greatest delight.'

The king heard what Edshu said. 'Take that man and bind him; he is a trouble-maker,' he said. They tried to catch Edshu and bind him, but he ran away very fast to a neighbouring hill, where he struck stones together. He went on doing so until the dry grass caught fire. He threw the burning grass down on to the town. The grass fell on the roofs, which burst into flames. He threw fire here, there and everywhere, and houses began burning all over the place. Everyone dashed about in confusion. Then Edshu went back into the town, and saw that everyone was trying to save what he could from the burning houses. One man would be carrying out a basket, another a sack, another a load of gourds and another cooking pots.

Edshu went among the people. He set to, and started taking the loads from them. Those who handed him things did not see who it was who took them, but dashed back into the burning houses to save more of their goods. But Edshu added the loads of pots to the belongings of gourd-owners, the gourds to those of the basket-owners and the baskets to those of the sack-owners. He carried the sacks to the owners of the pots. When the fire at last died down many houses had been burned to the ground.

After the fire everyone searched for his belongings. The man to whom the gourds belonged found them with the owner of the baskets. 'You're a thief,' he said. 'You took advantage of the confusion to steal my property.' The owner of the baskets denied stealing the gourds and accused others of robbing him. 'Now I've caught you, you thief. I've suspected you for a long time,' said the owner of the cooking pots to the man with whom he found them. In their fury everyone began picking up sticks and going for one another. They also went for the gourds and cooking pots and smashed them. This made their owners angrier, and they started fighting with the pestles of the women's mortars. What the fire had not destroyed was now destroyed by human fury. Several men lost their lives.

The king intervened and had the combatants separated. 'What has happened here?' he asked. Everyone denounced everyone else for robbing him during the fire. 'Are all my people thieves?' the king said. Edshu appeared and said: 'No, O king. Your people are not thieves. They are only stupid. I have only been having a game with them, and they played it very well indeed. Next time I want a good laugh I shall come here again.' He ran away, and nobody could catch him.

Initiation into the Ifa cult, and its ritual objects. – We shall now turn to the actions and customs associated with the *Ifa* oracle and try to gain an understanding of the original meaning of the system. I have already pointed out that *Ifa* really means only 'palm kernel', and that *Ifa* did not originate as a god but rather as an *orisha* system, or the basis for an *orisha* system. In the light of what we have said, it is a striking fact that *Ifa* is not the head of a totemic clan. Unlike Shango or Shankpanna or Oya and other deities, he has no descendants. On the contrary, anyone

181

can adopt the *Ifa* cult without involving himself in any relationship with any of the gods. Thus an individual fully initiated into its secrets is called, not *omo-ifa* (i.e., son of Ifa), but *babalavo* (father of the secret). Anyone can become a *babalavo* if, in addition to the necessary power of application, he has enough money and intelligence. Let us follow the initiation of a young man into the companionship of the *babalavo*.

The novice must in the first place procure the following: (1) *ikode*, parrot's tail feathers; (2) *boli*, a fish; (3) an *ekete*; (4) an *eku* (mouse); (5) *kanka*, a root used for washing. He will already have asked a *babalavo* to introduce him to his secrets and to be his teacher. He calls his teacher *oluvo*. The term *oluvo* generally refers to a high priest of *Ifa*, but every novice uses it to address his teacher. The *oluvo* takes his pupil, who has made a bundle of the five objects and carries it on his head, to the nearest river; in Ibadan they go to the Oshun. Both priest and novice are clothed completely in white. The priest takes his ritual equipment with him. At the riverside they lay their things down, and the *babalavo* washes the novice. Then they go into the bush, where there is a sacred place consisting of three broad clearings one after the other, the first of which anyone may enter. The novice's first instruction takes place in the second; only priests may enter the third, the most sacred of the three. The ceremonial begins with a meal. *Boli*, *ekete* and *eku* are cooked, made into an appetising dish, and eaten. The only persons present are the priest, the novice, and a member of the latter's family as witness.

The priest then opens his leather bag, the edge of which is generally decorated with cowrie shells, and takes from it sixteen palm kernels, which are the vital objects in the whole ceremony. The priest also has in his bag an *oqua-ifa*, or *Ifa board*, in the middle of which fine sawdust is scattered. Here the Ifa oracle is read in the novice's presence in the manner that I shall describe later. When the kernels are picked up, the straight or crooked way in which they fall forms a series of single or double lines, each four of which form an *odu*, and the vital question is whether the shapes thus formed in the white sawdust of the Ifa board announce the *odu*'s will that the novice should be accepted. If the answer is favourable, the most important issue of the day is settled. If the young man has any problem on his mind he can now put it, and for the first time he is able to see how the *babalavo* puts a question to the oracle and receives an answer. At all events, to use the Yoruba expression, 'the lord has looked with favour on his servant'. But once more it must be emphasised that the lord in question is not a god, an *orisha*, but one of the *odus*, the heads that speak from the signs of the palm kernels. The priest next rubs white into

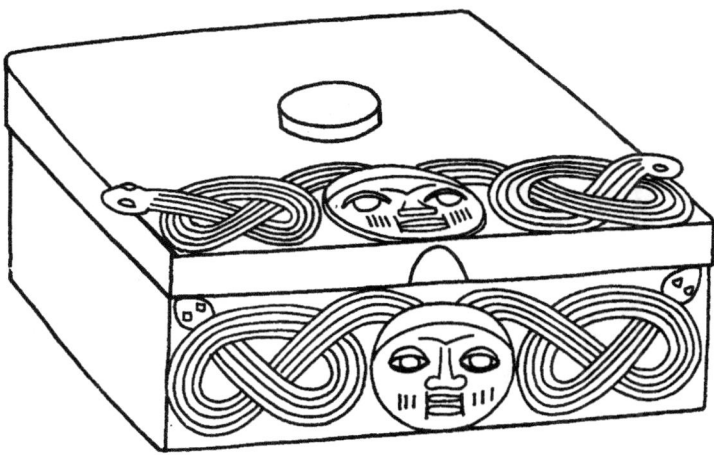

Fig. 52 Coffer for the sacred Ifa colours

the young man's hair, ties the parrot's feathers round him and puts the *oquelle* (see below) round him, with the middle over his shoulders and the ends hanging down in front. He gives the young man sixteen palm kernels and says to him: 'This is your Ifa.'

They then go back, the priest leading the way. The priest carries in front of him a knife with a bell hanging from it. They enter the priest's house and go to the place where the oracle is. When the novice crosses the threshold the priest casts white flour in front of him and welcomes him to the house in the *Ifa*'s name; for everything white, including white flour, is sacred to *Ifa*. Other *babalavo* now arrive. Everyone greets the novice, talks to him, discusses the profundity of Ifa's wisdom and the venerable nature of the cult. He is thus accepted into the community of the *babalavo*, which includes very many people who worship Ifa, daily consult the oracle and greet it every morning.

Initiation into the art of reading the oracle is a very slow process. Generally it takes three years. During the first the novice has only to learn the names of the *odu*. During the second he learns as many of the sacred truths as he is capable of understanding and memorizing. Not until the third year does he set about the real task of mastering the art of oracle reading. The devotees of the *Ifa* cult are divided into three grades. At the end of these three years of study those who aspire merely to the lowest grade, that of the ordinary *babalavo*, are qualified to divine each morning, from the way the *oquelle* or *Ifa* kernels fall, the significance

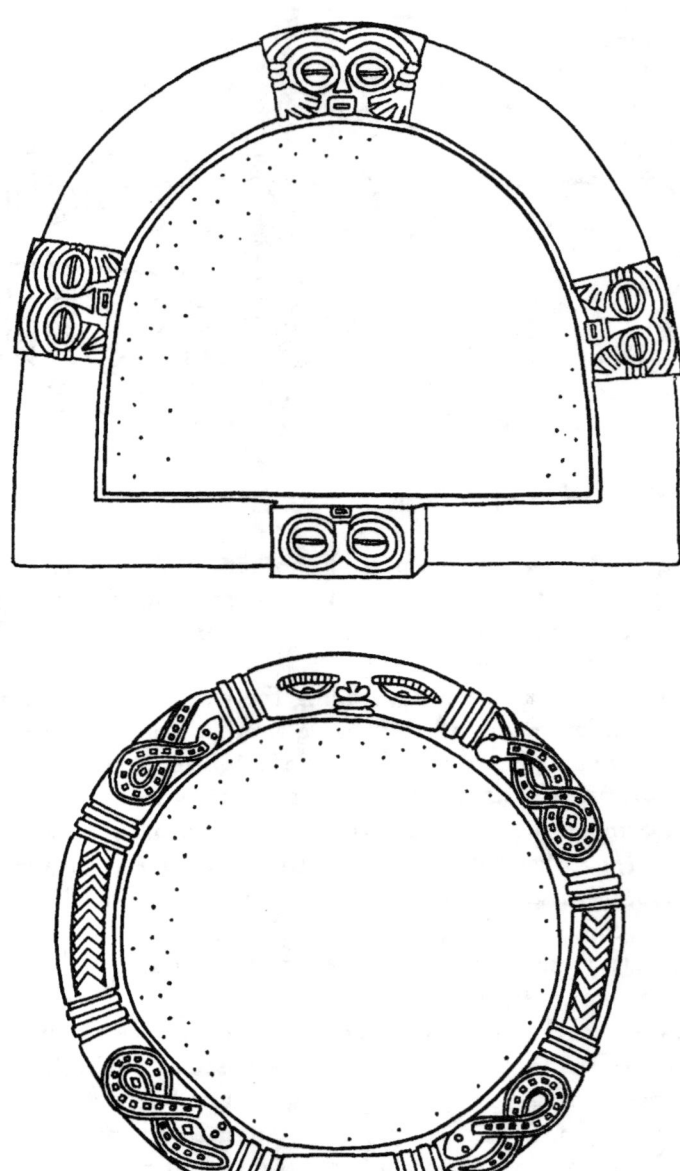

Fig. 53–54 Ifa boards

and meaning of the day for ordinary domestic purposes. Several more years of study are required of those who aspire to the higher prestige and still more intimate knowledge of the wisdom and truths and significance of the *odu* associated with the professional priests who constitute the second grade. The third and highest grade is that of the high priests, whom we shall discuss later. Because of the many truths and maxims associated with every *odu*, the art of reading oracles is very difficult to acquire. The basic knowledge required is said to consist of no fewer than 1,680 maxims for each of the 4,096 different *odus*. Obviously no-one could possibly remember such a vast number and, as the appropriate maxim always has to be considered in relation to the lie of the various *odus*, there is plenty of elbow-room for interpretation, and the oracle is consequently as mysterious as that of Delphi or the Sibylline Books. The novice sits at the feet of his instructor every evening; with the descent of darkness he plunges daily into the divine wisdom. He accompanies his master to various places, and watches attentively how he does his work and reads the oracle from the casting of the palm kernels or chain of palm kernels. Such instruction is obviously not given gratis, and a goodly income accordingly accrues to the priestly household.

The pupil has to buy an *adyelle-ifa*, or *adyelefa* for short. This consists of a bowl supported by a figure; these *ifa* bowls exist in extraordinary variety. Some are supported only by divided ornamental feet, others by doves, antelopes, hens with snakes in their beak, fish, etc. Those supported by an armed horseman are very handsome; the latter are sometimes armed with spears, and sometimes with ancient flints. One has a child impaled on his lance while with his other hand he holds a pipe that reaches all the way from his mouth to the ground. Large numbers of men and women and drummers carry such bowls about with them. The most popular show scenes from women's life. Two friends are seen sitting side by side, or a woman is feeding a child, or offering a bowl, or sitting at a loom, or carrying a child on her back in the African fashion. There is a tremendous vitality in all of them. The spirit that they breathe is not so much that of monumental representation of the divine as that of careful observation of human life. They are beautiful little carvings which, if we did not know their function, we should classify as African women's wares rather than sacred objects.

The sixteen palm kernels are kept in these bowls, into which palm oil and maize flour with water are also placed as offerings. The second essential item that the novice must procure is the *oqua-ifa*. This, as we have previously mentioned, is a board, which in the south tends to be square and in the north circular in shape. The ornamentation of these boards is exceptionally fine.

The top of the Ifa-board is dominated by a face that is sometimes extended into its bare inner surface, on which sawdust is strewn and signs drawn with the fingers; the face seems to preside watchfully over this process. The face is sometimes framed with hands on either side of it, or snake ears or simpler ornamentation. The board is carefully divided into four quarters, of which the face forms one. The other quarters are filled either with simple ornamentation or with relief work or with other faces, so that the whole is divided into four sections corresponding to the four cardinal points, as it were, covered sometimes with fine flat surface ornamentation, sometimes with something simpler, and sometimes with animals, scenes from everyday life, or other carvings. These are the most outstanding products of the ancient West African craftsmanship, and the specimens used by the real *oluvo* are distinguished by their exceptional fineness. If a *babalavo* reaches the high position of an *oluvo*, he is generally given the finest board in his family's possession. In the old days it was buried with him, and we acquired several such boards from old graves. They were the finest we found. To gain an understanding of the origin and development of the Ifa cult, we shall have to study the symbolism of these boards and return later to the question of their meaning and significance.

Yet another piece of Ifa ritual equipment is the *iroke*. This is a rattle, originally made of elephant's tusks, as I conclude, not only from the whole shape, but also from the fact that many are still made of ivory. The wooden ones are pointed in front and curved and hollowed out behind in such exact imitation of their ivory predecessors that it takes sharp eyes to discover that they are made of wood. A small lever or clapper is often inserted into the cup-like opening at the back which in elephants' tusks is provided by nature. When the middle part is held in the hand and the point is knocked on the Ifa board a wooden bell clapper is produced. The middle of the back part of the *iroke* is generally very tastefully decorated, either with a simple ornamentation or with a head or figure. Every morning at sunrise the *babalavo* knocks the Ifa board with the *iroke* and thus greets the god Edshu who presides over Ifa.

The rich also have an *okwong-ifa*, a kind of box with several inner compartments. In the middle of the central compartment there is a hollow in which the Ifa kernels are kept. In the great majority of cases the surrounding area is divided into four compartments containing clay, charcoal, lime and red wood dye. The exceptionally prosperous use *orun* (i.e., excrement of the sun, or sulphur) instead of clay. I shall return later to the meaning of these four substances. The outside of these boxes is generally very handsomely decorated with engravings or relief work. The decoration often includes a head, frequently surrounded by snakes, and sometimes there is a tortoise or a *varan* or warrior holding a captive. In the middle of the lid there is generally a knob which, I was told, is called an *ishiguang*.

Finally, there is the *oquelle*. This is a cord to which eight half palm kernels are attached, and the two ends generally consist of ornamental beads. The high priest at Ife had an *oquelle* provided with yellow pieces of nut instead of the half palm kernels; those used by the students of the art of oracle-reading generally had pieces of gourd instead of palmnut kernels. To consult the oracle the *oquelle* is held in the middle, so that there are four half palm kernels on either side. What matters when the cord is thrown is which of the palm kernels fall with the convex and which with the concave side upwards. This in itself produces an *odu*, or figure.

Consulting the oracle takes place in different ways, depending on the purpose. Every *babalavo*, i.e., every initiate into the secrets of the Ifa cult, throws the *oquelle* every morning, and the information provided by the *odu* refer to his private life and the events of the day. But whenever major undertakings of the community or locality are involved the high priest is called in. Every ruler, whether he is an *alafin* or *oni* or mere town chief, like the *bale*, has his own priests, often known by the title of *araba*. The term *araba* is used by the Yoruba of any outstanding object. If there are a number of kapok trees side by side, the tallest is described as *araba; araba* is not a term peculiar to the high priest. The priesthood consists of the following:

(i) The *oluvo*, or supreme *babalovo*. The *oluvo* is the high priest of the community, but every learner addresses his teacher as *oluvo*.

(ii) The *odofin*, or *oluvo's* deputy, who takes his place if for any reason he is unable to act.

(iii) The *aro*, or *odofin's* deputy, who takes over if both *oluvo* and *odofin* are prevented.

Furthermore, every *oluvo, odofin* and *aro* has his aides, who are called *adyigbona*. The so-called *asare-pavo* act as messengers, servants and pages, and these have *asavo* subordinate to them. The priests are again divided into *oluvo-otun-avo* and *oluvo-osi-avo*, who in turn have their *olopon-ekeyi*.

These priests read the oracle, and the ceremony of throwing the palm kernels is conducted as follows. The sixteen palm kernels are called *iki* or *aki*. A seventeenth object, an ivory carving called an *oluso*, is also used. It too is called an *iki*, but is not a round or shell-like object but represents a head, the head of Edshu, as is evident from the fact that it has a long pigtail. It is placed next to the *ifa* board and, so to speak, watches over the actions of the *babalavo* and the fall of the sixteen *iki*. The *babalavo* strews white sawdust over the *ifa* board, picks up the sixteen *ifa* kernels and throws them up in the air in the direction of his left hand, with which he catches them. What happens next depends on whether the number of kernels he catches is even or odd. If the number is odd, two vertical lines are drawn. If it is even, a single vertical line is drawn on the board with the forefinger of the right hand. The kernels are thrown four times, and corresponding marks are made underneath one another in the sawdust. The figure resulting from the four signs is described as a *medyi* or 'pair'. This process is repeated eight times, and two *medyi* are always drawn side by side, thus forming four pairs one below the other. The numbers written down form the *odu* presiding over the oracle of the day. The picture drawn in the sawdust is read from right to left. Each *medyi* represents an *odu* which is assumed to consist of sixteen *odus*, each of which is again composed of sixteen more *odus*, etc. The *odus* are the spiritual factor in the oracular process. The truths and maxims associated with every *odu* are for the moment a matter of indifference. To discover the origin and significance of the whole process it is necessary to establish the original meaning of these things.

The Ifa board and the four cardinal points. – To discover the original meaning that gave rise to this complicated system of divining, its individual elements must be compared with each other. I have previously mentioned the sixteen basic figures, the *odu*, or main heads. Each of these heads has a name and a symbolic sign. I have also described the Ifa boards and mentioned that they almost invariably indicate the four cardinal points in some way or other, often by four heads that divide the board into four. The priest who consults the oracle always faces east and always lays the board on the ground in the same way. There is at least one face on every board, and the praying priest always has it between himself and the sun. Now, this face is called *edshu-ogbe*. This accords entirely with *odu* No. 1. On boards decorated with four faces, that opposite the *edshu-ogbe*, i.e., with its brow towards the praying priest, corresponds with the sign *oyako-medyi*, that to his right the *evori-medyi* and that to his left the *odi-medyi*. Thus we are presented with a perfectly clear and straightforward system, which still seems to be generally recognised by the *babalavo*. At all events, I was given this basic explanation both in Ibadan and in Ife, as well as by Yoruba in Lokoya. As far as further information is concerned, my collaborators failed almost completely. Only an elderly *babalavo* in Lokoya had this to tell me about the four heads. 'Long, long ago, when everything was in confusion and young and old died, Olodu-mare (God) summoned Edshu-ogbe and said: "Create order in the region of the sunrise." To Oyako-Medyi he said: "Create order in the region of the sunset." Next morning Edshu-ogbe created order in the east, and in the evening Oyako-Medyi created order in the west.' That was the end of the legend, to which the venerable *babalavo* had nothing to add.

In fact the matter is not quite so puzzling as it seems at first sight. Having discovered that the four cardinal points are represented on the board and identified these with the most important four *odus*, and having noted that the board must always be placed and read in the same way, we can draw a number of parallels. The priest who explained to me the division of the board into four drew a picture in the sand. He joined four hills that stood, as it were, for east and west, north and south by two lines forming a cross, enabling Edshu-ogbe to cross over to Oyako-Medyi and Evori-Medyi to cross over to Odi-Medyi. He then described the line running from east to west as the 'main way' and that running from south to north as the 'second way'. When asked about the meaning of these ways, he explained that Edshu travelled along the main way to visit Shango and Obatalla travelled along the second way to visit Ogun. Thus it is clear that Edshu is the god of the east, Shango of the west, Obatalla of the south and Ogu of the north.

I mentioned above the Ifa boxes that contain sixteen Ifa kernels in the middle and four different substances in four hollows arranged in accordance with the four cardinal points. An *oluvo* in Ife explained to me that sacrifice for Edshu was put in the hollow filled with sulphur or clay, while that filled with charcoal was for Shango, that filled with lime was for Obatalla, and that filled with red wood dye was for Ogun. Thus there is complete unanimity about the cardinal points controlled by the gods. Once more we find Obatalla opposite Ogun (along the second way) and Edshu opposite Shango (along the main way). We can also add a third piece of evidence. When Edshu wanted to arouse strife he walked between the fields of two friends. He went in the direction opposite to that in which he seemed to be going, and wore a cap of four different colours. The legend says specifically that his cap was green in front, black at the back, red on the left and white on the right. Green can here be equated with yellow. Thus the picture that emerges is that of the god proceeding along the main way in the opposite direction and showing yellow to the east, black to the west and the two colours of Obatalla and Ogun to the gods in control of the two ends of the second way (joining north and south). Thus in this legend we are presented with a picture of a journey along a main way and in a reverse direction (the reversal being the cause of strife). Thus the conclusion would seem to be that the four cardinal points between which the two intersecting world paths run are governed by four gods.

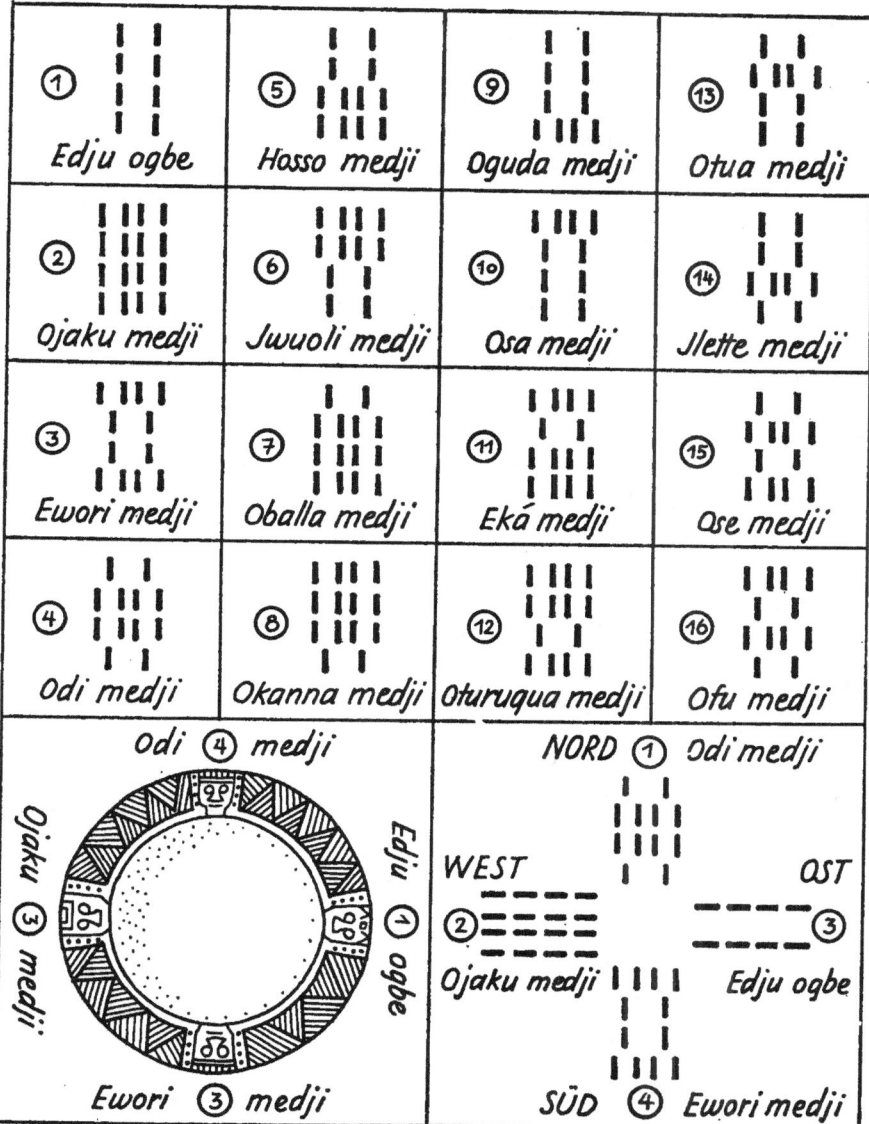

Fig. 55 Ifa ritual objects
Above, the 16 Odu signs. Below left, a board showing the distribution of the four head Odu. Right, the distribution and and disposition of the head Odu towards the four cardinal points. Main line from East to West, second line from North to South.

14. Zimbabwe and the Wahungwe Civilisation *

The king and his "venerable" court

The name of the mountain on the slopes of which the residence of the present-day Makoni ** is built is Sangano. On this mountain there lived, in ancient times, a people whose king was Madzivoa. Madzivoa did not have the title of "Mambo" ***, but he was a king none the less. Before the ancestors of the Wahungwe came, the people of Madzivoa led a miserable existence. They had no fire any longer and fed on raw fish.

Once, the people of Madzivoa had possessed fire. But they had lost the fire. The people did not have the fire drill, but they did have "moto we ngona" which consisted of a horn filled with magic oil and closed with a plug. This fire-making device, like fire in general, was the responsibility of the king's daughters (singular: Musarre, plural: Wasarre), and a Musarre looked after it. To make fire, the plug was pulled out of the ngona horn and the end, soaked in magic oil, was applied to dry grass which immediately burst into flames.

At the time when Madzivoa's father was king on Sangano mountain, the Musarre looking after the fire had a quarrel with one of the Machinda (princes). When the king died, the musarre hid the fire horn. Afterwards, she died without telling anyone about the secret hiding place. This was the reason why at the time when the ancestors of the present-day Wahungwe (or Waungwe) came to this country, Madzivoa's people had no fire and ate their fish raw. The fire horn (ngona) has not been found to this day.

The ancestors of the present-day Wahungwe were then living in the North. They first settled in Chipadze (NE of Makoni) and came to Mount Sangano as hunters. These ancestors were not yet called Wahungwe, but Wadzimba. The Wadzimba are not hunters really, but there would always be a few Wadzimba in all hunting expeditions. A Mudzimba is a man who is a successful killer of animals and warrior, a restless man who never feels at home for long anywhere. The cult of the Wadzimba and the art of making themselves strong consists in smoking. The pipe consists of a horn filled with water. A reed is inserted in it, which carries the pipe bowl called Chemana. Nothing is smoked in the pipe except

---

* From "Erythräa – Länder und Zeiten des heiligen Königsmordes", 1931, pp. 114–244.

** king. This is a title name.

*** sacral king.

192

leaves of the rumhanda tree. Ritual smoking makes the Mudzimba strong and fearless. When a Mudzimba is unsuccessful in the chase, one of his ancestral spirits (mizimu) often reveals himself in some other man and says to him: "Mudzimba so-and-so has left something undone and he must therefore make a sacrifice. Then he will be a successful hunter again." As soon as the Mudzimba is told this by his friend, he ties a mutcheka around himself, a black bandage, about 30 cm wide, which encloses the loins but covers nothing else. Then he has some beer brewed, he drinks, dances and sings.

One day, these Wadzimba warriors came to Sangano mountain as simple hunters. They saw the place and said: "This is a good place, let us settle here." The leader of this Wadzimba group (Sabarawara) had stayed on Chipadze mountain. His son (Muskwere) was leading the group. At first, the Wadzimba were afraid of Madzivoa's people. They were afraid Madzivoa's people would chase them away. But the Wadzimba had the fire drill and they gave the Madzivoa some fire. This was the first kindness they showed the Madzivoa.

One day the Wadzimba killed an elephant. They painted the teeth with black mud. Then the Wadzimba called the Madzivoa and his people. They showed the dead elephant to the people and said to Madzivoa: "You are the king of the country, which part of this animal do you want? Do you want the teeth, the breast, the back or the legs?" According to tradition, the chieftains were always given, of every kill, the breast from the neck to the stomach but not the loins, and also the ivory teeth. This is a tribute to the chieftain. However, Madzivoa said: "Give me the legs." Madzivoa wanted neither the breast nor the ivory.

The chieftain of the Wadzimba married Madzivoa's daughter. The chieftain of the Wadzimba said to Madzivoa: "First I brought you fire. Then I ate the breast of the elephant because you declined the ivory. Now I have married your daughter. From now on I shall be the Mambo here on the Sangano and you shall serve me in future." In this way, Madzivoa became the servant of Wahungwe-Mambo.

As soon as the Mambo had built his house on Sangano mountain, he spread the message throughout the land: "Come and get your fire from the new Mambo." All the people who had eaten their fish raw until then went to Sangano mountain to fetch the fire made with the fire drill. For this reason, the Mambo was called "Magone" which means the man skilled to make things. This is the origin of the title Makoni. All the people who lived in the distant areas of the land said to one another: "Let us go to the place of assembly to the Magone who is able to make the fire." In this way, the people of the Makoni constantly increased and his lands became more extensive.

It was at this time that the ceremony originated which is characterised by the proverb "the new king came with his new fire". As soon as a new king is installed, all fires and hearths must be put out throughout the land. The first official action of the king is to make a new fire with the fire drill. The people call the vertical rod musika, the horizontal rod chissikiro. The words are substituted for murume and mukadsi. The people say begetter and shaper, rather than man and woman, because shame prevents them from naming in public, by using these words, the sexual act which is expressed by this instrument and its original names.

The timber from which this ceremonial fire drill is made must be taken from the musamwi tree. The first wife of the Mambo, called the Wahosi, must assist the king during the fire-making ceremony, because it will only be a proper king's fire, if the Wahosi has been present as his wife. Moreover, the father of the Wahosi must also be present; after this, the elders come and get brands of the new king's fire and take them to their steading and the house of their wahosi. All the other people get the fire from the house of the Wahosi, and the whole people think of the time when the fire was made on the Sangano mountain by the Wadzimba for the first time and fetched by all the other people. When the fire goes out in any steading, a new flame must be borrowed from a neighbour, and it must come from a fire lighted from the new regal fire.

When the new king has lighted the fire, an ox is killed. The king despatches his messengers to all kings living near or far away and tells them that he, so-and-so, is now the Makoni, i.e. the Mambo in the Wahungwe region.

The group of steadings in which the king or mambo lives with his "family" is called Zimbawoye. The natives have no doubt about the meaning of this word. Zimba or Dzimba = house, and woye (uoye) = a term of veneration, to be translated "august". The "august house"! Present-day translation, adapted to the southern dialects, in which zimba = house, bwe = stones, is popular etymology, and can only be present-day popular etymology because even the old Portuguese invariably write the word as Zimbaoe. Zimbabwe as a house built of stone undoubtedly had a meaning different from Zimba-uoye = the venerated steading because the word was applied to graves in the rock, which are rightly called "houses of stone".

Surprisingly, the women at the court of a Makoni have more influence than the men. The huge, forceful men whom we encounter at other African courts of similar political structure, are completely absent, or are only pale shadows, at Zimbawoye. Nevertheless, the Wahungwe assert that this proportion of male and female participation in the "common weal" has always been the same.

Among the women of inner Zimbawoye, the highest place is taken by the Mazarira, who is also called Uomazarira (uo = the venerable, gracious lady). She is the mother of the king. Mazarira is her honorary title. After her elevation, she is not allowed to do any work. She need not concern herself with water, timber, cooking, working in the fields any more. Everything she requires is supplied by the king's wives third-class, and by the king's daughters. If the Mazarira and mother of the new king was the Wahosi (first wife) of the king's father, the new king is not allowed to see the Mazarira again after her elevation although she is his own mother. Apart from this, the Mazarira was considered to be the "mother of all kings" and was treated accordingly. When a Mazarira died, a new one was elected.

The relationship of the king's real wives was established by the arrangement of the dwellings. Previously, the Zimbawoye included three steadings or three centres. The first "house" was that of the king, the second was that of the Wahosi, the third was that in which the Wuarango cooked and which also served as eating place. The women were divided into three classes: the only member of the first class was the Wahosi, the first wife of the mambo. All visitors were received in her house, and cooking was done for visitors only, as far as preparation was concerned. All heavy work such as that associated with water, timber, cooking, washing and work in the fields was done by the many women in the third class, the Wuarango. Between the Wahosi and the Wuarango is the Wuabanda. If the Wahosi has a message for the Wuarango she sends the Wuabanda as her representative.

Now for the fourth group of royal women, the king's daughters, who are called Wasarre (singular: Musarre). For an appreciation of their abnormal way of life it should be emphasised from the start that the Wahungwe, like, apparently, all Wakaranga tribes, were formerly greatly concerned with the chastity of their daughters; from the time of the Matebele wars, this changed to the opposite. It was once customary to send all the young girls of a steading or village for a bathe in the early morning. When they returned from the bathe, one after the other had to lie on a mat. An old women then checked whether everything was in order. If premature and illicit intrusion was observed, the girl was bullied until she named the offender who was then severely punished. If a young husband later observed on the wedding night that his wife was no longer able to supply what he was entitled to demand, he got his mother to perforate the bottom of a pot and send the young woman back to her parents with this symbolic gift. It can therefore be said that, generally speaking, the chastity principle dominated among the Wahungwe and the Wakaranga as a whole, since these customs would seem to be fairly universal.

It is all the more striking to observe that this principle is not applied to the Wasarre, the king's daughters. The opposite could justifiably be alleged. The Musarre had the right at all times to dispose of her body as and when she wanted to. There is a proverb about them which mentions "the leopard's skin". This says two things. To wear the leopard's skin or to sit on it is a privilege of the royal family and the proverb intimates that free love is a royal privilege of the Musarre. The native wit characteristic of the Wakaranga tribes has, however, given a second meaning to the phrase which it is unlikely to have had at the beginning: the number of these sexual adventures is matched with the number of spots on the leopard skin.

There was, however, nothing immoral about this right of abandon. On the contrary: passionate abandon was mandatory. The sacral hymn (if the words were profane, the Wahungwe would consider them unpronounceable aloud in public) of the great rain sacrifice which all the dancers sing says: "When the Musarre yields her body to cohabitation, the rain will come". The vagina of the Musarre must never become dry.

However, the Musarre's obligation to indulge in sexual activity was not only outward-directed. Peculiar customs must previously have arisen in the heart of the Zimbawoye. I have been unable to obtain any definite information on this matter from the Wahungwe. A royal messenger of the previous Makombe, however, told me the following story: At the time of the reign of the older Makoni family, the custom among the Wahungwe had been for the Machinda, the heir apparent to the throne, to live with a Musarre, i.e. his sister. This relationship was not considered to be a marriage. When he became Mambo (king) and was given the title of Makoni, it was the duty of his sister and mistress to light the new fire with the Makoni. After this ceremony, the sister-mistress was given the honorary title Mwuiza and remained the keeper of the royal fire. My informant further alleged that the Mwuiza had at one time been the principal wife of the Mambo. After this, the Wahungwe had installed a Wahosi in accordance with the Barozwi custom and had put the Mwuiza among the Wuarongo. If the Makoni had previously had a son by the Mwuiza, this son was the first in the line of succession to the throne, and, in this case, the Mwuiza was promoted to Mazarira.

When two branches of the royal family were fighting for the office of Makoni, with their aspirants, there was a solution. One of the aspirants, A, married the daughter of aspirant B; A automatically became Mambo and Makoni, and B, the father-in-law who had to be present when the new fire was lit. The descendants of B admittedly lost claims to the royal crown once and for all. This custom is a last remnant of privileges resulting from the sexual relations of close blood relations.

A very important point is that the king's daughters really remained unmarried. In the view of the Wahungwe, first, marriage is sealed by payment for the bride (lobolo) and, secondly, a man may send his wife away, but a woman can only dissolve her marriage by arbitration of the elders. Neither of these institutions can be applied to the Musarre. The king accepts no payment for his daughters, he gives them away as a favour. Moreover, the Musarre owes no loyalty to her husband nor is she compelled to maintain a relationship. She can refuse the man the Makoni-father wishes to give her, or she may send him away eventually. The man will remain a simple Muranda in this case, i.e. an inhabitant of the Zim-bawoye not related to the royal family. Accordingly, the sons-in-law of the Mambo are not given the customary title (Mukwambo), but are called Wanehanda.

Like all Waranda (plural of Muranda) in the Zimbawoye, these Wane-handa constitute an important factor in the establishment of the Mambo. They could be described as the guards, the only reliable servants of the king. What is certain is that all the Waranda and, consequently, the Wane-handa are the only completely honest and loyal servants of the king in the Zimbawoye. Apart from them, the only male inhabitants of the royal village are the Machinda, i.e. princes, that is to say sons, brothers, nephews, grandchildren of the king. The Machinda, being blood relations are the opposite of the Waranda, who are not blood relations. All these are always involved in "court intrigues". The cause of these intrigues invariably is the eternal question: "Whose son will be the next Makoni"? which is tanta-mount to the other question: "Which woman will be the next Mazarira?" The problem is one for the old women, who will talk by the hour about their sons' attractions and claims, but will never express their hopes for the office of Mazarira. During such conversations, they will accuse one another of all conceivable crimes and nastiness. Poisoning and witchcraft are com-monplace.

The waters of origin

The myth concerning the origin of the Wahungwe refers to a ruler of the name "Madzivoa". They themselves derive this from dzivoa (lake, pond, ford). There are many of these on the southern Rhodesian plain, as would be expected in a granite landscape decomposed by weathering. According to a large number of myths and legends, many of the dzivoa are populated by 'beings' which live at the bottom of the lakes. Whether a dzivoa is inhabited can easily be seen from the rising of bubbles encircled by widening ripples. To illustrate this, the Wahungwe will make a drawing of such ripples in the sand. They are the same concentric ripples that form when a stone is thrown into the water. However, since they form without being caused by a stone and without any external influence, they must be caused by beings that live at the bottom of the lake. Moreover, whirlpools are sometimes found which engulf bathers. They tell the careful observer whether the lake is inhabited or not.

The generally accepted name of the spirits that inhabit the lakes is Wadzivoa among the Wahungwe and Manyika. This is what is stated in the legend about the origin of the Wahungwe. The preferred name of the underwater spirits among the Wahungwe, Barwe, Wateve, Manyika and Wazezuru is not Wadzivoa but Ndusu or Njuvi. Of these Ndusu, the Wahungwe tell that they live at the lake bottom like men, that they have fire in their huts, that smoke rises from their huts and that they love music.

"A man had a wife. He had two sons. When they were grown up, the father only had enough to pay the lobolo (bride-price) for one of them. Only one of the sons was able to marry. The younger son married. The older son had nothing to win a wife with.

The older brother said to himself: 'How am I to win a wife? I shall make a plan'. He prepared his mbira (a musical instrument made of sheet iron "reeds" attached to a wood box). He took his Mbira and departed.

As he went along playing his Mbira he met an army of rabbits (zuro). He said to himself: 'How can I get past the rabbits?'. He played his mbira. The rabbits began to dance. They raised much dust. When you could not see anything for dust, the lad escaped.

He continued his journey and met a troop of large animals. He played his mbira. The animals began to dance. They raised a lot of dust. When you could not see anything for dust, the lad escaped.

He continued along the road. After a while he met a pack of lions. He played his mbira. The lions began to dance. They raised a lot of dust. When you could not see anything for dust, he escaped.

The lad went on and on. At last he came to a mountain that was high and very, very long. At the foot of the mountain there was a dzivoa (lake) which was large and very, very long. The lad said: 'How am I to get across this dzivoa?' He sat on a rock on the bank of the dzivoa and started to play his mbira.

When he had played for a while, a man rose to the surface in the middle of the lake. This man, an underwater man, (Njuvi) stood on the water and listened to the lad playing. Then he went down, but soon returned with another man, and both listened to the music for a while and then went down. After this, many Njuvi came and listened.

Three Njuvi came up to the lad on the bank. They said to him: "Take this mushonga (charm). When you have taken it, you can live under the water like ourselves. Take it and come with us. We shall take you to our Mambo (king)". The lad said: 'All right'. He took the Mushonga. Three Njuvi escorted him to their Mambo at the bottom of the dzivoa. The Mambo of the Njuvi said to the lad: 'Play your mbira.' The lad played. He played his best. He played for three days and three nights. The Mambo was delighted. The Mambo ordered them to show the lad a large village with many people in it. The Mambo said to the lad: 'The village my people have shown you is yours. You can take to wife any maiden in it.'

The lad lived in the lake for several years. He had many wives and begat children. He said to himself: 'I must let my brother share in my riches'. The lad got ready. He left the lake and walked until he came to his brother. He said to his brother: 'I have a large village under the water. Come with me and share my riches'. The younger brother said: 'I am grateful to you, but I want to stay where I am'. The older brother returned to the dzivoa and never came back."

Some Wakaranga say that these beings that live in the depth of the water are the spirits of the dead. There are legends according to which these „Wadzivoa" ancestral spirits taught men to be blacksmiths, and gave them the tools from the depths of the water. Unfortunately, nothing remained but the memory of the existence of this tradition, the real import of which had been forgotten. A Barwe man gave me an excellent account of the presents given by the Ndusu: „From the Ndusu, men obtained 1. the knowledge of weaving and forging, 2. the knowledge of makona (medicines), 3. instructions on how to bury the Mambo (king), 4. instructions on how to offer sacrifices for rain, 5. the knowledge of the mukuabpassi (high priest), 6. the mbira (musical instrument) and the art of playing it."

The assertion about the relationship of these Wadzivoa to the primeval culture and about their nature as ancestral spirits may well be connected with a number of peculiar funeral customs which greatly deviate from the generally accepted form. Among the Wahungwe, these apply in particular to twins. They are called Wakuisa Makomo, i. e., allegedly, „those who climb up the mountain". This name is alleged to be due to the fact that they infringed the privilege of the king. Man should never have more than one child at a time. Of these, one must be killed, and the other thrown into the water in a pot and drowned. This sacrifice is intended to induce rain. Moreover, all infant corpses are placed in urns or wrapped in cloth and buried on the river bank or sunk in a pond. Again, there is said to be a favourable effect on rain. If a woman dies in childbirth, she is not buried in the cemetery but on the river bank.

The deeper meaning of these customs is reflected in the legends:

„A man had many wives. The wives had children. One wife had a child which went down with smallpox.

The other wives said: 'We do not want our children to become infected. Take your child and go away'. The other wives drove the mother and her sick child from the steading. The man built her a hut outside the steading next to the corral.

The husband said to his wives: 'When I die, bury me on the bank of the dzivoa where the hippopotamus live. If you bury me on the bank of this dzivoa, the dzivoa will dry out'.

The man died. His corpse was buried on the bank of the dzivoa in which the hippopotamus lived. All the women and children went, only the sick child and his mother did not go. When the corpse of the man was buried on the bank, the dzivoa began to dry out. The hippopotamus came out and ran away. The dzivoa soon became completely dry.

The sick boy said to his mother: 'When I die, bury me next to my father on the bank of the dzivoa. You will see that the water will return'. The boy died and was buried on the bank of the dzivoa. When the child was buried, the water began to rise again in the dzivoa. The dzivoa filled up and the hippopotamus returned to it."

There would therefore seem to be little doubt that there is a relationship between the children buried on the bank and thrown into the water, and the water level in the lake.

The dzivoa is always a water of origin. In the same way as the rain comes from it, as does the knowledge of the arts and sciences, so the ancestors of the original inhabitants of the land are descended, according to the Wahungwe, from Madzivoa.

"A man and a woman had two children, a boy and a girl. The boy's name was Runde; the girl's name was Munjari. The children grew up. The two children became adults.

One day, Runde went to his parents and said: 'My sister Munjari is so beautiful that I must marry her. I do not want another man to take her to wife'. The parents said: 'You cannot marry your sister Munjari. Only the Mambos marry their sisters. Otherwise nobody has ever married his sister.' Runde said: 'If nobody has done it before me, I shall be the first to marry my sister.' The parents said: 'We shall never allow you to marry your sister Munjari'. Runde said: 'If you do not allow me to marry my sister Munjari, I shall kill myself (ku vuraya).'

Runde had dogs. He called his dogs. He took his clothes. He took his spears. He went away with his dogs, spears and clothes. He went to a pond. He jumped into the water with his dogs, clothes and spears. Runde went on living with his dogs in the water.

The day after, an old woman came to the pond to draw water. The old woman washed her calabashes. She heard a voice. The lad was singing in the water: 'Dear grandmother' (customary mode of address for old women) 'washing your calabashes, go and tell them that Runde is in the lake; his clothes are the red colour of stagnant water; his dogs have turned into crocodiles; his spears have become reeds; he died for his Munjari'.

The old woman heard Runde's song. She ran into the village and went to Runde's parents and said to them: 'Runde has gone into the lake with his clothes, spears and dogs. He has done this because of his sister Munjari.' The parents became frightened.

Runde's parents said: 'Let us take another maiden to him whom he can marry so that he can return from the pond.' The parents went to the pond with a beautiful maiden. They called into the water: 'Runde, come out of the lake. Here is your sister. You can marry her.' Runde replied: 'This is not my sister. This maiden cannot help me. She is not Munjari. I will not come back.' The parents returned to the village with the girl.

Runde's parents came back with a maiden who was still more beautiful. The parents called into the water: 'Runde, come out of the lake. Your sister is here. You can marry her.' Runde replied: 'This is not my sister. This maiden cannot help me. She is not Munjari. I will not come back'. The parents returned to the village with the maiden.

Runde's parents said: 'The life of our son Runde is at stake. We must give him his sister Munjari'. The parents went to the lake with Munjari. They shouted into the water: "Your sister Munjari is here whom you want to marry. We will allow you to'. Runde heard these words and saw his sister. Runde was content. He came out of the lake with his dogs, clothes, and spears and married his sister Munjari".

When this story had been told, an elderly woman from the Eastern Wahungwe area said that the story was rather different and certainly not something one should tell in front of children. She gave me the "authentic" version afterwards. It ran as follows:

"Once upon a time there lived a man and his wife. They had a son who was called Runde and a daughter who was called Munjari. The two children grew up together.

One day, Munjari saw her brother in the bath. She saw her brother naked. Munjari said to herself: 'Runde is more than all other men. I want to sleep with Runde'. Munjari went to a Nganga* and said: 'Make me a mushonga (magic charm). What I desire is a man.' The Nganga made a mushonga. The mushonga was a small grain. The Nganga gave the mushonga to Munjari.

In the evening, after eating, Runde said to Munjari: 'I am thirsty, give me something to drink.' Munjari put the mushonga under a finger nail. She brought a calabash of water and held it in such a way that her thumb nail was in the water. Runde drank. The mushonga had fallen into the water. Runde drank the water. He swallowed the mushonga.

The next day Runde went to his parents and said: 'No-one shall marry my sister Munjari. I want to marry her myself.' The parents said: 'You are getting above yourself. Only the Mambos marry their sisters'. Runde said: 'I must marry my sister.' The parents said: 'You are not a Mambo and you are not an animal. We do not allow you to marry your sister'. Runde said: 'If you do not give me my sister Munjari for a wife I shall kill myself'. The parents said: 'We shall not give you your sister Munjari for a wife.' Runde left.

He took his white clothes, his spears, and his dogs, and went to a lake. He went into the lake with all his possessions. His clothes became the red sheen on the lake surface. His spears became reeds, his dogs turned into crocodiles, he himself lay on the lake bottom in the shape of a lion.

The day after, an old woman came to the lake shore. She washed her clothes. The old woman's clothes became red. The old woman was startled. Runde sang: 'Dear grandmother, you are washing your clothes. Go and tell them that Runde is in the lake. His clothes are as red as the stagnant water. His dogs have become crocodiles. His spears have turned into reeds. He has died for his Munjari'.

* priest.

The old woman heard Runde's song and ran to the village of the parents and said to them: 'Your son Runde has gone into the lake. His clothes have become the red sheen on the lake surface. His spears have become reeds. His dogs have turned into crocodiles. He has died for his Munjari.' The parents took fright. They said: 'We must do anything we can for Runde'.

The parents went to the lake with a beautiful maiden. They shouted: 'Your Munjari is here'. Runde called from the water: 'If you are my sister Munjari, jump into the lake'. The maiden took fright and ran back to the village. Runde shouted: 'This was not my sister Munjari'. The parents went back to the village.

The parents went to the lake with another fair maiden. The parents shouted 'Your sister Munjari is here'. Runde called from the water: 'If you are my sister Munjari, jump into the lake.' The maiden took fright and ran back to the village. Runde called: 'This was not my sister Munjari'. The parents went back to the village.

The parents said: 'We only have one daughter'. The parents called Munjari. They went down to the lake with Munjari. The parents shouted: 'Your sister Munjari is here'. Runde called from the water: 'If you are my sister Munjari, jump into the water'. Munjari took off her dress. Munjari took off her anklets and her bracelets and took the pearls out of her hair. Munjari went into the lake.

When Munjari went into the lake, the reeds became spears, the crocodiles dogs, the red sheen turned into white clothes, and Runde rose from the water dressed in white clothes, and Munjari followed him. Munjari put on her pearls, her bracelets, her anklets, and her dress. Runde and Munjari went to the village. Runde and Munjari married. Runde became the first king of Madzivoa land."

Finally. the woman explained to me why the story should not be told in the presence of children and young people: Because it was the story of the origin of all Wadzivoa and of the first kings.

The last part of the legend is reminiscent of the description of the funeral rites of the second wife murdered after the king. It is said that before her sacrificial death, the second wife "was painfully deprived one by one of all articles of clothing and jewelry", so that she was naked at the moment of death and was only robed again when the corpse entered the funereal cave. — Since this legend is taken for history describing the origin of the royal family, we gain the impression that the peculiar way of life and the life and death ceremonial of the princes followed a mythological model.

Again, the dzivoa appears as the water of origin. Derived from the dzivoa is all knowledge of engineering, the science of the mukuabpassi, the ritual of regicide. It is the source of rain and, it now appeared, the origin of the first kings, of the first dynasty.

The fertile rain and procreation

There is an odd piece of evidence to show that the concept "rain" is of paramount importance to the inhabitants of Southern Africa. In all the Bantu peoples between Benue and South Africa I found a word for water (mai, maji, mazi etc.) and another word for rain (vula, mwura etc.). The peoples of this region, however, only know the word mvura for rain, which they apply also to the water from brooks, wells, and rivers, having completely given up the other word.

Among all the peripheral peoples, such as the tribes on the Limpopo and the Waremba in the South, the Batonga and the Wataware who live in the north on the Zambesi we were able to record descriptions of dances and celebrations and hymns of the rain cult. The fundamental principle is the same in all of these. Mostly, a round dance is performed, encircling a hill, a tree, a house, etc. and "holy" beer is drunk, and hymns with monotonously repeated texts are sung. These are litanies directed mostly at the king or the ancestors as mediators between man and God (Moari). These dances are continued for days, frequently until the prayers are heard and rain falls.

In the central area of Southern Erythraean culture* the ceremony also involves songs and dancing. One or two priests celebrate to start with. Then a sacrifice is offered up and finally a holy area is defined, which constitutes an open-air temple. Among the Wahungwe the rain sacrifice to be performed in the case of persistent and ominous drought was not originally called Mbila but Masingo. The superficial observer fails to identify any special priests. The suggestion that a sacrificial feast should be held probably comes from the Wasikiro, the mediums of the dead kings. During the ceremony no-one is allowed to walk in the bush or the fields because the Mondoro, the spirits of the dead kings incarnated as lions, which follow the Wasikiro like dogs, scour the area around the site of the sacrifice.

The place of the priest is taken by a Machinda, a son of the royal family. The rite is performed under a tree with widespread branches. The

* In Frobenius' terminology the Southern Erythraean Culture was the southern form of an African culture which had sacral kingship as its most important trait.

people assemble in masses. All bring beer. The officiating Machinda prays: "Ndemba woye, do ti pai mwura. Iwe u wa sika chimge ne chimge. Ti no pa bgabga ne ngombe. Yako iyi." ("Gracious God, grant us rain. Thou and thou only hast created the world. We give beer and an ox. Let this be Thine"). The women then give their shrill shouts of joy and the men clap their hands. Beer is drunk and a black, hornless bull is killed.

Round-dances are then performed about the site of the sacrifice. The conventional hymn is as follows:

"Ku chira musarre, mvura no vuya" ("when the king's daughters cohabit, the rain will come"). This song is very interesting in that normally the Wahungwe are very reserved and chaste in daily speech. For example, they do not refer to the two components of the fire drill by their proper names, murume (man) and mukadsi (woman), but refer to them obliquely as musika = the maker, generator, and chikiro = the shaper, so that the parallel to the sexual act is not unduly close. Nevertheless, the drastic sentence quoted above is repeated by the whole congregation at the ceremony. The old people also told me that there would certainly be no rain if the Musarre (king's daughters) did not cohabit lustily.

At first sight, this would seem to suggest that prayer and sacrifice were addressed directly to God and that the intermediaries, the Mizimu, were excluded. Closer investigation, however, shows that this is not the case. In former times at least the officiating Machinda, i.e. the member of the royal family, had to be a Sikiro, a medium of a dead king. This means that it was after all a Muzimu in person who sent prayers and sacrifice on their way to Ndemba. Like all other sacred acts, the Masingo rite would appear to have been in the hands of the Sikiro. They gave advice, they asked for the views and intentions of the Mizimu, they selected the victim, and it is interesting to note that they had one further function: all the bones of the sacrificial ox "with a little meat on them" had to be thrown from the place of sacrifice into the bush for the Mondoro (royal spirit lions) to eat.

The first rainy season sacrifice, Masingo, was demanded every year by the priest (Mukuabpassi) in the month of Kuwumbi. This month is approximately the same as the month of April. It is also called Madsudsu or Makoni, the latter, allegedly, because the ceremony was celebrated in the homestead of the Makoni. The exact time was determined by the Mukuabpassi by observation of the stars. When he had determined the proper date, he went to the Makoni and said "Changamire Mambo! The day of the Masingo is such and such a date. Let beer be brewed". Beer was then brewed in the steadings of the Makoni. All the people assembled to drink the beer. The prayer was said by the Mukuabpassi. It went as follows: "bgabga vuyu baba wangu" ("this beer for our father"). After that, there was beer drinking and dancing, and a song was sung which went as follows: "Ti no tevera magora pa nyama. Ti no lya wuchi ne nyama" ("We follow the vultures to the carcass. We eat honey and meat"). An ox is then killed. Previously, this is alleged to have been followed by a hunting expedition during which it was important that every huntsman should cut off the tail of the animal he killed and make a knot in the hair "because otherwise all those who eat of his meat would get a stomach ache".

According to the Batonga, Waremba and Manyika, it was the custom among the Wahungwe previously to sacrifice maidens, that is to say daughters of the king, at the big rain ceremonies. This was done in a consecrated space which had two large entrance gates and was surrounded by a fence. The Wahungwe themselves denied this.

Corresponding to the first regular Masingo festival there is another which is arranged around the "Chizozo". The Chizozo is a sacred grove situated on the northern slope of Sangano mountain with an oval area of dense trees and bushes surrounded by a wide, bare strip of ground. This track is cleared of grass and vegetation every year. In this grove there rest the very old women of the royal family, the "Mazarira", Wahosi, Wabandsi, Worongo and Wasarre. The central undergrowth contains very old graves only.

The date of the purification festivals was also determined by the Mukuabpassi, after observation of the stars. The festival was celebrated in the month of Wuwu or Mawuwu (also called Betsa Mamepo) which coincides approximately with our month of September. This is the month in which the grass was burnt off and spring digging for agriculture began. At the request of the Mukuabpassi, beer was brewed in Zimbawoye. The people assembled, and beer was drunk.

It could be said that this Chizozo spring festival, held at the beginning of the rainy season, corresponds or would correspond to the Masingo autumn festival, begun in Zimbawoye. There is, however, a very major difference which reveals the apparent similarity as to some extent the opposite. The Masingo festival is celebrated every year, the Chizozo festival once every two years. Previously, the performance of both depended on the observations of the stars carried out by the Mukuabpassi priest, whose present-day successor knows nothing much about it. It is therefore impossible to obtain from direct accounts any indication of the way in which the date was fixed. However this may be, one of these festivals gives the impression of being an initiation and integration sacrifice, the other a conclusion and thanksgiving sacrifice, or, the one could be a sacrifice for the period of rain and vegetation, and the other a sacrifice for the dry period and hunting period. There must be some profound significance in the fact that the rain and vegetation festival is only celebrated once every two years.

Now for the report of the old "high priest" of the Barozwi or Barotse in Southern Rhodesia, who is called the "Mawutse" and is the inheritor of the religious ideas of the past.

If no rain comes, beer is brewed. A circular fence of stakes is built which is called Rushanga. In its centre there is a tree which is called Muhadscha. The place fenced off is called Mutoro. The fence, Rushanga, has two gates in the south, the left-hand one for the Mukaranga, the right-hand one for the Mawutse himself. The rain sacrifice festival is called Mbila.

On the day of the Mbila all the people assemble at the Rushanga. All the heads of families bring beer. The Mukaranga enter the Mutoro from the left, the Mawutse from the right through the appropriate gate. The Mawutse is dressed in a dark blue toga. Under the tree, the Mawutse takes off the toga and spreads it out. He himself is naked. After this, the Mukaranga kneel on the left, the Mawutse on the right, in the centre of the area, facing the entrance with heads lowered.

The Mawutse prays as follows: "Madzibambo wangu wa ndi kumbirira kuna Moari, a ndi pe uyo mvura, a chengete sakanaka zildyiwa ne ku ndi pa uyo ku cheka." ("Ancestral spirits, graciously pray for me to God that he may grant us rain and blessing on food and harvest"). The Mawutse prays aloud. The Mukaranga remains silent. When the prayer has finished, the people clap their hands. The people then begin to dance around the Rushanga. One of several songs is: "Ti no da wazhinyi" ("We ask for much"). All these many people pray unceasingly like a single soul for that which they need, until it is granted. The dancing must be continued for a very long time. A black ox is sacrificed, which has been killed with axe or spear and is not slaughtered. This is done under the tree. There is neither a sacred fire nor inspection of entrails. Fires are lit outside the Rushanga. Those whose homes are a long way off boil their meat there and then, whereas the others take their share of the sacrificial meat home. They all drink the sacrificial beer.

This Mbila festival is held both when there is too little rain and when there is too much. The officiating priest is called Mawutse. The office of Mawutse is hereditary. He is considered to be "the mother of the people". He has to perform two sacrificial ceremonies: 1. The Mbila described above, and 2. the Rukoto which is held after the harvest prior to thresh-ing. Every head of a family brings a basket full of his grain. This is boiled and a beer festival held in which all take part. A lot of beer must also be brought to the Mbila: it is a religious observance.

The Mawutse is a rain priest whose power extends as far as the Wan-djandja in the Charter district. He is a great priest, and yet there is one who is even greater, to whom he is subordinate in difficult rainy seasons and whom he only assists in the rain sacrifice. He is the rain priest Man-gongo in the Korekore area near Sinoya. He is a particularly strong me-dium, who conducts the Mbila and celebrates using exactly the same ceremonial as the Mawutse. The Mangondo also has the title Nehanda. – The Mbila of the Mangondo priest differs from that of the Mawutse in that the Mukaranga is absent. The place of the silent kneeling figure of the Mukaranga is taken by the Mawutse. Mangondo and Wawutse take off the black toga and spread them under the tree. Before starting his prayer the Mangondo observes the stars through a gap between the tree-tops.

On this, a man from Sinoya commented that previously, when famine threatened due to lack of rain, the woman priest called Nehanda had to sacrifice the Mawutse himself, i. e. hang him from the tree on the Mtoro, to bury his corpse later under the roots. In ordinary life, only a maiden would be sacrificed.

The old Bazoe was one of the few members of the old priesthood whose knowledge had survived. He said that his family had originally lived in Zimbabwe where his ancestors had performed the sacrifices in ancient times. They had been the funeral priests of the great kings until the Mutapa came to the land at the time of Banya Mwuetsi. Mutapa had abolished the sacrificial death of the kings, which was the reason why the reign of the Banya Mwuetsi had disintegrated. The kingdom could, however, be restored if the sacrifices were correctly performed and ceremonies were held in a Rushanga.

In Zimbabwe, the west gate had been called the "Mukaranga gate". This is where the princesses (Musarre) had lived their life dedicated to love. This love life had involved not only men but a large snake which lived in the "dzivoa" of Zimbabwe. If the Musarre had not lived in this way and cohabited with the snake, there would have been no rain and the dzivoa would have dried up. This was precisely what had hap-pened: since Zimbabwe had been destroyed and the Musarre driven out, the dzivoa had disappeared and there had been no proper rainy seasons. –

208

According to tradition, there lived in the large temple of Zimbabwe, in addition to other women, those daughters of the kings whose duty it was to practise the art of love particularly at times of shortage of rain. If the drought became ominous in spite of their endeavours, one of them was buried alive in the Zimbabwe valley.

All these girls were daughters of kings or at least came from the royal family. One group of these girls lived chaste and modest lives. These had to look after a fire which was put out when a king died and was lit again when a successor was chosen. These women performed a festive dance with songs, when the morning star could be seen for the first time.

Another group was that which practised ritual "whoredom". Rain sacrifices were never selected from the former but always from the latter group.

The valley in which the Zimbabwe temple is now situated was previously largely occupied by a large lake, i.e. a dzivoa. From this lake, the Zimbabwe temple, which was later situated in the centre of the dzivoa rose by itself. The Zimbabwe temple was, therefore, not built by human hands.

As long as the people observed the sacrifices and in particular killed the kings, Zimbabwe continued to rise from the dzivoa and to sink again after a lapse of time. With each re-emergence Zimbabwe brought many jewels and gold and Ndoro (shells). After this, there was the evil king Mutape who prohibited the sacrifices of kings, made many laws, and made the people work hard. The dzivoa dried up and the Zimbabwe temple was on dry ground and increasingly decayed. –

It is inevitable that an immense ruin like Zimbabwe should give rise to myths and legends. The strands of ceremonies, legends, and traditions are woven into a fabric which is made even more substantial by a valuable final group of traditions.

In ancient times, no rain fell for a whole year. The Wanganga (priests) therefore ordered a Mukaranga to be sacrificed. The Wanganga said: "It must be a nubile Musarre (king's daughter) who has never slept with a man. The Musarre must be innocent." The Mambo called his first wife and said: "Find among the Musarre a nubile and innocent one to be sacrificed as a Mukaranga". The first wife of the king went. She asked all the Wasarre to come and enquired: "Which one of you has never had anything to do with a man?" The king's daughters laughed and said: "Is it the business of the king's daughters to live like other girls?" The first wife of the king said: "Lie down on a mat". The king's daughters laughed and lay down on a mat. Among the nubile daughters of the king the first wife of the king found not one who had never had anything to do with a man.

The first wife of the king went to the Mambo and said: "Mambo, among the nubile Wasarre there is not one who has never had anything to do with a man." The Mambo called the Wanganga together and said to them: "Among the Wasarre there is not a single one who has never had anything to do with a man. Tell me what is to be done". The Wanganga said: "Mambo, the Mukaranga must be sacrificed. If no untouched nubile Musarre can be found, find the oldest Musarre of those who are not as yet nubile. She must be locked up at the place of sacrifice and remain there until she is nubile. Then she can be sacrificed as a Mukaranga". The Mambo called the first wife and said: "Find the oldest of the Wasarre who are not as yet nubile and who has had nothing to do with a man". The first wife of the king called together the little girls of the Simbawoye. She found a child that had had nothing to do with a man. The little girl had no breasts as yet.

The little Musarre was taken to the place of sacrifice. The place of sacrifice had a high wall (the man explained: circular like the wall of a hut with a door but built not of timber and clay but of stone). In the centre there was a termite hill. On the termite hill there was a tall tree. The girl was taken to the sacrificial chamber. The entrance was sealed with stones. The grown-up Wasarre took food and water to the Mukaranga every day. They passed it down across the wall. The Wakaranga ensured that no man went near the place of sacrifice.

The girl grew up at the place of sacrifice. It took two years before she was grown up and had breasts. No rain fell during these two years. All the cattle died. Many people died. The rivers dried up. The grain did not germinate. The day came when the girl was nubile.

The Wanganga went to the king. The Wanganga said: "The Mukaranga is nubile. The Mbila can be held." The king called the people together. The people assembled around the place of sacrifice. The Wanganga opened the door to the place of sacrifice. The Wanganga dug a pit in the termite hill between the roots of the great tree. The Wanganga strangled the Mukaranga. The people danced around the place of sacrifice. The Wanganga buried the girl between the roots of the great tree in the termite hill. The priests called the Mizimu. The people danced around the place of sacrifice.

When the Mukaranga had been buried between the roots, the tree began to grow. The tree grew and grew. The tree grew all through the night. The people danced all through the night. The tree grew for three days. The people danced for three days. When day came, the top of the tree reached the sky. The morning star appeared in the sky for the first time. The top of the tree spread across the sky. The stars and the moon could no longer be seen. A great wind arose. The leaves of the tree became clouds. It began to rain. It rained for 30 days.

The cosmic god and the earthly king

What moves me most deeply of all these things is the idea of the god-king who in the high endeavour of creating an ultimate symbol is first chosen as a man without blemish, is then invested with all conceivable powers and privileges, only to end his life by being sacrificed. This applies to the Musarre, the princesses, but it becomes even more manifest in the great kings themselves, the Mambos who were preceded, surely not only in legend, by a great prototype, a kind of emperor. We will now proceed to deal with "ritual regicide".

Reports that under certain circumstances the kings were put to death reached the Portuguese a long time ago. In the 80's, the ancient Mpossi, the Waremba chief in the Belingwe district and the grandfather of the present chieftain, told Harry Posselt that previously the Wakaranga kings were put to death once every four years. Mpossi added that good kings were spared by the priests and went into exile.

Among the Walowedi (or Lovedu) the sacred fire of state was still guarded. In addition to the king, there was a "Mojaji", a female regent whose husband was only prince regent and whom nobody was allowed to see face to face. Ritual murder of kings "was practised by Bahungwe and Manyika. A chief ruled for not more than five years and was then killed by a claimant method: the youngest wife (Mukaranga) of the ruling chief was secretly approached and bribed with presents in the stillness of the night. On a given date she would assist the claimant to enter the hut of the chief, who had his throat cut whilst asleep. The new chief would then proclaim his ascendancy and the tribe be summoned to pay homage."

From the Marandellas district it is reported that succession is regulated according to birth. The king is succeeded by his brothers in order of age. When there are no more brothers, it is the turn of the sons. When the king has become so old that he has lost his regal vigour, he is killed. The murder is decreed by his successor, who acts on his own judgement, without consulting priests, oracles, etc. The murder is done by men instructed to do so, at the time of the new moon. The king is blindfolded with a piece of black calico, and is then strangled.

The last Mambo of the Barozwi was murdered as follows: About 1780

211

there reigned the Mambo (king) Rupenya Mpengo; he was called "the mad" because he was so cruel. The Barozwi lacked the courage to murder this king because he was very powerful. The priests, whose business it was, approached the people of Selukwe and arranged a simulated war-like expedition which proceeded as planned. The Selukwe people insulted the Barozwi, the Barozwi complained to the Mambo Rupenya, who straightway started an expedition against the Selukwe. The warriors marched in front. The Mambo followed in a litter. When the enemy was sighted, all the warriors and the royal litter bearers of the Barozwi ran away. The Selukwe charged the litter, captured the Mambo and strangled him with a black cloth which the Barozwi priests had given them for this purpose. The Selukwe left the king's corpse lying in the field and returned to their villages. The Barozwi priests soon stopped running and returned to the "battlefield". They found the corpse of their king strangled in accordance with the proper rites and carried him home. The Mambo's corpse was buried with due ceremony.

On the subject of the ritual murder of kings, the Barwe told me that previously they had killed their kings every two (?) years. Concerning the way in which the assassination was done, there were two different views. Some said he was strangled, others said he was stabbed and his throat cut. It seems to me that strangling was the earlier form of assassination. Some of the Barwe told me the name of the cloth used for strangling; it was musangwua. It appears that the king's principal wife, the Imasonge, took part in the assassination. Shungano told me that in recent times the king was frightened of death and fled to a ruin where he hid himself. He had not been pursued there because the ruin had been considered as a place of asylum. I obtained no definite proof that there was a connection between the cult of Venus and ritual murder of kings. I was however told that the king was only murdered when Venus and the moon had not yet risen, and when the seed corn had been consecrated but not sown. The old king always conducted the seed ceremony, and never the new king, because the new king first had to grow into his office, together with the seed.

Now, best of all, a story told in December 1928 by a Barwe man on Messica farm:

Once upon a time there was a Makombe king who was more powerful and stronger than all other Mambos who lived before him or after him. This Makombe subjugated all peoples. He was the only king. All other kings served him. He was king of Zimbabwe too.

The Makombe became ill. The day arrived on which he was to be killed.

All great kings must be killed. The four Morongo (regents of the four cardinal points) went to the Makombe and said: "Mambo! Choose the man who shall be Makombe after you". The Mambo said: "My eldest son shall be king after me".

The day on which the Makombe was to be killed approached. The Makombe asked: "Has there ever been a Mambo who was not killed?" The four Morongo went to a Nganga and said: "Has there ever been a Mambo who was not killed?". The Nganga cast the Hakata (dice). The Nganga cast the Hakata three times. The Nganga said: "There has never been a king who was not killed; but a king can return if his own sister takes his illness upon herself".

The king was killed. The king was wrapped in cloths. After three days, the people came to squeeze the corpse dry. The dead Makombe had a wife who was his sister. The wife said to the people: "Leave it to me; it is my business". The woman squeezed the Makombe's corpse. She did it every day for twelve months. She would not let anyone help her. After twelve months, the king's corpse had dried out completely. The grave diggers carried the corpse of the king to the cave in which the corpses of the kings were laid.

When the corpse of the king was laid in the cave, the sister said: "Leave the cave. Close the cave. I shall stay with the Makombe". The sister lay down next to the corpse of the king. The grave diggers placed rocks in front of the cave and left. The sister of the Makombe remained lying next to the corpse. Her hair dropped out. Her fingernails and toe nails dropped off. Her teeth dropped out. All her flesh dropped off.

The day after, the guardians came to the cave. They took the rocks away from the entrance and entered. They looked for the corpse of the king; they looked for the sister of the king. The corpse of the king and the body of his sister had crumbled to dust. The guardians were frightened; they ran to the Morongo and said: "The corpse of the Makombe and his sister have crumbled to dust". The Morongo went to a Nganga. They said to the Nganga: "The corpse of the Makombe and his sister have crumbled into dust. What does this signify?" The Nganga cast the Hakata. He cast the Hakata three times. The Nganga said: "Wait four days. Then you will see what happens". The Morongo left.

The Morongo waited four days. Four days passed. When it got dark on the fourth day, the Morongo for the first time saw the new Mwuetsi (moon) rise and saw the Marinda (evening star) follow it. —

Further, there is a fragment recorded among Mpossi's Waremba which probably came from the Nganga of the Piri mountains. It was difficult to extricate the meaning of this fragment, which ran as follows: A young lad fell in love with the evening star and wished to marry it. He asked the Hakata dice how he could obtain the object of his desire. The answer given by the Hakata was: "You must steal the corpse of the king". He cast again, and the Hakata replied: "You must steal the corpse of the king and take a horn from its head". The lad said: "What use will that be to me?" The Hakata said: "You will find out".

The man went to the funeral cave of the king. The people had just finished mummifying the last king. The corpse was ready to be carried away. The corpse had two horns on its head. The lover of the star of Venus wanted to break off one of the horns of the corpse, but the king's corpse jumped up and, carrying the daring lad on its back, ran off until it reached the evening star.

This description brings to mind the image of the corpse of the Mtoko which is concealed in the skin of a bull and lies in state in this form – or of the fool who riding a bull with the moon on his chest rises from the dzivoa to royal estate. We are reminded of the horns of the moon which are animal horns; we are told of a boy with a birth mark in the shape of the moon who later becomes king. Bull, moon, king on the one side, star of Venus and the king's daughters on the other. All of these apparently images of the night sky. The night sky seen as a picture book.

Let us now turn our attention to what popular legend has to say of the stars. There is first of all a statement which is known to practically all the peoples of this civilisation and which I shall now report in its most comprehensive form, as told by a man of the Wahungwe:

"When the moon is full he is exactly opposite to his principal wife, the sun, and she makes him ill because she is jealous of the moon's second wife, the Nehanda (Venus). The moon prefers the latter. The sun with its rays makes the moon ill so that from then on it wanes until at last it dies. Nehanda who loves him follows him into death and saves him. The moon becomes well again and rises in the sky as a very small and still sick man. Nehanda follows him as his loving mate."

It seems important to me that we found people in all tribes to whom knowledge of the identity of the evening and morning star is a matter of fact. This means that the stars must have been observed attentively in past ages.

The most important feature of these views and traditions is contained in a cluster of tales which as a whole represent the products of decay of a large uniform myth; this we succeeded in discovering in a fairly good original condition.

Let us report the most important item of this fabulous material:

A man married a woman. The woman conceived. A boy was born. When the father saw the boy, he said: "The boy has a birth mark (wuarra-ndaema) on his forehead". The mother said: "Let us ask the Hakata whether the child is to stay alive". The father said: "Let us ask the Hakata".

The father went to a Nganga. The father said to the Nganga (magic priest): "My son has a birth mark on his forehead shaped like the moon. Shall we let the child live or shall we expose him on the bank of the dzivoa?" The Nganga asked the Hakata. The Nganga said: "Do not take the child to the dzivoa. The child will become a great Mambo, but, one day, the Mambo will be bitten by a snake and killed." The parents did not take the boy to the dzivoa. The boy grew up.

When the boy was grown up, he said to his father one day: "I shall go away and seek a wife." The father said: "You do that". The boy with the birth mark went away. He went a long way.

One day he came to a land where no rain had fallen for a long time. Everything had dried up. The cattle died. The people died. Along the road, the boy met a daugther of the king guarding the last cattle of the land. The boy spoke to the girl. The lad saw that the girl was very beautiful. The boy said to the girl: "I want to take you to wife". The girl said: "I will gladly go with you. The Mambo, my father, will however only give me for a wife to the man who gives rain to the country". The lad said: "Go to your father and tell him that I shall give rain to the land. I can do it".

The girl went to the Mambo and said: "I have met a boy who can give rain to the land". The Mambo said: "If the boy gives the land rain, I shall give you to him for a wife". The girl returned to the boy and said: "The Mambo agrees. Give the land rain".

The boy with the birth mark like the moon on his forehead went to a cave. In the cave there was a snake. The boy said: "I am the boy with the birth mark shaped like the moon on my forehead. Crawl from the feet up across my body and across the birth mark on the forehead." The snake said: "I will". The snake crawled over the body of the boy from the feet to the birth mark.

When the snake was crawling across the boy's feet, the horizon began to turn grey. When it crawled across his body, large clouds came. When it crawled across his forehead and the birth mark, which was completely covered by the body of the snake, it began to rain. It rained for five days and five nights.

The boy went to the king's daughter. The boy asked: "Has there been enough rain?" The king's daughter said: "Yes, there has been enough rain. My father will give me to you for a wife. I shall become your wife. But do not forget the thing I now tell you. As long as I am your wife you must eat nothing except the porridge I cook for you. You may take a second and a third wife, but you must never eat the porridge they cook for you." The boy said: "I agree".

The boy with the birth mark in the shape of the moon on his forehead married the girl. Every time the rain failed the boy went to the cave and said to the snake: "I am the boy with the birth mark shaped like the moon on my forehead. Crawl across my body from the feet and across the birth mark on my forehead". The snake did this. Then it rained.

From the day on which the boy came to the country all the fields had enough rain and the people had enough food. One day, the king died. The Machinda wanted to make a son of the dead king the new king. The women however said: "The boy with the birth mark in the shape of the moon on his forehead must be the new Mambo". The boy with the birth-mark became the Mambo of the country.

One day, there had been no rain for a long time. The king went to the cave where the snake was. Near the cave there was a small steading in which lived a woman and her daughter. The king passed the steading. The king was thirsty. The daughter stood in the door of her hut. The king said: "I am thirsty, give me something to drink". The girl went into the hut and brought the king a cup of water. The king drank. The king saw that the girl was very beautiful.

When the king had drunk, he went into the cave. When he returned from the cave, it was raining. The king entered the house of the woman. The king said to the woman: "I want to marry your daughter". The mother said: "You can marry my daughter, but the father of my daughter is a Mondoro (spirit lion). Therefore, you must eat the meat my daughter prepares as mulivo (side dish)". The king said: "I agree".

The king took the daughter of the Mondoro to be his second wife. Every day, the king ate the porridge prepared by his first wife and the side dish prepared by his second wife.

One day, the first wife said to her husband: "Ever since you took a second wife, you have not tasted of my side dish. The side dish I prepare is not meat but it is good and I want you to eat it." The king said: "I have promised my second wife". The first wife said: "If you do not eat my side dish today, I shall go into the dzivoa". The king got frightened. The king ate the side dish prepared by his first wife.

Next day the king entered the hut of his second wife. The second wife said: "Yesterday, you did not eat my side dish". The king said: "Forgive me, I did it so that my first wife would not go into the dzivoa." The second wife said: "No, I do not forgive you. I shall return to my mother". The king said: "Forgive me". The second wife said: "No, I do not forgive you. I want a husband who lives with me and eats my mulivo." The second wife got her things together and returned to her mother.

The second wife returned to her mother's house. The second wife then went to the cave where the snake lived. The second wife said to the snake: "I want a husband who lives with me and eats my mulivo". The snake said: "I shall come with you". The snake went to the hut of the second wife. The second wife lived with the snake.

One day, the king said to himself: "I love my second wife. I must visit my second wife and be with her." The king went to the hut of his second wife. The second wife said: "Mambo, what do you want of me?". The king said: "Forget the quarrel; let me stay with you until tomorrow." The second wife said: "It cannot be done, go away". The king went up to the second wife and wanted to embrace her. The snake jumped out from under the bed of the second wife and bit the king.

The king became ill and wasted away. The second wife said: "I want to see the Mambo once more before he dies". The second wife went to the steading of the king. The second wife went up to the bed of the king. The king died. The second wife lay down next to him and also died.

Further, I report, without any lengthy introduction, the myth told me by a Mukaranga, an old Nganga from the Mpiras region:

Moari (god) made a man who was called Mwuetsi (moon). He made him at the bottom of a dzivoa and he gave him a Ngona (= a horn containing ointment). Mwuetsi first lived in the dzivoa (lake).

Mwuetsi said to Moari: "I want to go on land". Moari said: "You will regret it". Mwuetsi said: "Nevertheless, I want to go on land". Moari said: "Well then, go on land". Mwuetsi went from the dzivoa to the land.

The land was bare and empty. There were no grasses. There were no bushes. There were no trees. There were no animals. Mwuetsi wept and said to Moari: "How am I to live here?" Moari said: "I told you before you started. You have chosen the path at the end of which you will die". Moari said: "Even so, I shall give you what belongs to you". Moari gave Mwuetsi a girl who was called Massassi (morning star). Moari said: "Massassi shall be your wife for two years". Moari gave Massassi a fire drill.

In the evening, Mwuetsi went into a cave with Massassi. Massassi said: "Help me, let us make fire. I shall hold the Chimandira (horizontal stick);

you work the Rusika (the vertical drilling stick)." Mwuetsi did what Massassi asked him to do. Massassi held the horizontal stick. Mwuetsi worked the drill. When the fire was lit, Mwuetsi lay down on one side of the fire. Massassi lay down on the other side of the fire. The fire was burning between them.

Mwuetsi thought: "Why has Moari given me this girl? What am I to do with the girl Massassi?" When it was night, Mwuetsi took his Ngona horn. He moistened his index finger with a drop of oil from the Ngona horn. Mwuetsi stood up. Mwuetsi said: "I cross the fire from one side to the other". Mwuetsi stepped across the fire. Mwuetsi went up to the girl Massassi. Mwuetsi touched Massassi's body with the anointed finger. Then Mwuetsi returned to his bed and slept.

When Mwuetsi woke up towards morning, he looked across at Massassi. Mwuetsi saw that Massassi's body was swollen. When it was day, Massassi began to give birth. Massassi gave birth to grass. Massassi gave birth to bushes. Massassi gave birth to trees. Massassi did not cease to give birth until the earth was covered with grasses, bushes and trees.

Thereafter, the trees grew and grew until their tops reached the sky. When the tops of the trees touched the sky, it started to rain.

Mwuetsi and Massassi lived a full life. For food, they had fruit, roots, and seed. Mwuetsi built a house in which he lived with Massassi. Mwuetsi made iron and a spade. He made hoes and dug a field. Mwuetsi made fabrics out of bark and bast. Massassi made baskets and caught fish. Massassi brought water and wood. Massassi cooked. In this way, Mwuetsi and Massassi lived for two years.

After two years, Moari said to Massassi: "Massassi, the time is up". Moari took Massassi from the earth and returned her to the dzivoa. Mwuetsi lamented.

Mwuetsi wept and said to Moari: "What shall I do without my Massassi? What shall I do without my wife? Who will hew wood and draw water for me? Who will cook for me?" Mwuetsi lamented for eight days.

Mwuetsi lamented for eight days. Then, Moari said to him: "I told you at the beginning that you were on the way to death. I shall give you another wife. I shall give you Morongo (the evening star). Morongo will stay with you for two years, and then I shall take her back." Moari gave Morongo to Mwuetsi.

Morongo came to Mwuetsi's hut. When it was evening, Mwuetsi wanted to lie on the other side of the fire. Morongo said: "Do not lie on the other side of the hut. Lie next to me." Mwuetsi lay down next to Morongo.

Mwuetsi took the Ngona horn and was about to use the index finger and the ointment. Morongo however said: "Do not do this. I am not like Massassi. Anoint your belly with the Ngona oil. Then anoint my belly with the Ngona oil." Mwuetsi anointed his belly with Ngona oil. Mwuetsi anointed Morongo's belly with Ngona oil. Morongo said: "Now have intercourse with me". Mwuetsi had intercourse with Morongo. Mwuetsi fell asleep.

The next day, towards morning, Mwuetsi awoke. Mwuetsi saw that Morongo's belly was swollen. At day break, Morongo began to give birth. On the first day, Morongo gave birth to chickens, sheep and goats.

On the evening of the second day Mwuetsi again had intercourse with Morongo. In the morning, Morongo gave birth to elands (nuka) and cattle.

On the evening of the third day Mwuetsi again had intercourse with Morongo. On the fourth day, Morongo gave birth, first to boys and then to girls. The boys who were born in the morning were grown up by evening.

On the evening of the fourth day, Mwuetsi again wanted to have intercourse with Morongo. A thunderstorm threatened and Moari said: "Leave off. You are approaching death". Mwuetsi was frightened. The thunderstorm passed. When the thunderstorm was over, Morongo said to Mwuetsi: "Make a door and block the entrance so that Moari cannot see what we do. Then have intercourse with me." Mwuetsi made a door. Mwuetsi closed the entrance of the hut. Mwuetsi then had intercourse with Morongo. Mwuetsi fell asleep.

The next day, towards morning, Mwuetsi awoke. Mwuetsi saw that Morongo's belly was swollen. When it was day, Morongo began to give birth. Morongo gave birth to lions, leopards, snakes and scorpions. Moari saw this. Moari said to Mwuetsi: "I warned you".

On the evening of the fifth day, Mwuetsi wanted to have intercourse with Morongo again. Morongo however said: "Behold, your daughters are grown up. Have intercourse with your daughters." Mwuetsi looked at his daughters. He saw that they were beautiful girls and that they were grown up. He had intercourse with them. They bore children. The children who were born in the morning were grown up by evening. Mwuetsi became the Mambo (king) of a great people.

Morongo, however, had intercourse with the snake. Morongo did not give birth any more. She lived with the snake. One day Mwuetsi came back to Morongo and wanted to have intercourse with her, but Morongo said: "Leave off". Mwuetsi said: "I will not". Mwuetsi lay down next to Morongo. The snake lay under Morongo's bed. The snake bit Mwuetsi. Mwuetsi fell ill.

When the snake bit Mwuetsi, Mwuetsi fell ill. The day after, there was no rain. The plants dried up. The rivers and dzivoa (lakes) dried up. The animals died. Men began to die. Many people did die. Mwuetsi's children asked: "What shall we do?" The children of Mwuetsi said: "Let us consult the Hakata." Mwuetsi's children consulted the Hakata. The Hakata said: "The Mambo Mwuetsi is ill and wasting away. Send Mwuetsi back into the dzivoa".

Mwuetsi's children then strangled Mwuetsi and buried him. They buried Morongo together with Mwuetsi. Then they made another man Mambo. Morongo had lived two years in the Zimbabwe of Mwuetsi.

This creation myth provides a key to a number of doors. Most of the accounts we were given later, on life, on death, on the spirit life of the kings, on the Ngona horn and the fire drill, on the creation of nature, on the rain rite and the circumcision ceremonial, on star gazing and on hierodule princesses, are gathered together in this great myth which I do not hesitate to number among the most impressive that have come down to us from the great age of the "cosmic view". It would be presumptuous to offer interpretations and explanations. A man who, like myself, has devoted a lifetime's study to these subjects, acquires very high opinion of the significance of the major achievements of a civilisation. He will therefore never lay clumsy hands on that which the human spirit was enabled to bring forth as a superb product of that age, and which can only be experienced in moments of grace but can never be captured by processes of ratiocination.

What has been put into words is however sufficiently clear and transparent to provide a glimpse of a vast picture. We are face to face with a past which, with profound piety and sudden vision has discovered the mystery and puzzle of nature's procreation and fertility, interpreting them in accordance with the creative powers of the mythological age, powers which it is so difficult for ourselves, the impious children of a materialistic age, to comprehend. We must "understand" with the intellect what the mythological age described in pictures. We write and read little books in dusty corners, whereas their vision encompassed the universe, the earth, flora and fauna, and the heavens in their purview and created "understanding" from the cosmos, in humility.

The great mystery and puzzle of procreation and fertility is thus symbolized by the movement of the celestial bodies. The moon becomes the symbol of human greatness and yearning, the evening star the symbol of fulfilment, but both are subject to the tragic fate of all that lives, i.e. to death and rebirth, leading to a new dramatic existence. The moon and the evening star and their rhythmically repeated changes of image reflect the mystery and riddle of life, the ultimate problems of which are procreation, fertility and death.

At this time when the myth flourished, this vision of the cosmos was projected on to the earth. Human beings lived their lives in accordance with the self-created vision of the universe. Life was made into a drama. The royal court, the Zimbawoye originally defined by its fence, became a symbol of the sky touching the earth at the horizon, the king became Mwuetsi, and his wife the Nehanda. Just as the moon rises, waxes, wanes and dies, the king became visible, blazed forth in lavish splendour and then receded into complete obscurity and was executed. He disappeared like his great exemplar, until his sister and wife redeemed him and delivered him in his new and young incarnation to the light of day before the eyes of the people. The brightness of the young stars (chisi, also meaning holiday) is represented symbolically by the sacred ceremony of fire making and fire distribution. The hierodule nature of the princesses signifies the sacred function or life-giving water. Circumcision of the boys is connected with the cult of the goddess of love, of dedication, of procreation.

All this presents itself as a projection onto the earth, in the form of a cult, of the movements of the stars in the night sky, down to the details. Just as in the popular legend the boy with the birth mark in the shape of the moon on his forehead and with the moon on his chest riding the ox emerges from the lake and returns to it, the reigning king is likewise adorned and his corpse lies in state in the skin of the black ox, on the forehead or between the horns of which a white mark must be placed.

There can be no doubt that no amount of hard work and dedication has been able or will be able to recover all the images of mythical perception.

This is how the mythical vision is projected: from the sky to the earth, from the earthly to what is under the earth. This is how, in particular, the cosmic god became the earthly king, in order to act out the role of his exemplar in his life and death, in all its awesome drama.

Editor's Postscript

To the true and convincing words of Leopold Senghor in the foreword to this anthology the Editor would like to add a few remarks. He would like to give some kind of introduction to the life and work of Leo Frobenius for those who have not been so familiar with his writings. He also wants to say how the different parts of this anthology were selected.

Leo Frobenius has suffered the fate of many other important men: often named, seldom quoted, and even more rarely read. Most of his books – the first were published in the last years of the last century – have not been re-issued. Few of them were translated into English or French. This does not make it easier for those who are interested in his works. This is regrettable, and it is most genuinely regretted by those for whom the dialogue between Africans and Europeans is task and concern.

The centenary of his birth now offers the welcome occasion, if not for an edition of his collected works, then for an anthology with quotations from his most important works, in order to give those who cannot read German the possibility to become familiar with his thought.

Leo Frobenius was born in 1873 in Berlin, where his father was an officer in the Prussian army. At the early age of 21, he astonished the scientific world with a weighty volume "Secret Societies in Africa" in which he made statements about the culture of the black continent that were quite unorthodox at that time. In accordance wih his very independent nature, Frobenius, as a scientist, was nobody's pupil. He was an apprentice at various museums and universities although – as he himself put it – the sources were his real teachers. His doctoral thesis on "The origins of African culture" was rejected by a German faculty, and he turned his back on the Universities for good. From then on, he went his own way. It is true that, as an older man, he received an honorary professorship from the University of Frankfurt, but he never held public lectures, although the number of those who call themselves his pupils is considerable. We admire his achievements all the more when we consider that he was not only a scientific genius, but was equally gifted as an administrator. His entire life-work, his research institute with its many collaborators, his numerous research expeditions, his extensive scientific archives – these he supported during his lifetime with funds he raised himself.

His growing perception and his intuitive understanding of the meaning of culture, Frobenius associated with his "experiencing" of foreign cultures and peoples. A series of twelve great expeditions, beginning in 1904 and ending, shortly before his death, in 1935, took him to the Congo and the

Kasai, to West Africa which he covered in two trips of almost four years' duration, to Morocco, Algiers, Tripoli, and into the deserts and mountains of the Central Sahara, to Egypt, to the Sudan, to the shores of the Red Sea, and to South Africa. Thus, he spent many years of his life in the bush, in the savanna and the tropical forest. It were essentially these travels that established his fame, as well as the numerous books he wrote about them, in his very memorable style. At that time, Frobenius was quite properly called the real scientific discoverer of African culture in Europe. Hardly any ethnologist, before or after him, devoted himself so passionately to the clarification of cultural inter-relationship, on both the largest and the smallest scale. Only direct contact with the actual ways of life of the African, only close, even intimate contact with African people made it possible for him to fulfil his work as we now have it before us. Frobenius was a tireless worker whose diligence almost approached fanaticism. This is proved not only by his numerous publications, but also by the treasures he left behind in his archives, most of them by his own hand, comprising several hundred thousand notes in which he systematically catalogued all the most important features of the African culture of his day. His great archives of mythology remained a torso – here, he catalogued not only the myths of the entire world, according to their most important themes, but also collected representations of myths in the arts of the world. His premature death left these, as well as many other tasks he had initiated, unfinished. Given the opportunity of looking through these archives, one is astonished at the universality of the collections – next to Greek vase paintings, one finds African sculpture and Oceanic ornaments. Frobenius' lifework was crowned officially when the city of Frankfurt took over the sponsorship of the African Institute which, up to then, he had supported by his own efforts, and appointed him Honorary Professor of the University of Frankfurt, and a Director of the Ethnographical Museum of the same city. Frobenius could now work more freely, and devoted the last years of his life principally to training his students as the successors to his work, and sending them on several great expeditions under his supervision, the finest fruits of which were the discoveries of the Sahara rock art.

Frobenius' premature death, the anti-intellectualism of that time which made many of Frobenius' ideas suspect, the war that destroyed the Africa Institute and the Ethnological Museum in Frankfurt with many of their treasures, and brought the death of a number of students – are reasons why his great achievements did not produce the effective results they deserved.

It was only after the second world war that a new concern with Frobenius and his cultural humanism could arise. The Africa-Institute, renamed the Frobenius-Institute, attracted a great number of students who – in many cases – are today well-known representatives of African cultural anthropology and history.

The vast collection of the Africa-Archives was the basis for the work that issued from it: the doctrine of culture as an independent entity. Frobenius was one of the first cultural anthropologists who did not confine himself to an ethnographic description of the facts, but elaborated a method for organizing, in respect of space and time, the confused welter of observations about the world's non-literate peoples.

As a historian, Frobenius endeavoured, through his research, to provide an historical background for the civilizations that had formerly been regarded as having no history, because their past was not illuminated by any written records; and thereby to incorporate them into the current of old world history. This work stimulated an expansion of the historical perspective which, at the turn of the 20th century, had been almost exclusively confined to the advanced and literate civilizations of Europe and the Near East. The historical field of vision was thus expanded, not only in spatial-geographical terms, by the inclusion of previously neglected parts of the world, but in anthropological terms as well. Many African cultures have preserved forms of thought, of behaviour, and of general cultural patterns that are obviously much older than those of the earliest advanced and literate civilizations of the Near East. In his works on the philosophy of history and civilization, Frobenius sought to comprehend not only a particular culture, but culture as such, and with it the entire history of the world. He tried to grasp and to explain the forces and motives that lead to the origin of a culture, the laws governing its course, the interrelation between man and culture, and the meaning and goal of his historical development. The broad scope of his research contributed in sights and findings of fundamental importance to historically oriented cultural anthropology, as well as to the cultural history of extra-European peoples.

I can only pick out the most important of Frobenius' countless contributions to African studies. I will refer only in passing to his great representative twelve-volume collection of myths and fairy tales. His great documentation of rock paintings was a pioneering achievement. These rock paintings – especially in the Sahara area and in South Africa – were in part already known when he examined them. But he was the first to photograph and copy them with scientific exactness, and to increase the number of known pictures to a considerable degree by new discoveries. For this purpose he had trained in his Institute a whole generation of painters who accompanied him on his travels and, from the middle of the thirties on, made expeditions of their own to preserve the treasures of South West European and African rock paintings and engravings. In view of the unexpected wealth and the range of style of his discoveries, Frobenius cherished the hope that extensive further photography – which was prevented by the war – would produce so many new pictures of revealing content that, like a tremendous picture-book, they would illustrate the world history of the non-literate peoples. This hope was not to be fulfilled, nor is the dating of many rock-paintings by Frobenius accepted today, and we are not able to produce a correct chronological order for lack of archaeological data.

May I sum up: at a time when Europe was still caught up in the prejudices of the superiority of the white race and its culture, Frobenius opened the door to an inclusive cultural historical view of the entire world. The Eurocentric historical perspective was thus overcome. All the cultures of this earth from then on appeared to be equal unities in their own right. The difference is gradual, and they think in different categories. Frobenius would say: they have a different "Paideuma", a different cultural soul. But this implies no values.

Leo Frobenius not only conceded to all the cultures of this earth their historicity, he tried to follow the actual course of their development, regardless of the lack of written sources. It is unimportant that today many of his philosophical speculations are rejected, or that many of his historical constructions require revision. Keep in mind that he had only very little source material available, mostly collected by himself during his travels. We must also consider that he had no absolutely reliable instruments to date his materials, such as archaeologists have today. This fate he shares with many other great pioneers. Nevertheless, his insight will remain the foundation for the study of African cultural history. Only subtle intuition and tremendous industry – the two characteristics of genius – made possible his vast life work, upon which we can only look in admiration.

Leo Frobenius was in many respects a child of his time as was true of other great minds both before and after him. The high priests of the sociological sciences and ideologies so widely celebrated today made statements even after the turn of the century about non-Europeans and "primitive peoples" which today bring a blush to the cheeks of any European. They can hardly be used as evidence with which to condemn a great humanist who was in many respects decades in advance of them.

But it is distressing that Frobenius, who more than anyone before or after him recognized, defended, and made known the importance of traditional African culture, remained detached from the problems of colonialism, the emancipation of the African, and the liberation of Africa. He disregarded the evolution of young Africa, at that time entering its early phase. His stance was that of the great seer and interpreter of the past, if such epithets do him justice at all. There are in fact few personalities who more stubbornly elude clear definition than Frobenius. Friends called him "Proteus" because of his glittering "form" which changed constantly. He was never afraid of dissociating himself with a *pater peccavi* from certain of his thoughts and conclusions which he came to believe were wrong or had been superseded. It was without doubt only his early death which kept him from doing the same with the works of his later years. If 35 years after his death we now ask the perhaps premature question: "what remains?" – a vital question in assessing the moral and scientific significance of such a man – then we have the right to call him not only the founder of the historical and cultural study of Africa in Europe, but also a humanist, free from the prejudices of his time, who proved that culture exists wherever human beings are to be found. He was at all times a courageous man, independent of the politics of the day, who dared to state publicly, at a period when the racism and the arrogance of the white races had reached their peak, that race had nothing to do with culture.

*

It was not easy for the editor of this anthology to make his selections. What is typical of the "real" Frobenius? What should be the criteria in making a selection from his innumerable works? Indeed, who should and who will read this book? To begin with, let it be said that this anthology is by no means intended to be a scholarly edition: that must remain the task of a later generation. What we want is to make the largest possible range of readers, above all Africans, familiar with Frobenius' most important ideas and to give a general view of the whole range of his work. In doing this we run the risk of censure from strictly textual critics, as a cross-section such as we offer here must necessarily have as its basis the discretion of the editor. We have not hesitated to make cuts in the interest of greater readability and clarity of Frobenius' thought processes. Even during his life-time the verbosity of his diction and often overblown quality of his style received criticism, and it seemed advisable on occasions – for example the fourth chapter of this selection – to cut whole sections of the original. The citation of sources enables the critical reader to make comparisons with the German original.

We have divided the anthology into three main sections, in order to highlight the three main topics of Frobenius' research: Philosophy and Methods; African Art (in which the "Rock Art" assume an important place); African Cultures (given the abundance of material we have selected what seemed representative of the best).

The first chapter – a schematic introduction and examples from the "Atlas Africanus" – offers the reader better than any preface an impression not only of the cultural-historical method as Frobenius understood it, but also of the almost incredible thoroughness with which he carried out his work. What, however, these generously scaled maps do not reveal are the archives of over 100,000 file cards written by Frobenius himself which contain classified data extracted from publications. Until his death, Frobenius was continuously engaged in making extracts from all the literature on Africa available at the time.

The second chapter presents the substance of a discussion in the year 1905, in which for the first time Frobenius expounded the principles of the cultural-historical method. He repeated it in expanded form in the appendix to his book *Erythräa,* in which he attached great importance to co-operation among the historical disciplines, words which are still valid today. This comprises the *third chapter.*

While these three chapters are concerned with the methods of cultural research, the *fourth,* which includes a large part of his work *Paideuma,* gives Frobenius' conception of culture as "a living essence endowed with form" (Kulturmorphologie). It is at this very point that Frobenius proves himself to be the last representative of the "romantic school" which had for nearly a century held an important position in Germany and which today is so deliberately misunderstood and misinterpreted.

The "African Art" section is made up of four chapters. *The fifth chapter* ("African Art") shows Frobenius as the master of the general survey. His remarks on the significance of African art and its relation to the whole culture and history should not be forgotten, the more when we consider that they were written at a time when Europeans were prepared at most to accept the aesthetically bizarre aspects of African art and not the functional aspects.

Chapters Six to Eight present extracts from the great works on the rock art of the Sahara-Atlas, the Fezzan, and of South Africa. They should give an idea of the immense value of Frobenius' discoveries, which to this day have not been surpassed. He was the first to bring them to the attention of the world. These extracts should also make clear how Frobenius, in contrast to practices still common today, did not interpret the rock art abstractly as "l'art pour l'art", nor allow himself to be carried away into fanciful attempts at explanation. Rather he tried to reach an understanding of the content of the rock art in terms of the traditions of modern African man. This method may well be regarded as questionable, and certainly it is hazardous to assume continuity over thousands of years. On the other hand this approach – that is, explaining phenomena in African culture in terms of Africans – is incomparably more consistent than undertaking explanations from a Eurocentric viewpoint. Though we may have certain misgivings with respect to Frobenius' interpretations of the rock art of the Atlas and Fezzan, in South Africa his method has been confirmed in the most convincing way. Here he succeeded in establishing the relations between the rock paintings, the Zimbabwe buildings, and certain myths which were still current in his time.

In the third section we have brought together selections from Frobenius' writings on African cultures. On his extensive journeys – from Senegal to the Red Sea and from Algiers to the Cape – he gained an acquaintance with African cultures which has scarcely been equalled. A complete edition of these writings, most of which have not yet been translated into English or French, would be an invaluable legacy for Africa – above all the 12 volumes of tales, myths, and religious traditions. We regret that for reasons of space it has not been possible to offer more of these tales.

Chapters Nine and Ten give examples of the oldest African culture in terms of cultural history, namely that of the hunting people. We owe to Frobenius' intuition the carefully compiled description of the hunter culture, the basis of which was the many reports he gathered personally throughout the Sudan. He gave it an African name: the "Mahalbi" culture. In addition, what he wrote about the Bushmen, the original inhabitants of South Africa (who today have either died out or have been forced to retreat to arid areas) seemed important enough to reproduce here as did the great myths about the bush spirit "mantis". One can distinguish here very old layers of human culture.

On his journeys to Morocco and Algiers, Frobenius not only collected three large volumes of traditions and folk-tales of the Berbers, he also made attempts to establish the characteristics of their old folk-culture and to expound their basic differences from the Arabs who arrived later. Extracts from this appear in the *eleventh chapter*.

Chapter Twelve presents three tales which were selected from hundreds, and they give an impression of what Frobenius called "the splendour of the Sudan". In west Sudan, where he remained for over four years, Frobenius not only recorded the spiritual („geistige") culture, but established extensive archives with records of the material culture: architecture, dress, ornaments, weapons, pottery, etc. (cf. Pl. 19–21 and fig. 43–44).

Among Frobenius' sensational finds and discoveries belong the terracotta-plastics (pl. 8–9 excavated by him in Ife, Nigeria, which opened up a totally new and unexpected chapter in African art. As always Frobenius did not consider this find as an isolated archaeological artifact, but placed it in the living context of the Yoruba culture which he regarded as the heir to Ife art. Even if we entertain severe doubts about his theory of the "Atlantic" origins of this culture, still his description of the Yoruba religion, presented here in the *thirteenth chapter,* is a magnificent contribution to the culture and history of this people, which occupies such an important position in West Africa.

Finally, in *Chapter Fourteen,* we bring selections from the results of Frobenius' research in South Africa, which he set down in his book *Erythräa* (cf. also Chapter 8 of this anthology which treats the South African rock paintings). At their centre stand both the sacral kingship of the Wahungwe, heirs of the great culture of Zimbabwe, and the interrelationship between fertility and rain, which was of such crucial importance for the people of this region and the whole of Africa.

The editor would like to conclude with some words of thanks. Thanks above all to S. E. Leopold Sedar Senghor, President of the Republic of Senegal, who as a great friend of Leo Frobenius has written the forword to this anthology. Thanks are due to all those whose financial support has made the publication of this book possible. Finally, the editor extends warm thanks to all the members of the Frobenius Institute who have contributed to the success of this book: for the advice in the selection of texts, for the typing of the manuscript, for the selection of plates and illustrations, for the preparation of the illustrations and photographs for the press, and for the proof-reading of the text.

Main works of Leo Frobenius

1894   Die Geheimbünde Afrikas: Ethnologische Studie. Hamburg.

1897   Der westafrikanische Kulturkreis. Petermanns Geographische Mitteilungen, 43: 225–236, 262–267.

1898a   Der Ursprung der afrikanischen Kulturen. Zeitschrift für Erdkunde zu Berlin, 33: 111–125.

1898b   Die Masken und Geheimbünde Afrikas. Leipzig.

1898c   Der Ursprung der afrikanischen Kulturen. Berlin.

1899–1901 Probleme der Kultur. 4 vols. Berlin. 1: Die naturwissenschaftliche Culturlehre. 1899. 2: Die Mathematik der Oceanier. 1900. 3: Die Schilde der Oceanier. 1900. 4: Die Bogen der Oceanier. 1901.

1907   Im Schatten des Kongostaates: Bericht über den Verlauf der ersten Reisen der D.I.A.F.E. von 1904–1906. Deutsche innerafrikanische Forschungs-Expedition, Nr. 1, Berlin.

1910   Der schwarze Dekameron: Liebe, Witz und Heldentum in Inner-Afrika. Berlin.

1912–1913 Und Afrika sprach. Bericht über den Verlauf der 3. Reiseperiode der D.I.A.F.E. in den Jahren 1910–1912. 3 vols. Berlin.

1916   Der Kleinafrikanische Grabbau. Praehistorische Zeitschrift, 8: 1–84.

1921   Paideuma: Umrisse einer Kultur- und Seelenlehre. Munich.

1921–1928 (Ed.): Atlantis: Volksmärchen und Volksdichtungen Afrikas. 12 vols. Munich. 1–3: Volksmärchen der Kabylen. 4: Märchen aus Kordofan. 5: Dichten und Denken im Sudan. 6: Spielmannsgeschichten der Sahel. 7: Dämonen des Sudan: Allerlei religiöse Verdichtungen. 8: Erzählungen aus dem West-Sudan. 9: Volkserzählungen und Volksdichtungen aus dem Zentral-Sudan. 10: Die atlantische Götterlehre. 11: Volksdichtungen aus Oberguinea. 12: Dichtkunst der Kassaiden.

1922–1933 Frobenius, Leo and Wilm, Ludwig von (Ed.): Atlas Africanus: Belege zur Morphologie der afrikanischen Kulturen. 8 parts. Munich.

1923   Das unbekannte Afrika: Aufhellung der Schicksale eines Erdteils. Munich.

1925　　　　Frobenius, Leo and Obermaier, Hugo: Hádschra Máktuba: Urzeitliche Felsbilder Kleinafrikas. Munich.

1925–1929 Erlebte Erdteile. 7 vols. Frankfurt am Main. 1: Ausfahrt: Von der Völkerkunde zum Kulturproblem. 1925. 2: Erschlossene Räume: Das Problem Ozeanien. 1925. 3: Vom Schreibtisch zum Äquator. 1925. 4: Paideuma. 1928. 5: Das sterbende Afrika. 1928. 6: Monumenta africana. 1929. 7: Monumenta terrarum. 1929.

1931a　　　Erythräa: Länder und Zeiten des heiligen Königsmordes. Berlin and Zurich.

1931b　　　Madsimu Dsangara: Südafrikanische Felsbilderchronik. 2 vols. Berlin and Zurich.

1932　　　　Schicksalskunde im Sinne des Kulturwerdens. Leipzig.

1933　　　　Kulturgeschichte Afrikas: Prolegomena zu einer historischen Gestaltlehre. Zurich.

1937a　　　Ekade Ektab: Die Felsbilder Fezzans. Leipzig.

1937b　　　Frobenius, Leo and Fox, Douglas C.: Prehistoric Rock Pictures in Europe and Africa. New York.

1937c　　　Frobenius, Leo and Fox, Douglas C.: African Genesis. New York.

1938a　　　Die Waremba: Träger einer fossilen Kultur. Zeitschrift für Ethnologie, 70: 159–175.

1938b　　　Das Archiv für Folkloristik. Paideuma, 1: 1–18.

Works on Leo Frobenius

Leo Frobenius: Ein Lebenswerk aus der Zeit der Kulturwende, dargestellt von seinen Freunden und Schülern. 1933, Leipzig.

Hahn, Eduard, 1926, Leo Frobenius. Preußische Jahrbücher, 205: 205–222.

Ita, J. M., 1972, Frobenius in West African History. Journal of African History, 13, No. 4: 673–688.

Jensen, Adolf E., 1938, Leo Frobenius: Leben und Werk. Paideuma, 1: 45–58.

Kalous, Milan, 1970, Leo Frobenius' Atlantic Theory – a Reconsideration. Paideuma, 16: 27–51.

Lowie, Robert H., 1913, Und Afrika sprach . . . A Book Review. Current Anthropological Literature, 2: 87–91.

Mühlmann, Wilhelm, 1939, Zum Gedächtnis von Leo Frobenius. Archiv für Anthropologie, N.S. 25: 47–51.

Niggemeyer, Hermann, 1939, Leo Frobenius. Ethnologischer Anzeiger, 4: 268–272.

Norkaitis, Jonas, 1955, Kulturphilosophie und Kulturpsychologie von Leo Frobenius. Tübingen.

Petri Helmut, 1953, Leo Frobenius und die kulturhistorische Ethnologie. Saeculum, IV, No. 1: 45–60.

Ratzel, Friedrich, 1904, Geschichte, Völkerkunde und historische Perspective. Historische Zeitschrift, 93, No. 1: 1–46.

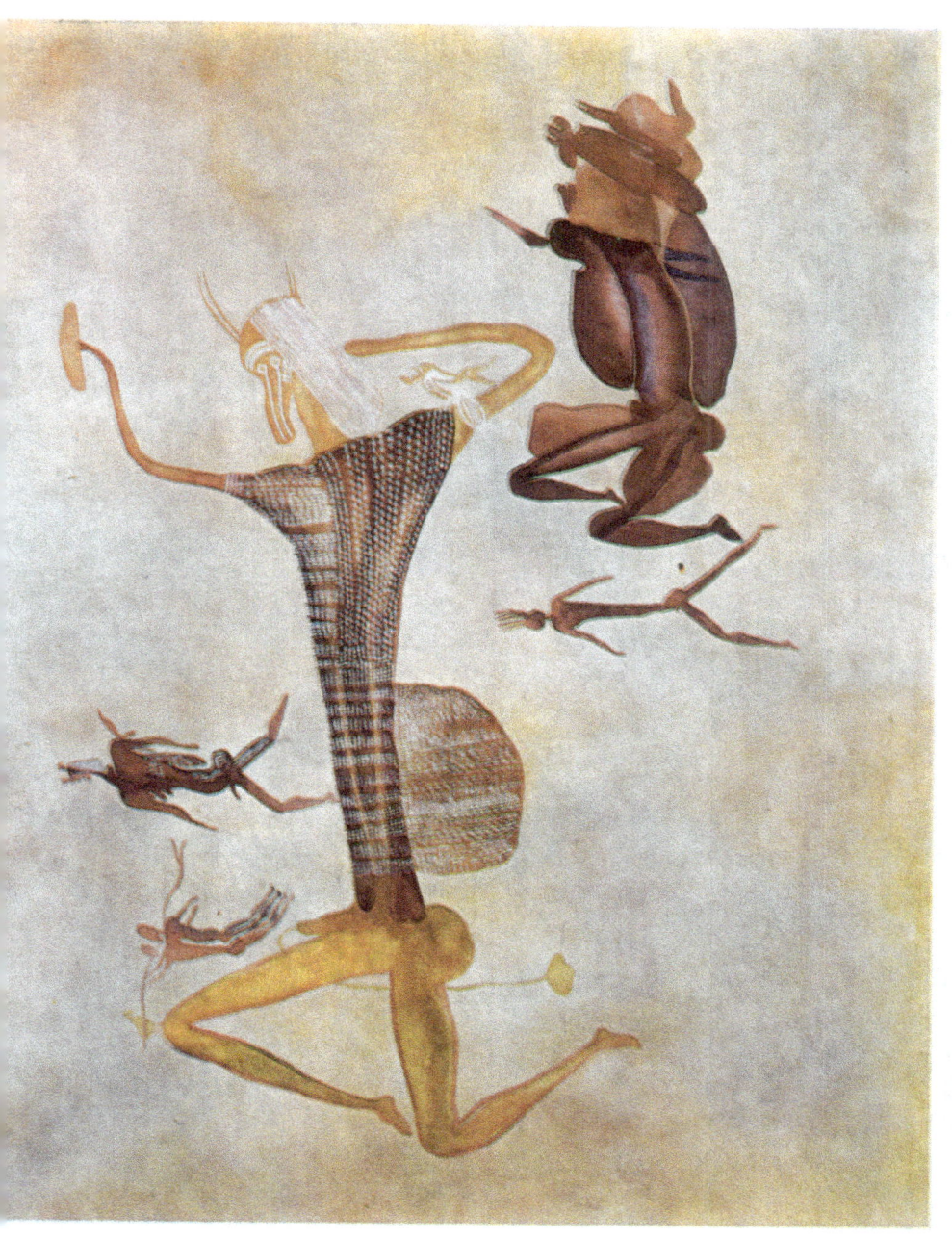

Pl. 1. Dead king (rock painting, Rhodesia)

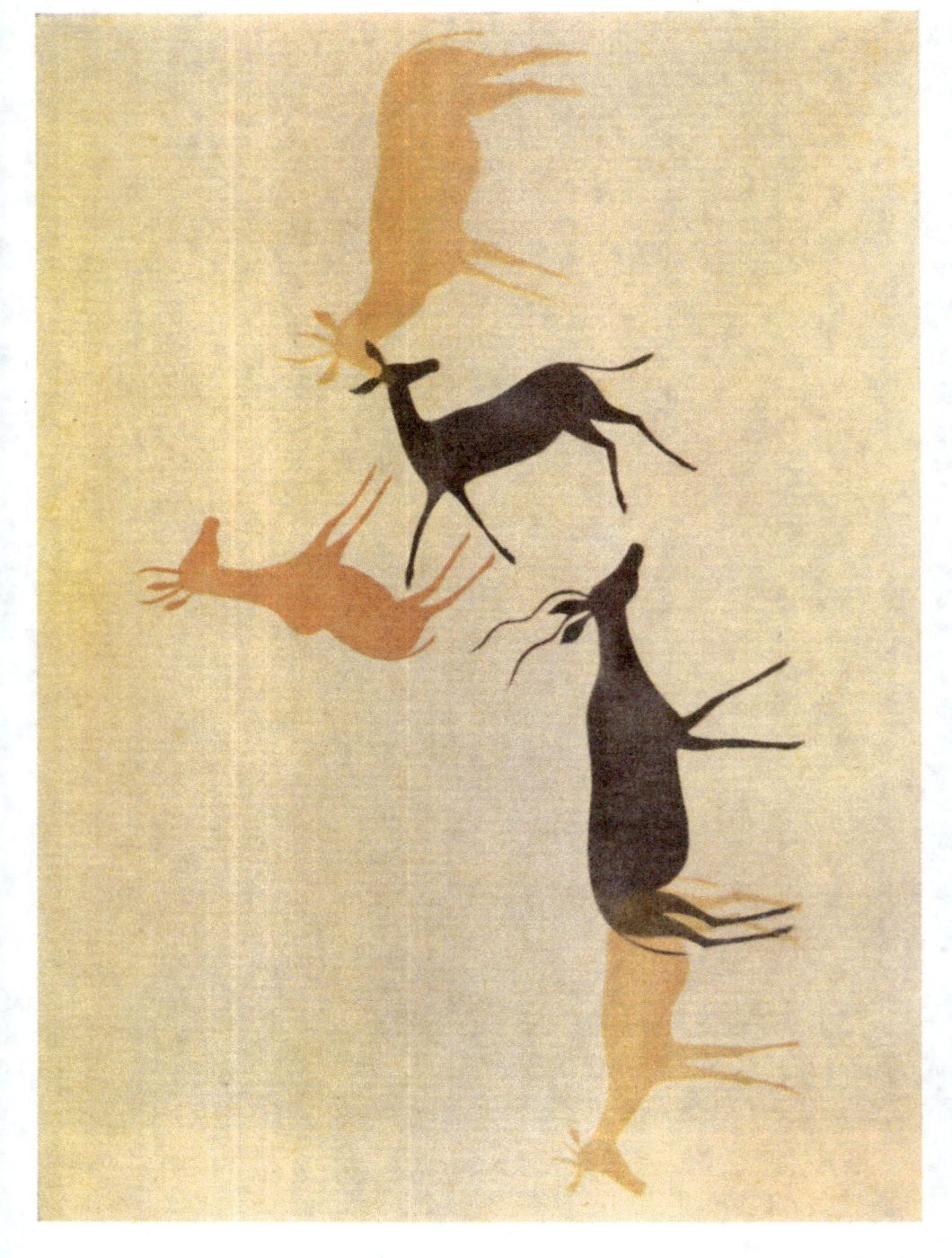

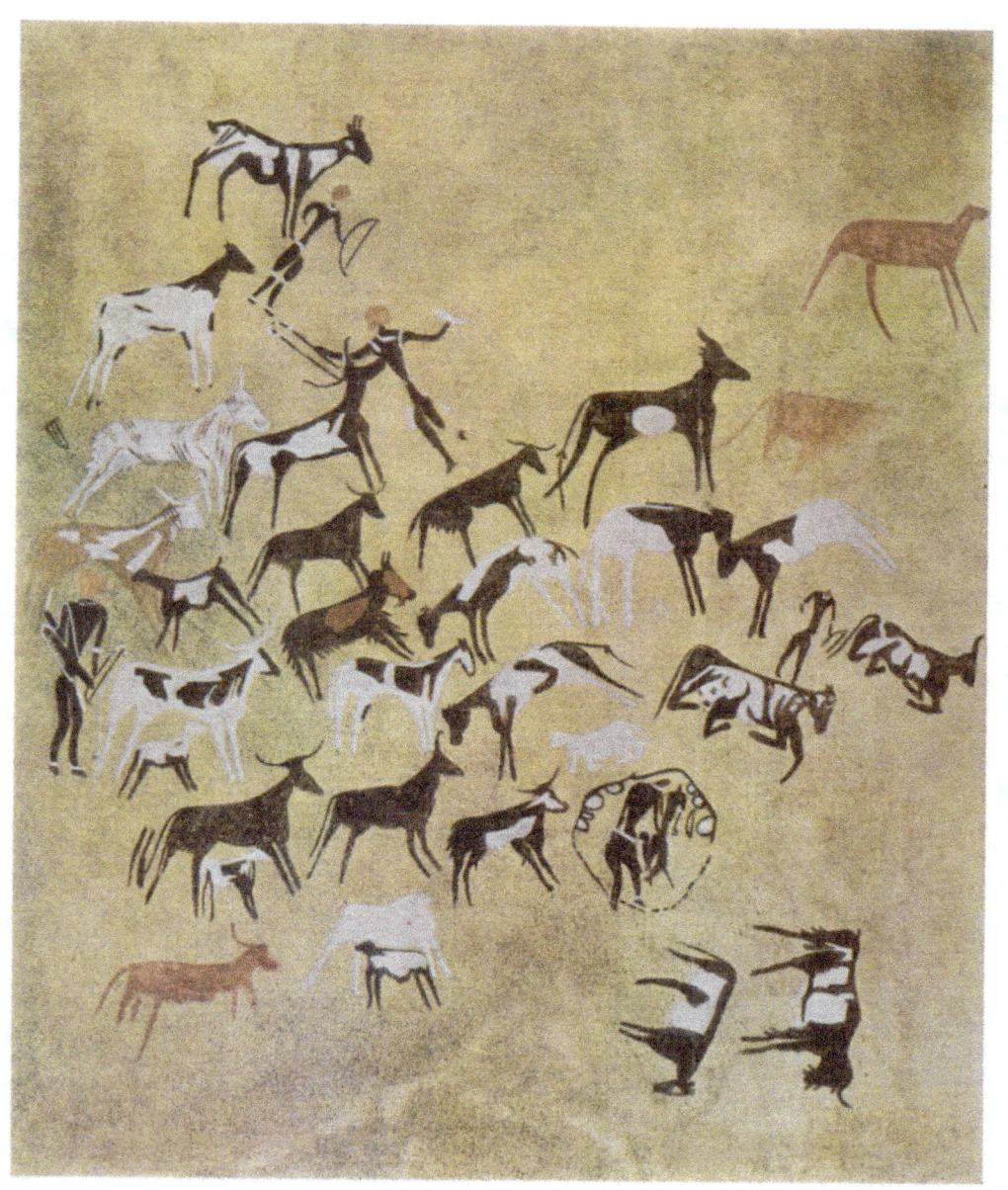

Pl. 3. Herd of cattle and herdsmen (rock painting, Libyan desert)

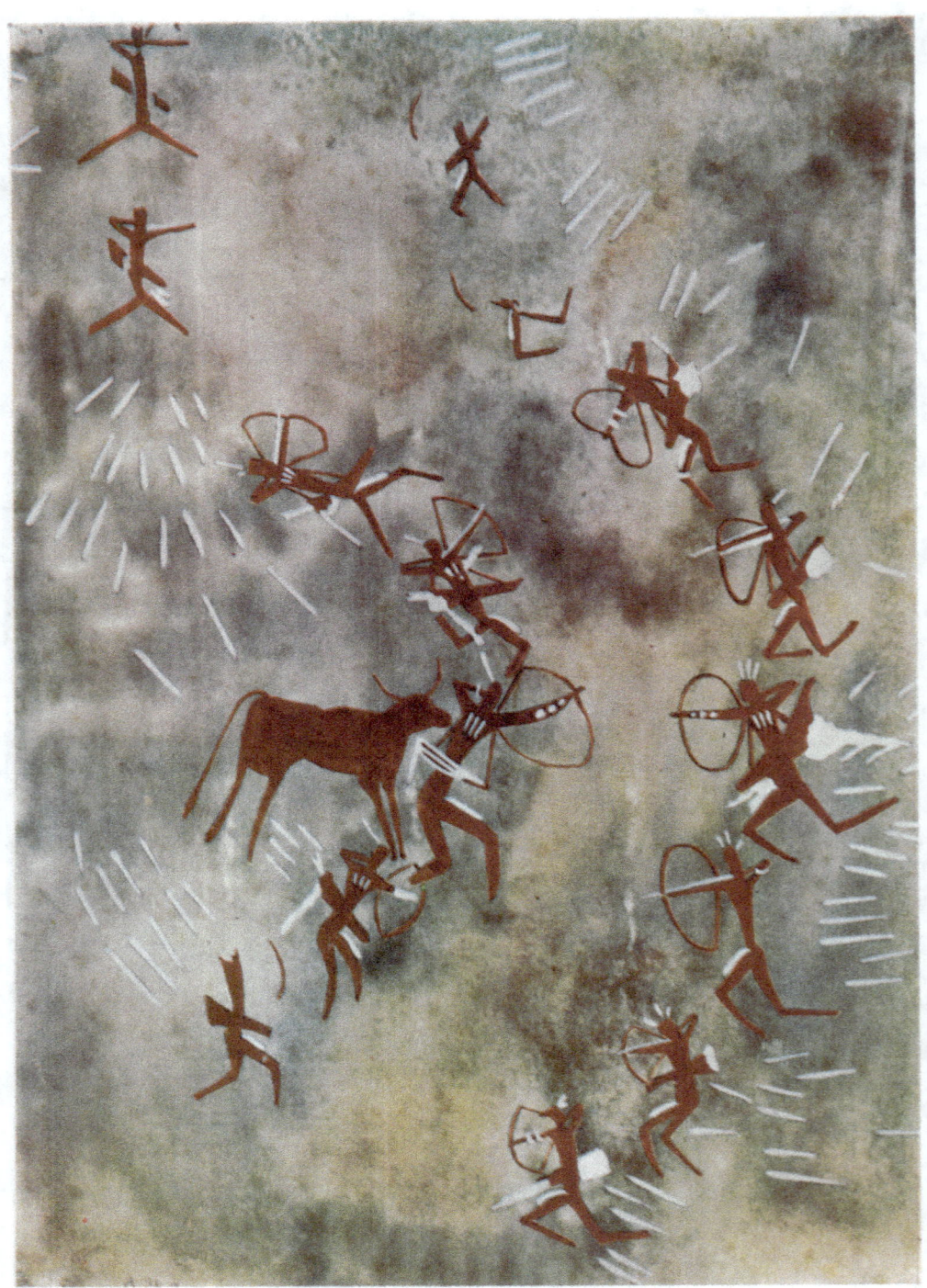

Pl. 4. Battle for an ox (rock painting, Libyan desert)

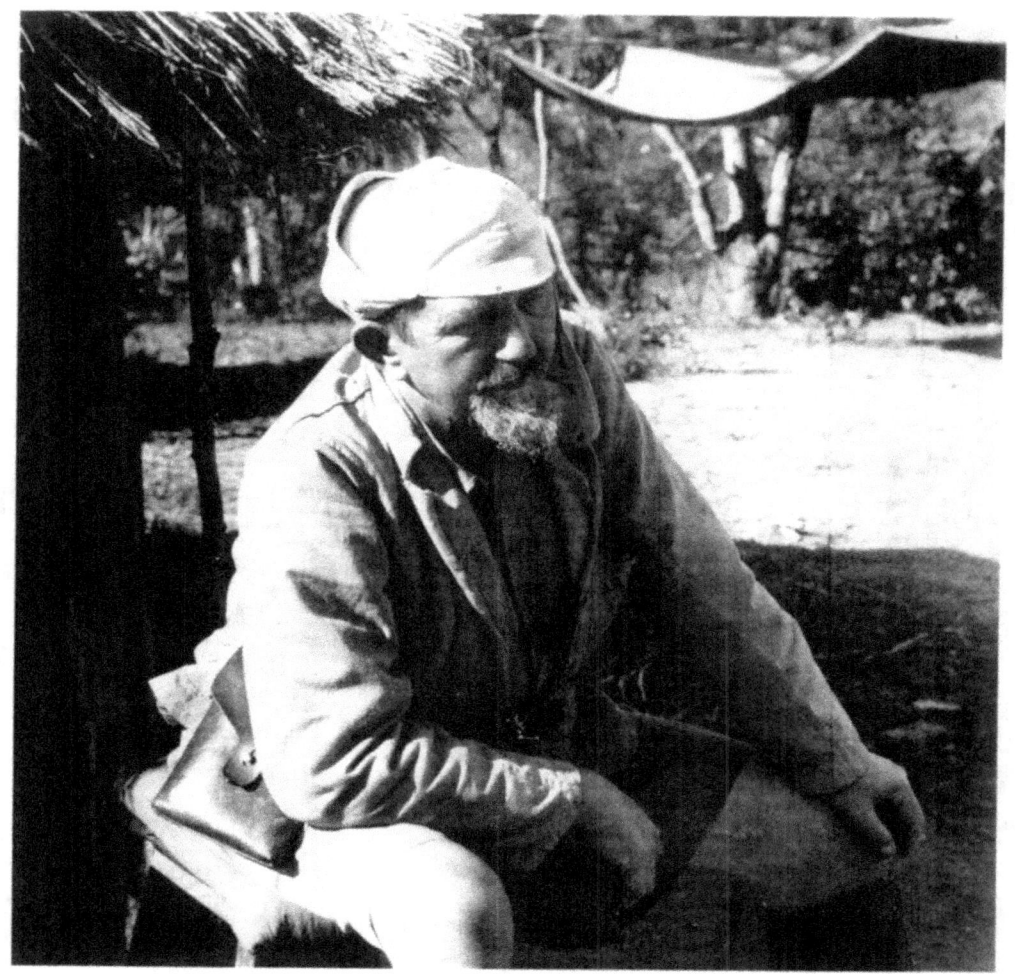

Pl. 5. Leo Frobenius about 1930

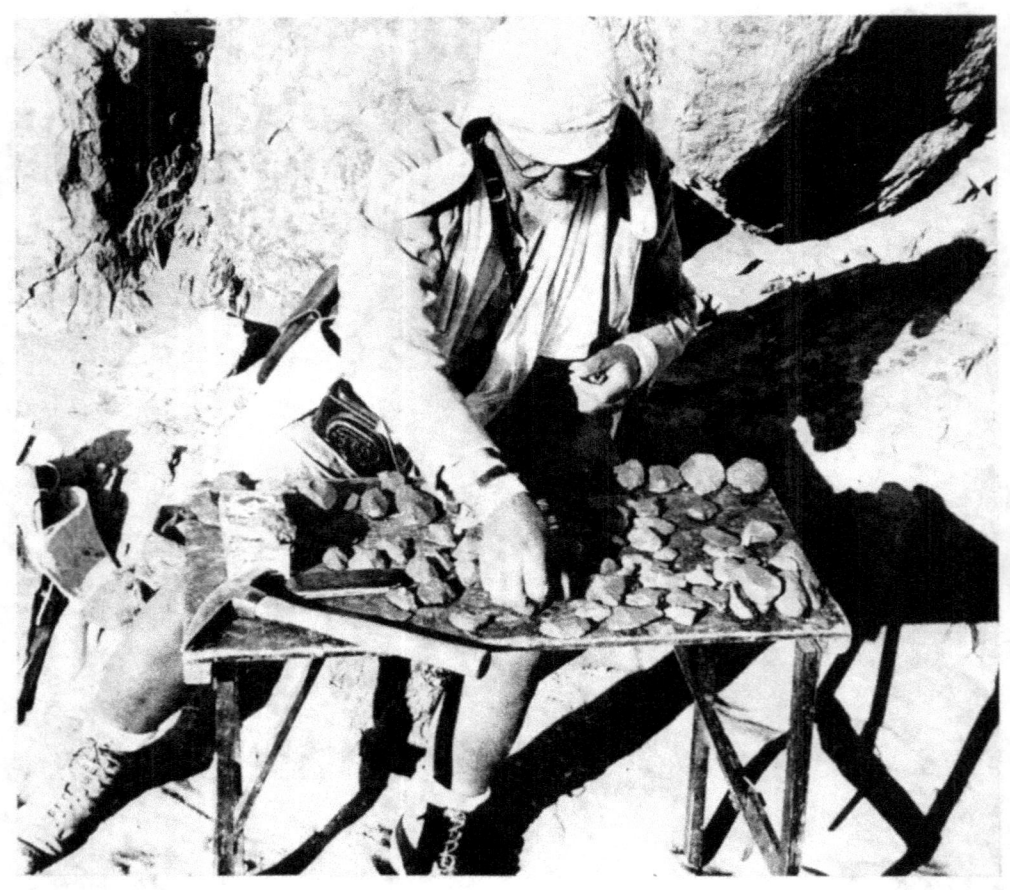

Pl. 6. Leo Frobenius in the Sahara towards the end of his life

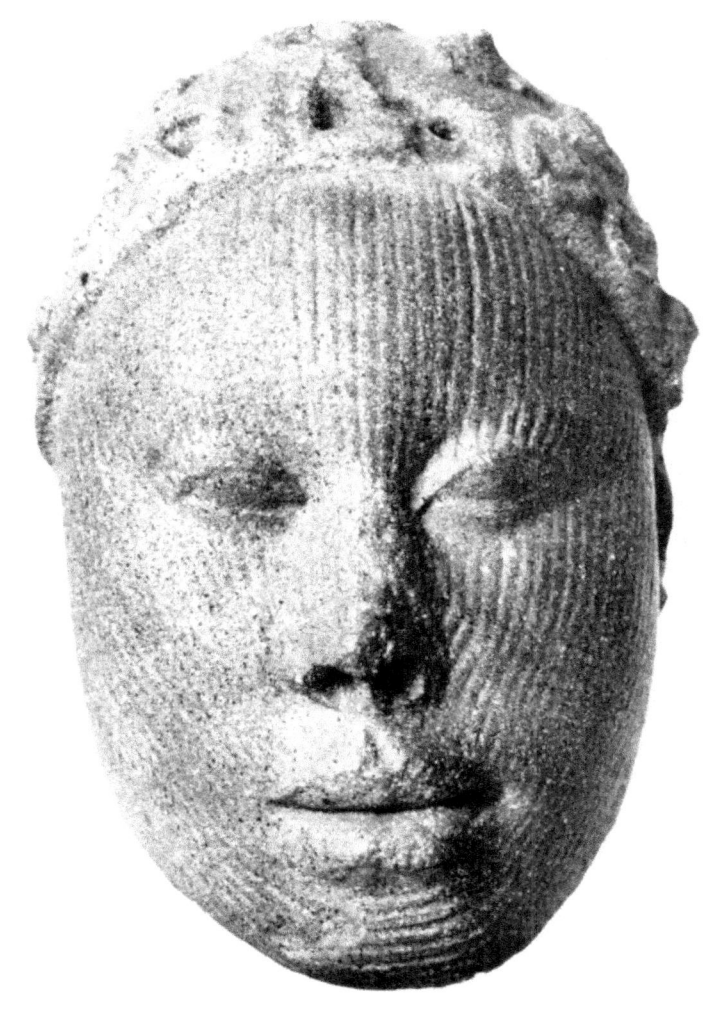

Pl. 8. Terracotta head excavated by Frobenius in Ife (Nigeria)

DER URSPRUNG

DER

AFRIKANISCHEN KULTUREN

VON

L. FROBENIUS

Mit 26 Karten von Afrika nach Entwürfen des Verfassers,
9 Tafeln in Lichtdruck, Buntlichtdruck, Autotypie etc. sowie ca. 240 Textillustrationen
von L. Hugelshofer, Arthur Thiele, H. Frobenius, Conrad Schultz,
dem Verfasser und Anderen

BERLIN

VERLAG VON GEBRÜDER BORNTRAEGER

1898

Pl. 7. Title page of the programmatic book "Der Ursprung der afrikanischen Kulturen"

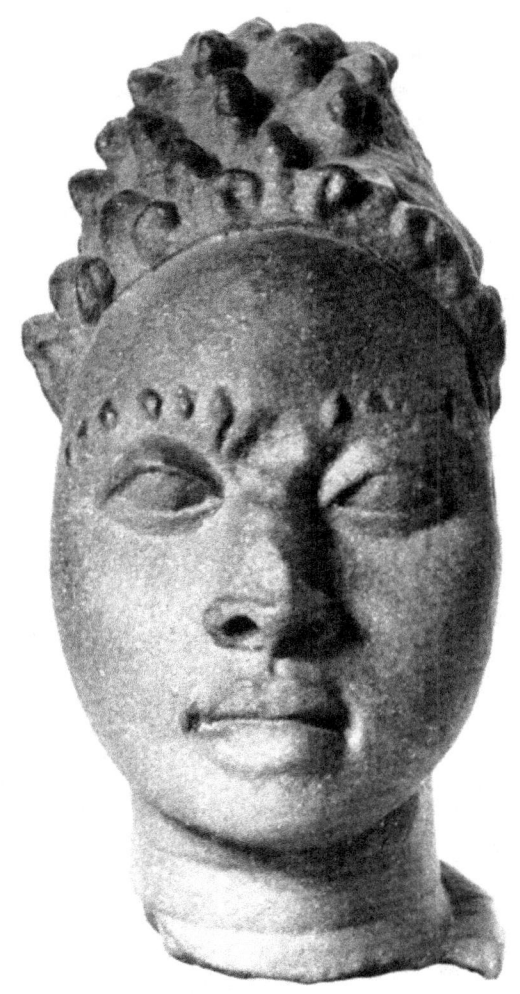

Pl. 9. Terracotta head excavated by Frobenius in Ife (Nigeria)

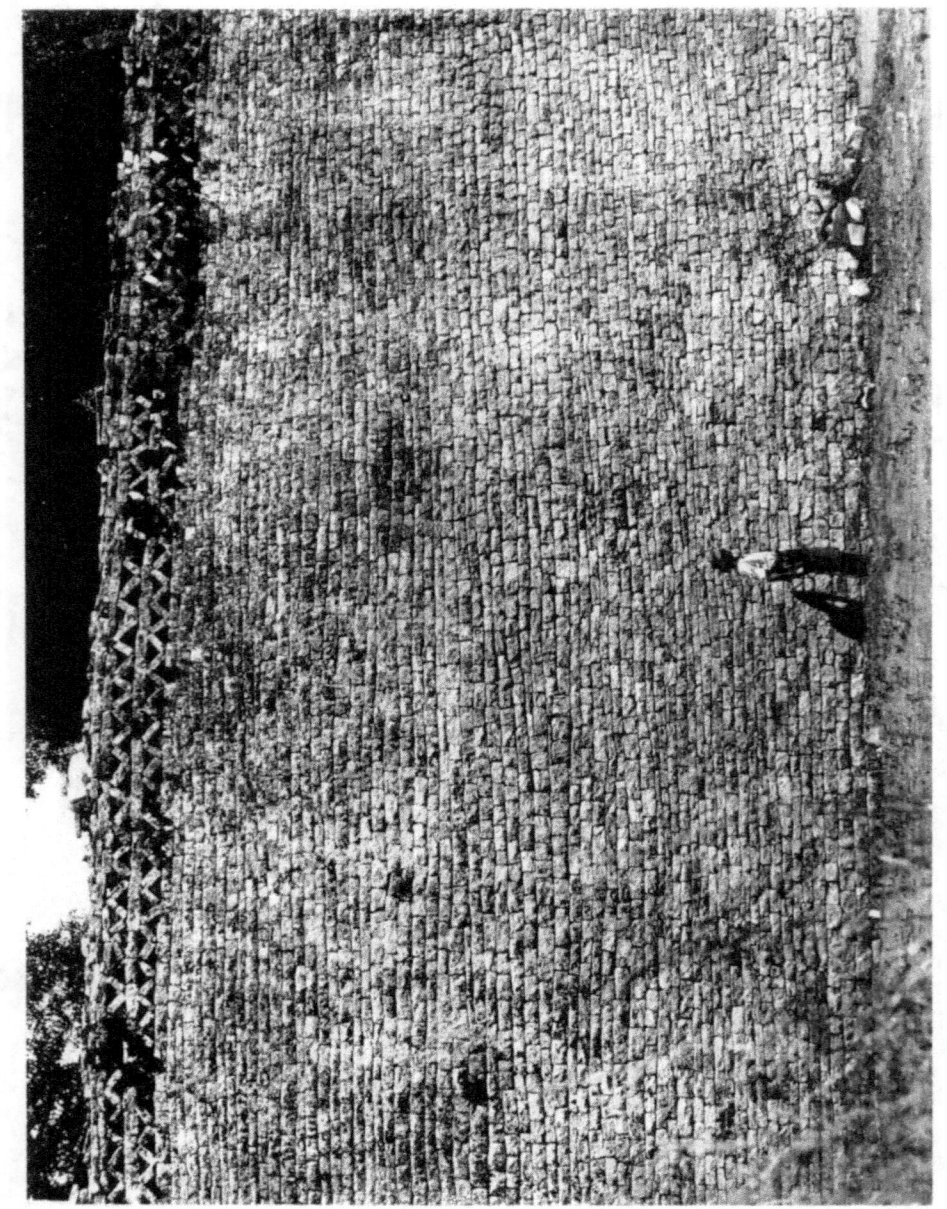

Pl. 10. Outer wall of the great temple of Zimbabwe

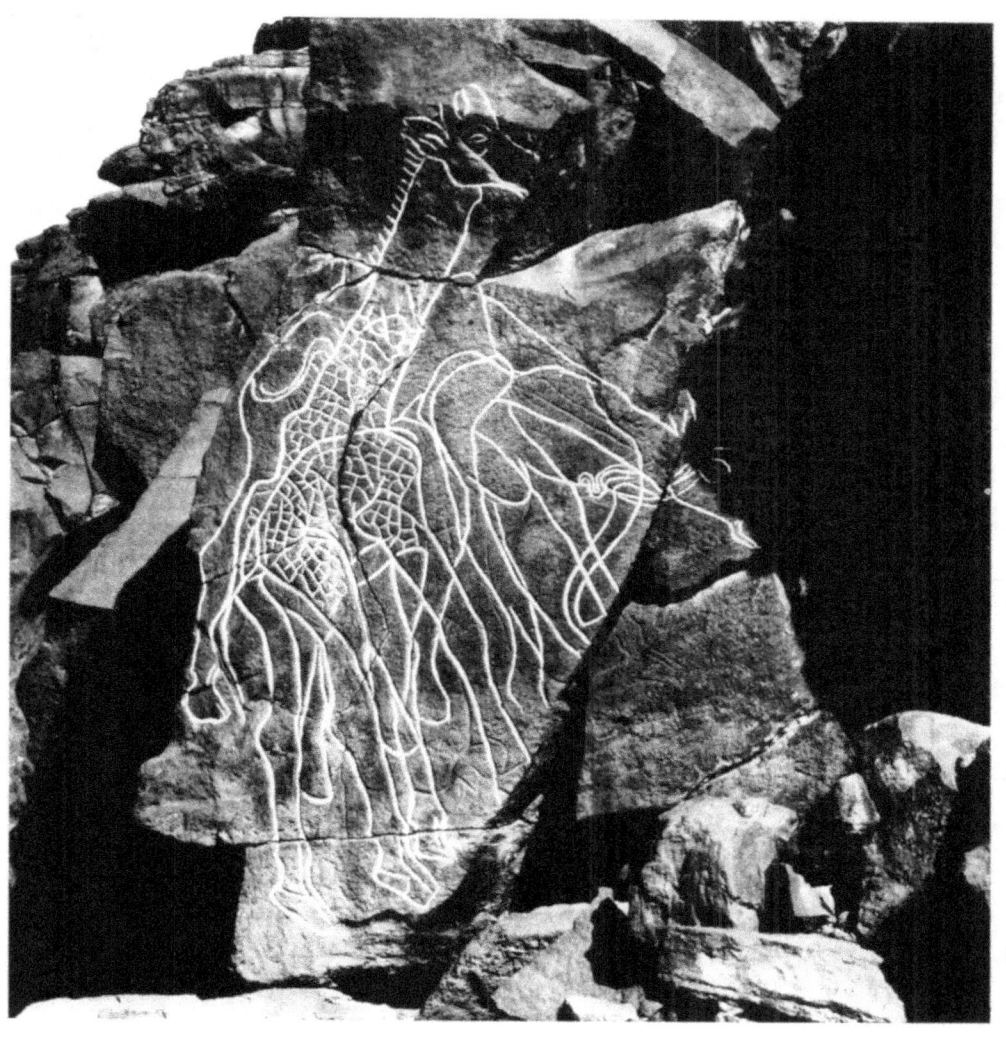

Pl. 11. Overlapping engravings of giraffes and elephant on a rock face (Fezzan)

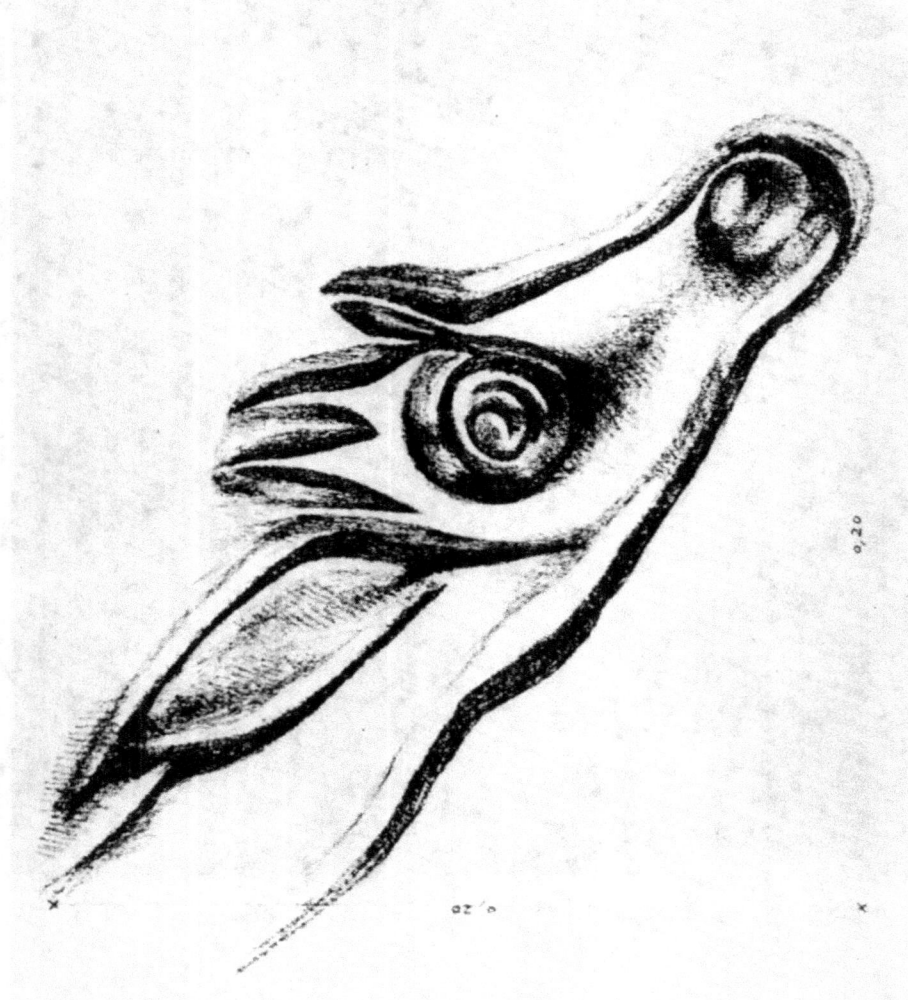

Pl. 12. Head of a giraffe (rock engraving, (Fezzan)

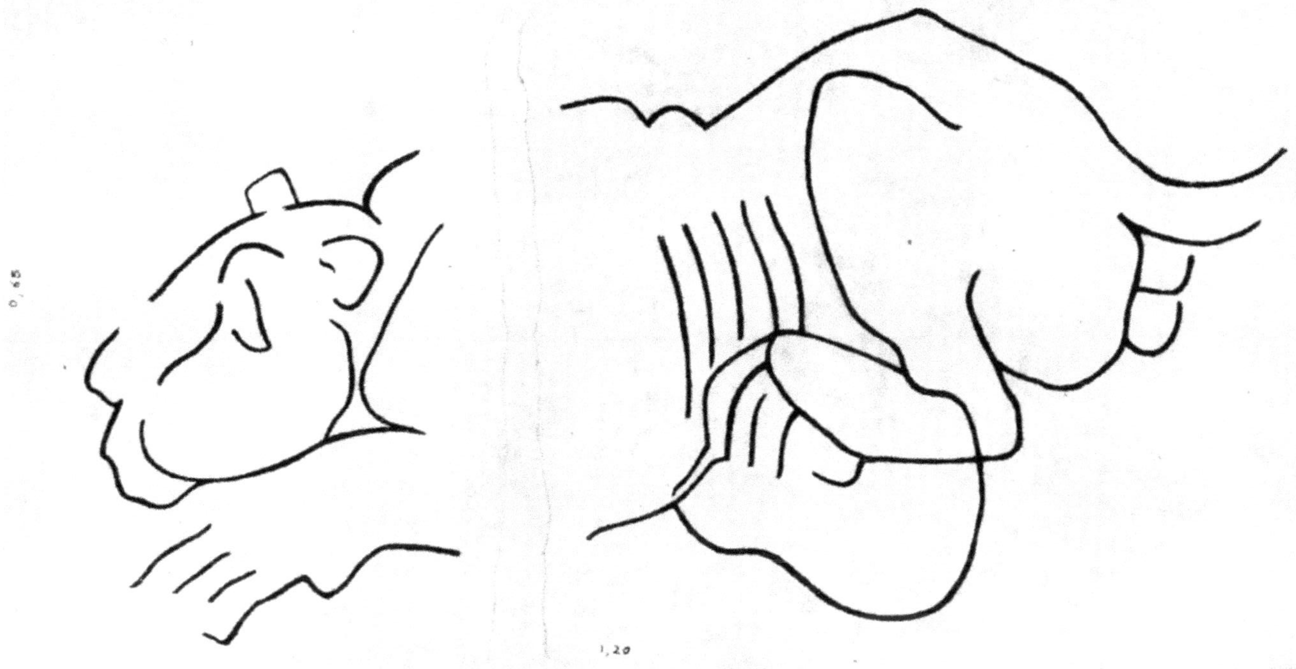

Pl. 13. Lioness (?) (rock engraving, Fezzan)

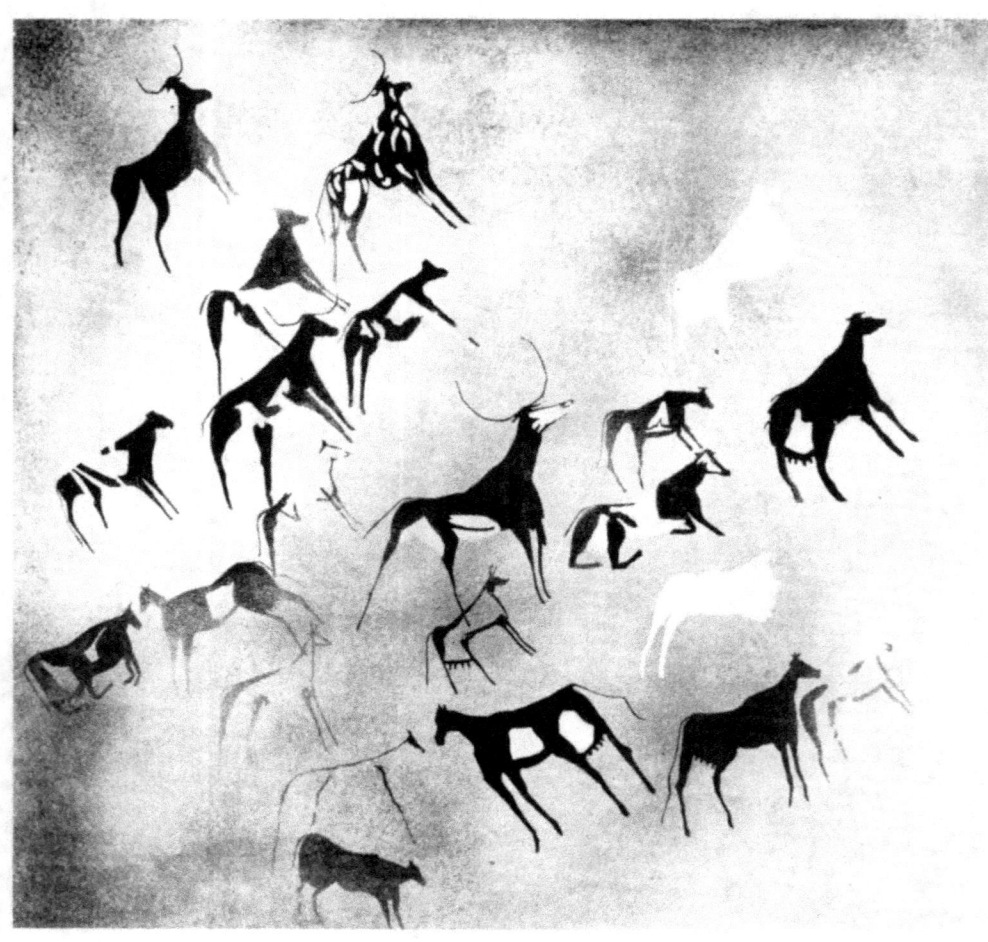

Pl. 14. Cattle (rock painting, Libyan desert)

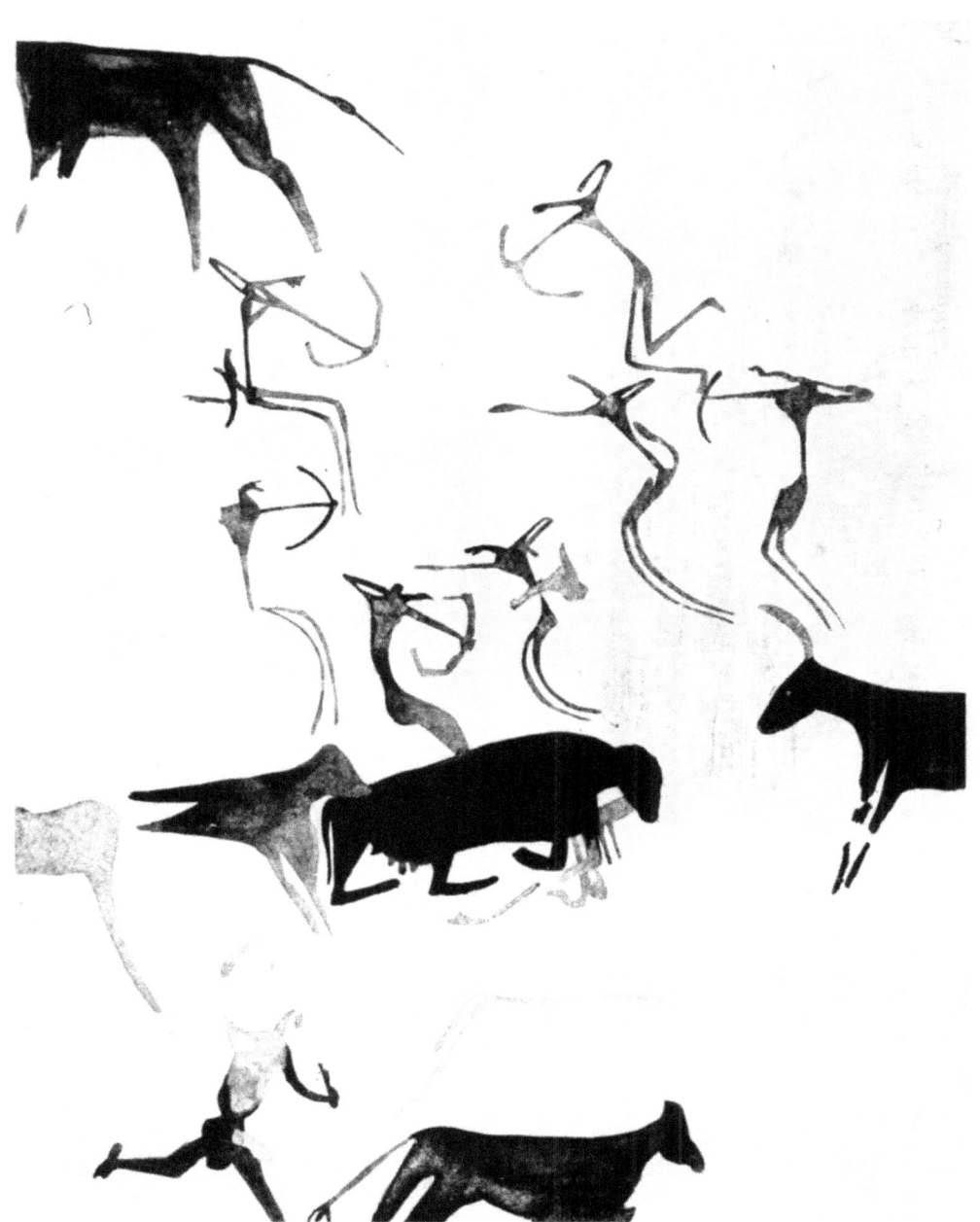

Pl. 15. Cattle and bowmen (rock painting, Libyan desert)

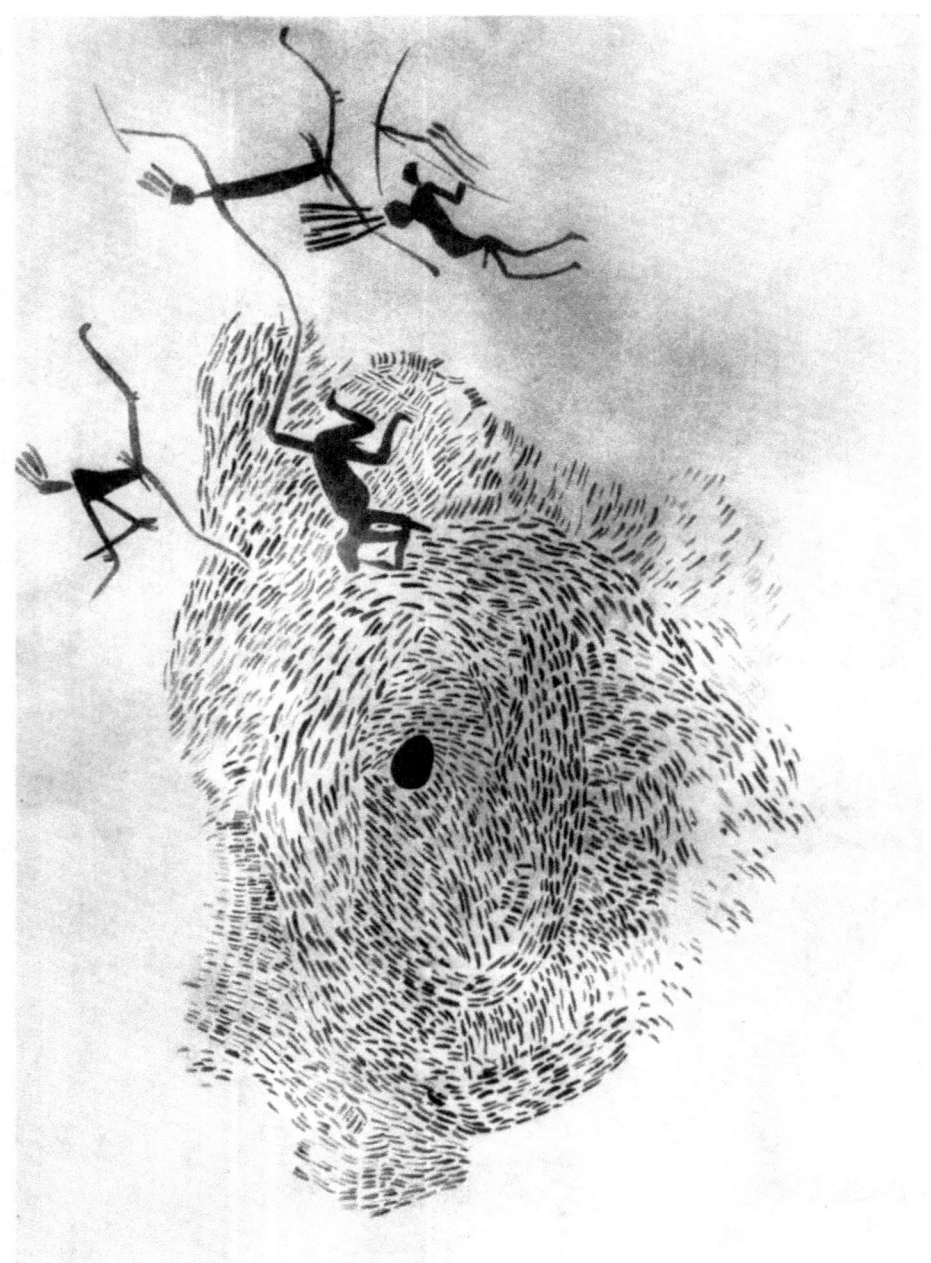

Pl. 16. Monkey pursued by huntsmen plunges into a lake (rock painting, Rhodesia)

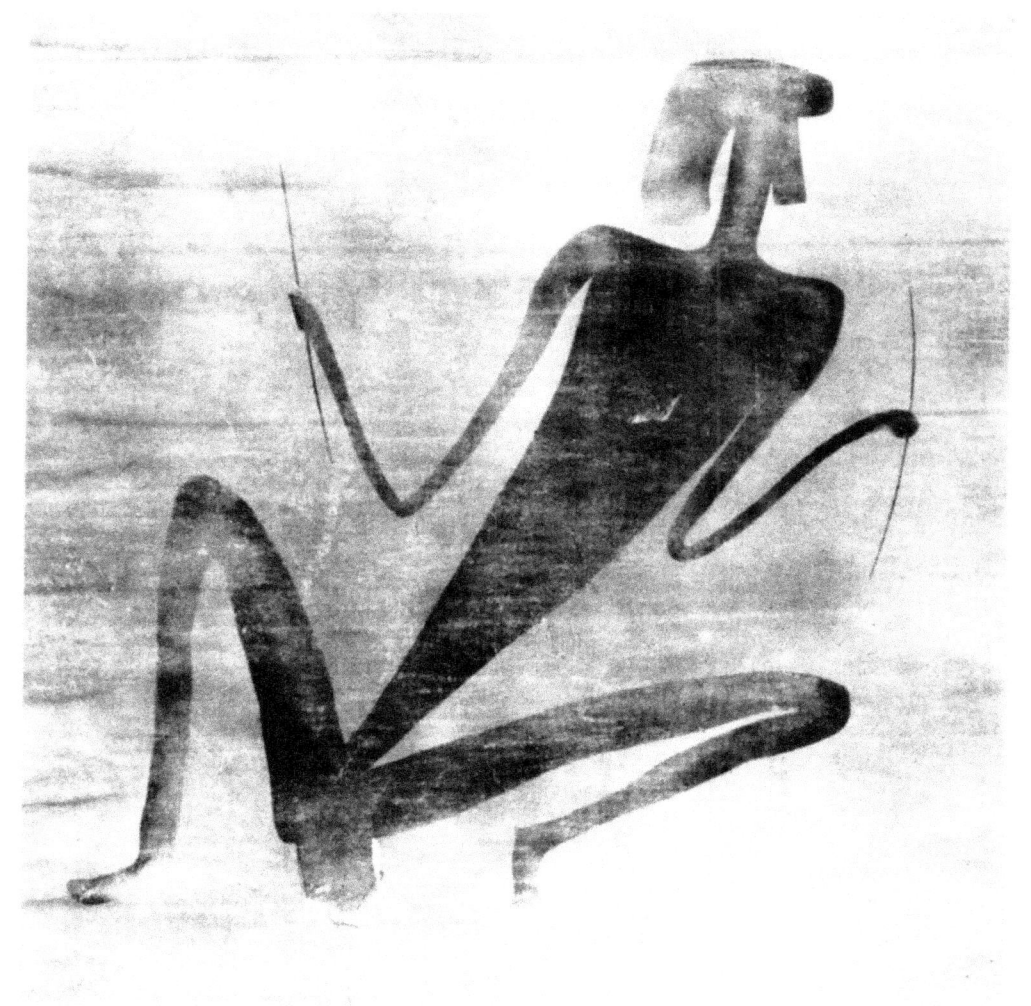

Pl. 17. Large seated man (rock painting, Rhodesia)

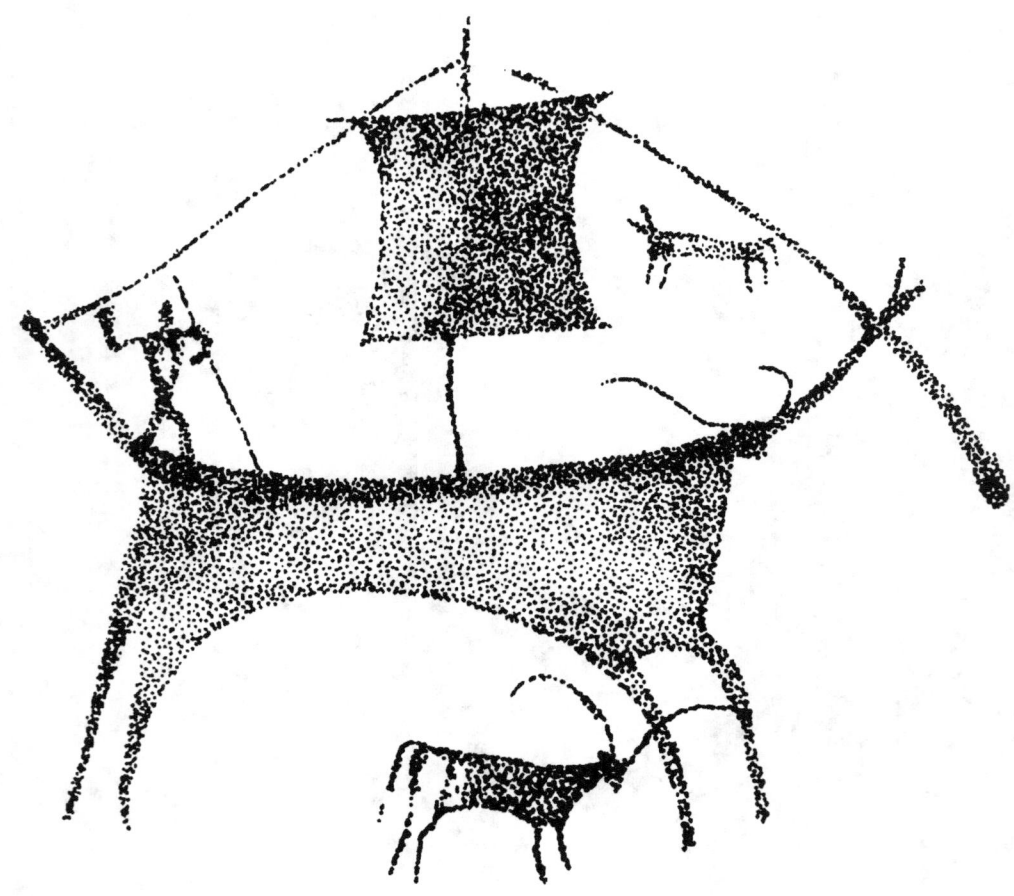

Pl. 18. Cattle and ship (rock engraving, Nubian desert)

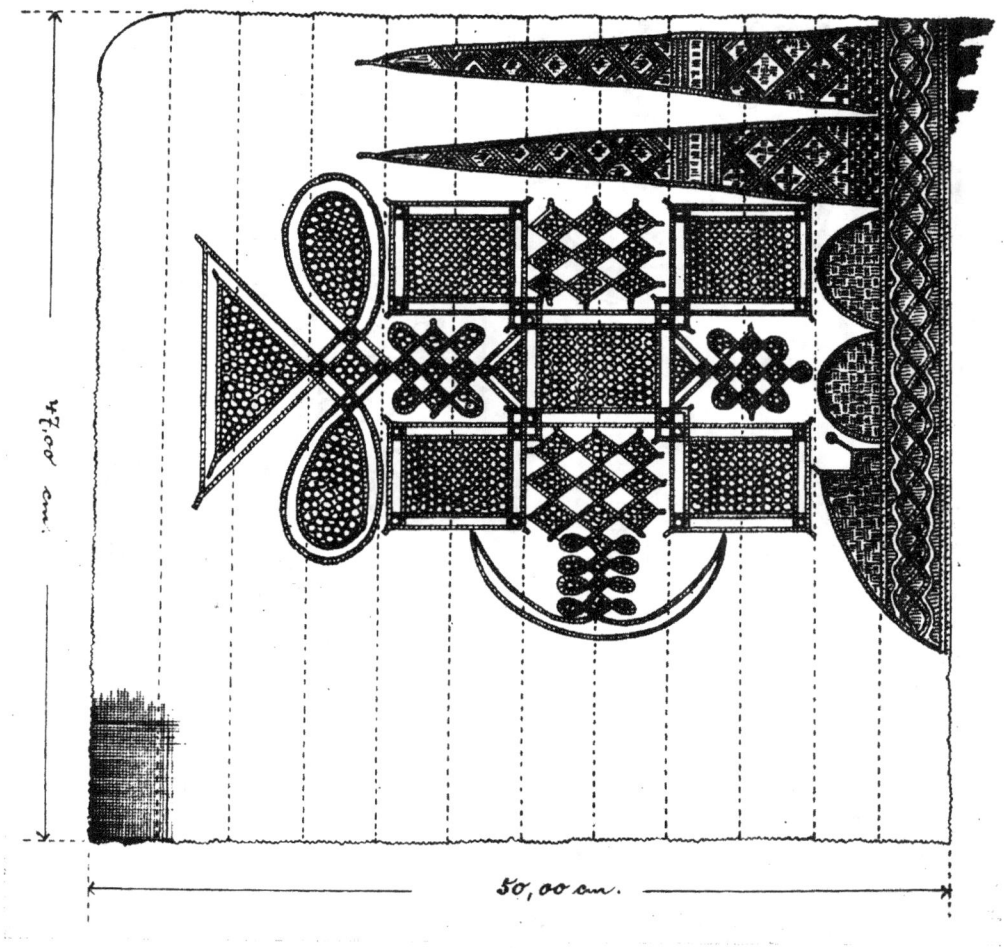

Pl. 19. Embroidered tobe (cloak) (Nupe, Nigeria)

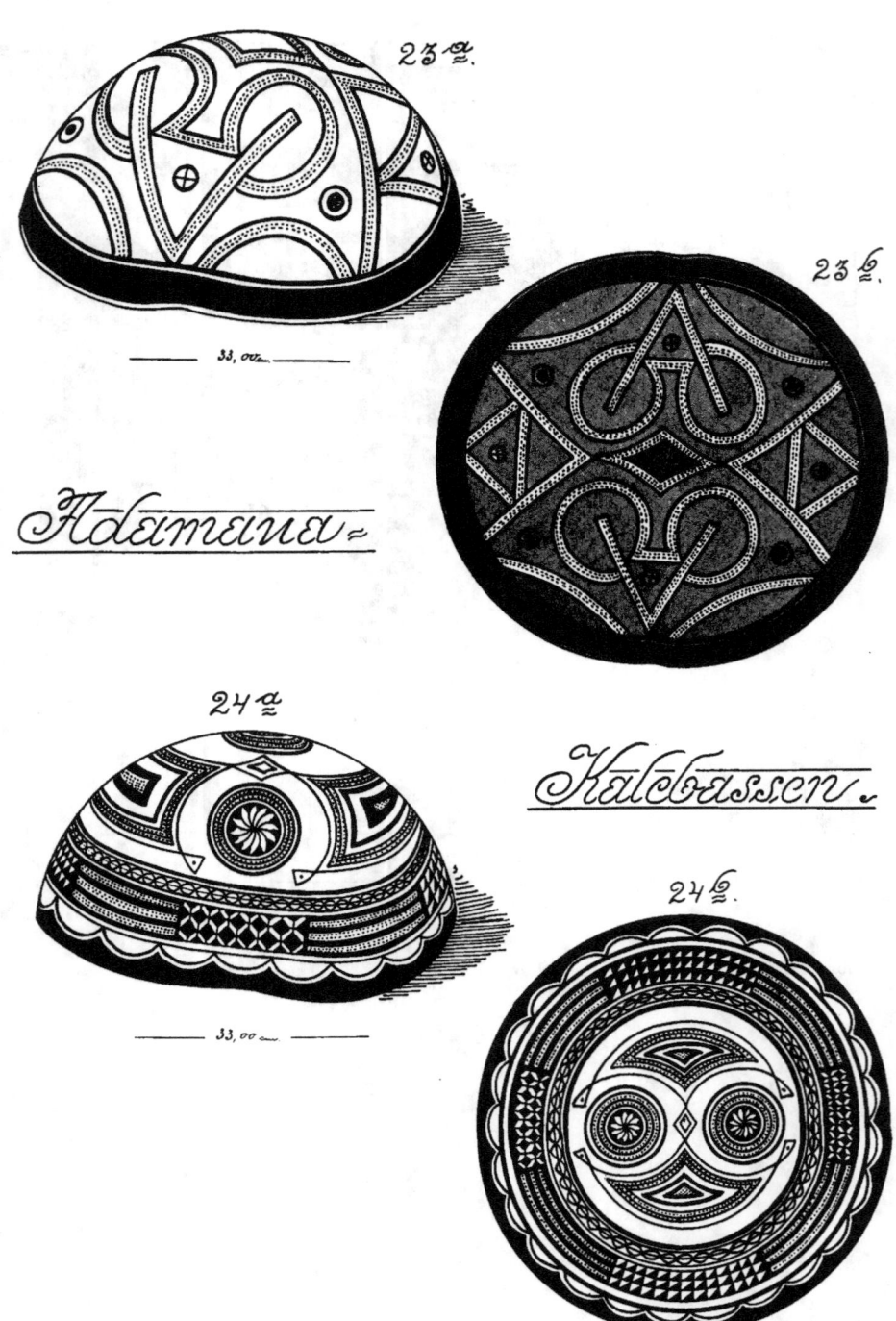

23 *a*.

23 *b*.

Adamaua

24 *a*.

Kalebassen

24 *b*.

Pl. 20. Gourds (Adamawa, Cameroun)

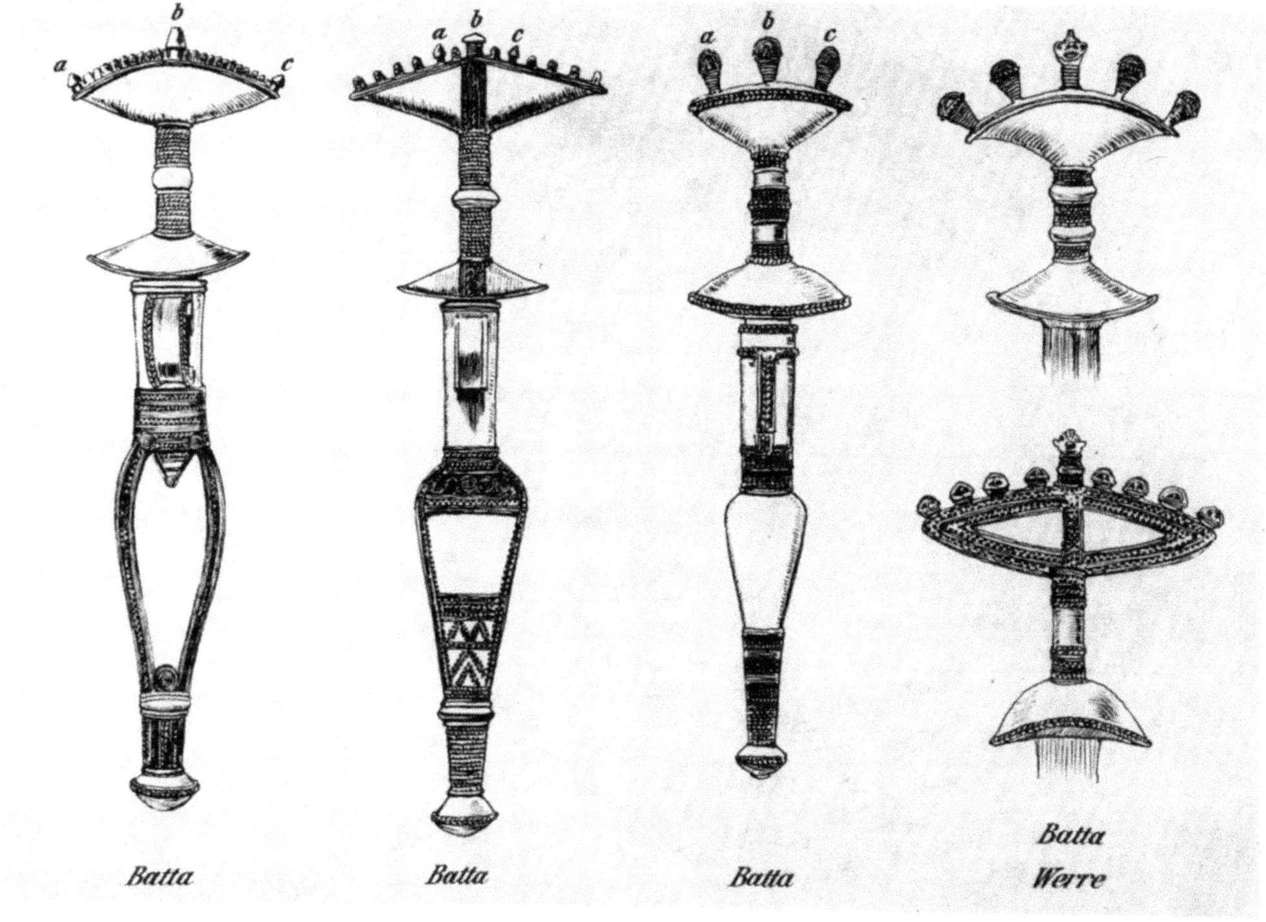

Pl. 21. Knife designs (Nigeria)

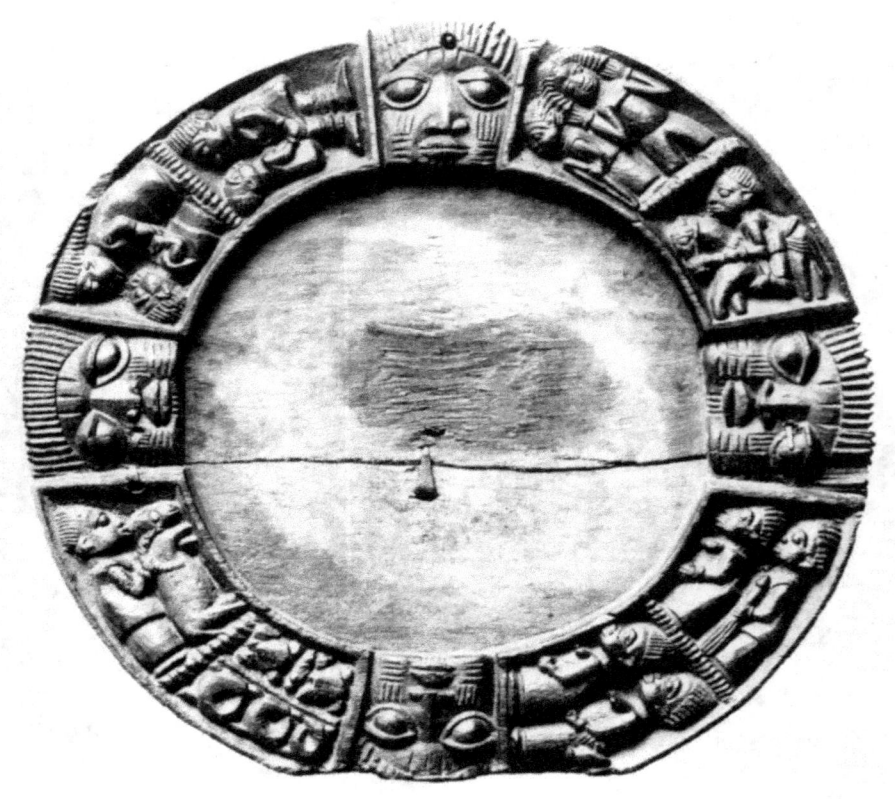

Pl. 22. Oracle board (Yoruba, Nigeria)

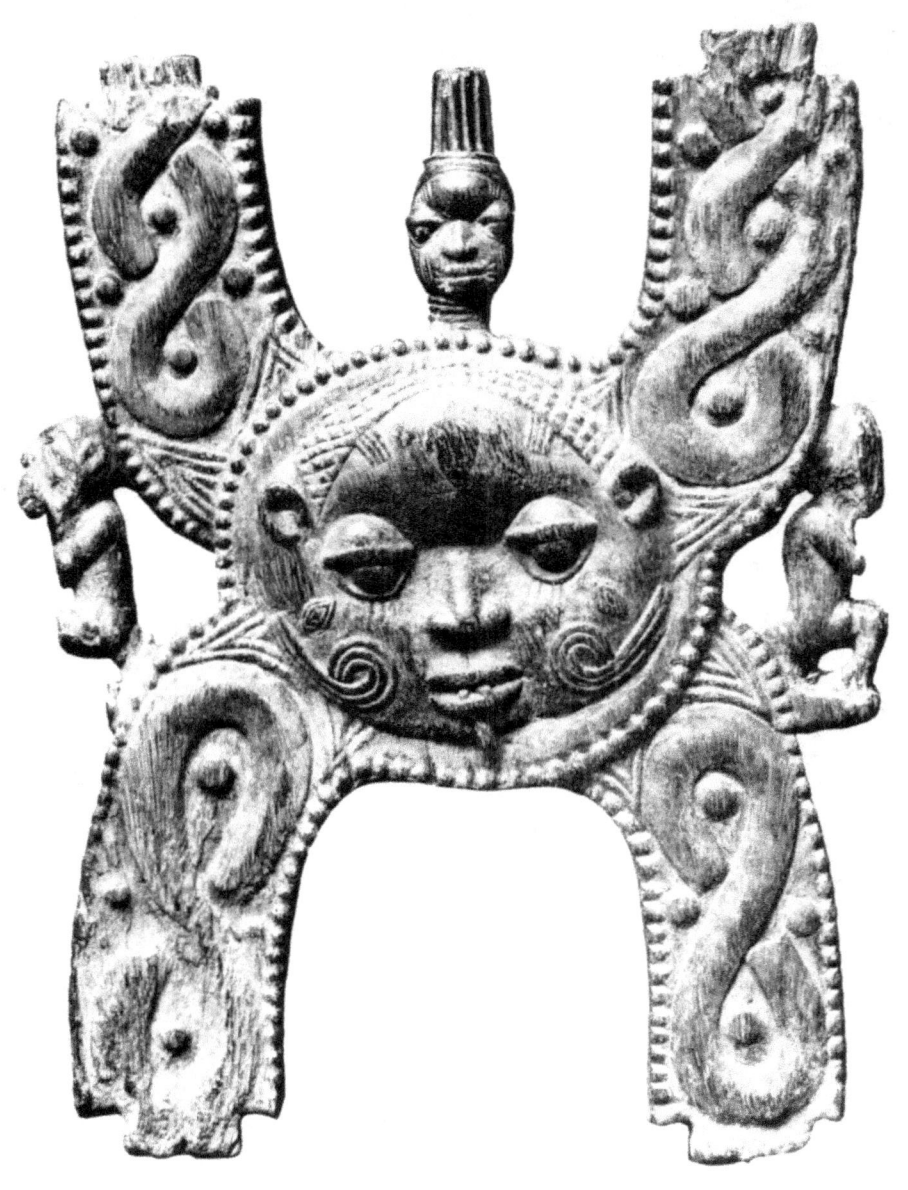

Pl. 23. Wood carving (Yoruba, Nigeria)

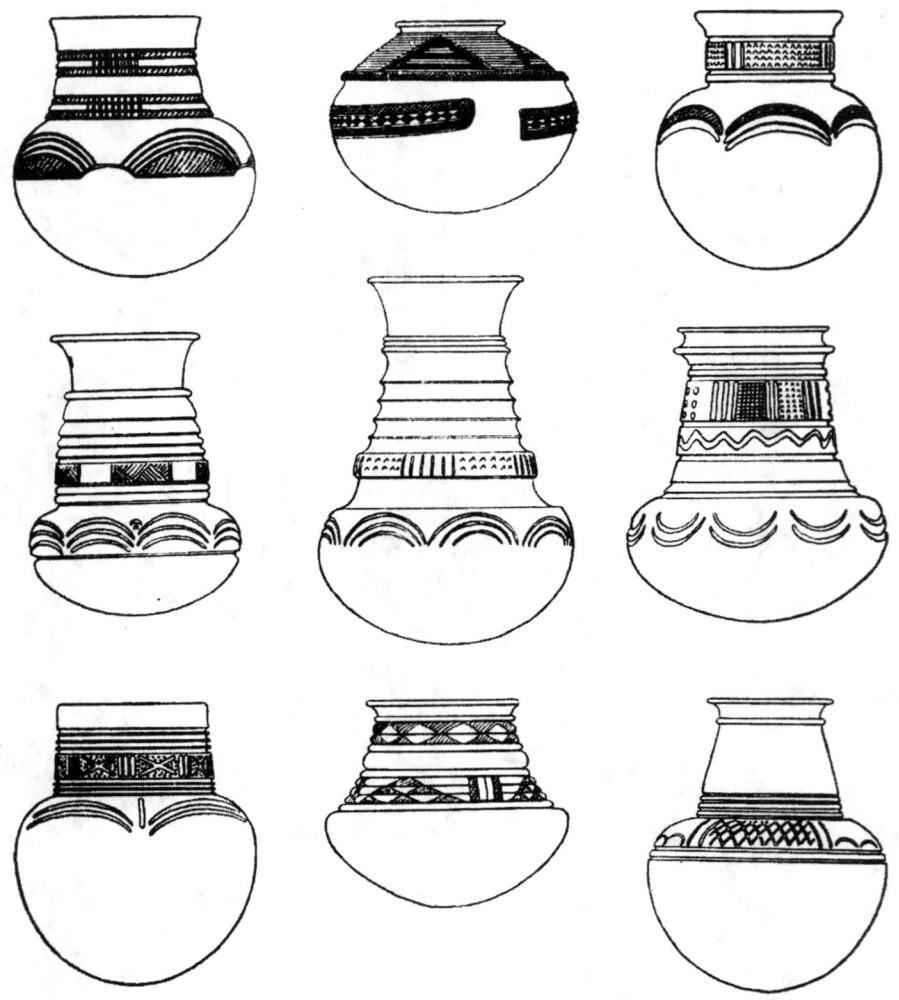

Pl. 24. Earthenware vessels (Basonge, Zaire)